EXPLORING NATURE
IN WINTER

The Naturalist's Bookshelf

The Naturalist's Bookshelf is a contemporary series of new and original works on environmental concerns, gardening, and nature study. Innovative in both design and content, volumes in this series are for your personal library reference and use in the field.

Exploring Nature in Winter

A Guide to Activities, Adventures, and Projects
for the Winter Naturalist

ALAN M. CVANCARA

Illustrations by DANIEL F. RICHARDS

Walker and Company

NEW YORK

First published in the United States of America in 1992
by Walker Publishing Company, Inc.

Published simultaneously in Canada by Thomas Allen & Son
Canada, Limited, Markham, Ontario

Library of Congress Cataloging-in-Publication Data
Cvancara, Alan M.
Exploring nature in winter: a guide to activities, adventures, and projects
for the winter naturalist / Alan M. Cvancara: illustrations by Daniel F. Richards.
    p.   cm. — (The Naturalist's bookshelf)
Includes bibliographical references and index.
ISBN 0-8027-7385-0
1. Natural history—Outdoor books. 2. Winter. I. Title.
II. Series.
QH81 C88   1992
508 — dc20   92-12560
CIP
Book design by Ellen Lavine

Printed in the United States of America
2   4   6   8   10   9   7   5   3   1

As before, now fourthly, to ELLA:
Without whose help and support this book
would not have been completed.

C O N T E N T S

CONTENTS

P R E F A C E

This book is a guide for anyone who wishes to learn more about the natural world during the cold season—whether a winter walker or snowshoer, cross-country skier, winter camper, animal watcher, or armchair naturalist. It focuses on those places that experience tingling cold and receive appreciable snow during winter but is useful elsewhere as well. In North America, "real winter" exists in the northern half of the United States, Canada, and Alaska.

Many winter-related topics are covered in this book. It explains what winter is and how you might learn to like it—if you are among the many who don't. You'll learn about winter weather and how to forecast it. The book delves into the many kinds of ice and snow: for example, rime and frost—two kinds of ice that people often confuse. It gives you useful tips on traveling in winter, in your vehicle or on foot. You'll learn how to recognize plants and animal sign in winter, and how plants and animals adapt to the cold and snow. This book is chock-full of helpful advice on winter activities, including preserving snow crystals,

building snow shelters, winter birding, winter stargazing, winter photography, and winter exploring for nature in your home area and while on winter excursions in open terrain, and woods, and along ponds, lakes, and streams. In addition, you will find a winter survivalist's handbook tucked away as an appendix; this will materially help you should you find yourself in cold-season trouble. Numerous drawings and photographs illustrate the book.

I've used the following conventions in this book. Technical or unique terms, where defined or described, are italicized. Informal pronunciations are given for words likely to be unfamiliar, with the stressed syllables in capitals. Using my difficult-to-pronounce last name, Cvancara, as an example, I would provide you with this aid: SWUHN-shuh-ruh.

Besides my wife, Ella, acknowledged in the dedication, I wish to give special thanks to two persons. Mary Kennan Herbert has guided and materially aided me with this book—as with my previous three. John W. Hoganson assisted me with darkroom photography.

EXPLORING NATURE
IN WINTER

Looking from under an icefall—a frozen waterfall—to the frozen stream below.

ONE

Winter in Perspective

What Is Winter?

If you live in a cooler temperate region, you recognize winter as a time of cold temperatures—often well below freezing for long periods, extreme wind chills, short days, frequent demands on your time for snow removal, slick roads and streets, sloppy entryways, and the logging of more TV hours. You know, too, that it follows autumn and precedes spring. Some residents, experiencing rigorous climates, however, complain of the inequitability of the seasons: "a lot of winter, a little summer, and no spring or autumn!"

As astronomers view it, though, winter in the Northern Hemisphere is a cold season extending from the winter solstice—about December 21—to the vernal equinox. Solstice, from the Latin *solstitium*, meaning "the sun stands still," is one of two days in the year when the sun is farthest from the equator. (Notice *sol*, "sun," in the word *solstice*.) At the winter solstice, the day with the fewest hours of daylight, the sun ceases its apparent south-

ward migration ("stands still"). During this day the sun rises and sets at its most southerly positions. Daylight lengthens after the winter solstice, but days of longer daylight are not really noticeable until mid-January.

Astronomers declare that winter ends at the vernal equinox. Equinox, from the Latin *aequinoctium*, meaning "equal nights," is one of two days of equal daylight and night hours when the sun apparently crosses the equator. The vernal (spring) equinox occurs on about March 21.

The winter explanation holds true only for the Northern Hemisphere. In the Southern Hemisphere the timing of winter is reversed: It extends from the summer solstice (about June 21) to the autumnal equinox (about September 22). Don't forget to pack your long johns if you are planning a trip to temperate Australia in July!

In spite of the astronomers' definition of winter, we may experience winter well beyond their limiting guidelines. Depending on the place, severe cold may rush in during October and November and snow may last into April or

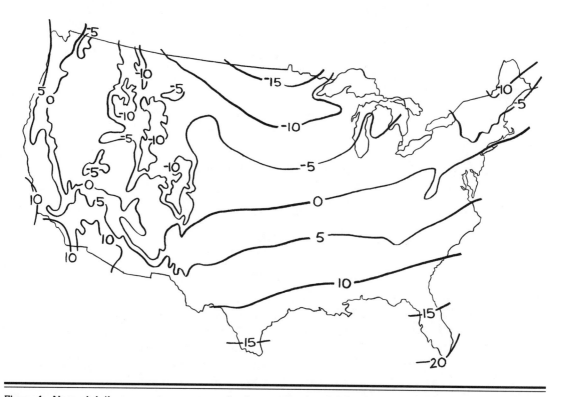

Figure 1. Normal daily average temperatures (in degrees Centigrade) for January in the United States for 1931–1960. (Modified from *Climates of North America*, by R. A. Bryson and F. K. Hare, eds., Amsterdam: Elsevier Publishing Co., 1974, p. 242. Adapted with permission.)

even May. At higher elevations, of course, winter may last even longer.

Marked wintry effects in North America extend throughout Canada and Alaska and engulf about the northern two-thirds of the United States. You can realize this from maps depicting average daily temperatures for January and average snowfalls for the wintry season. January temperatures in the coterminous United States east of the Rocky Mountains regularly decrease northward, with lowest values in northeastern North Dakota and northwestern Minnesota (Figure 1). Temperature values vary irregularly in the western mountains and moderate along the West Coast. In Canada, temperature values show similar patterns as those for the United States—but continue to decrease northward—with lowest temperatures in the north-central part of the country; they moderate, however, along both the eastern and western coasts. Average snowfall in Canada (Figure 2) generally increases from the Canadian Arctic southward to the eastern and western coastal areas, with considerable variation in the western mountains and western coastal areas. In the United States appreciable average snowfall extends across about the northern two-thirds of the nation with heavy concentrations in the northeastern states. Little snowfall occurs along the West Coast and is highly variable—with substantial amounts in places—in the western mountains.

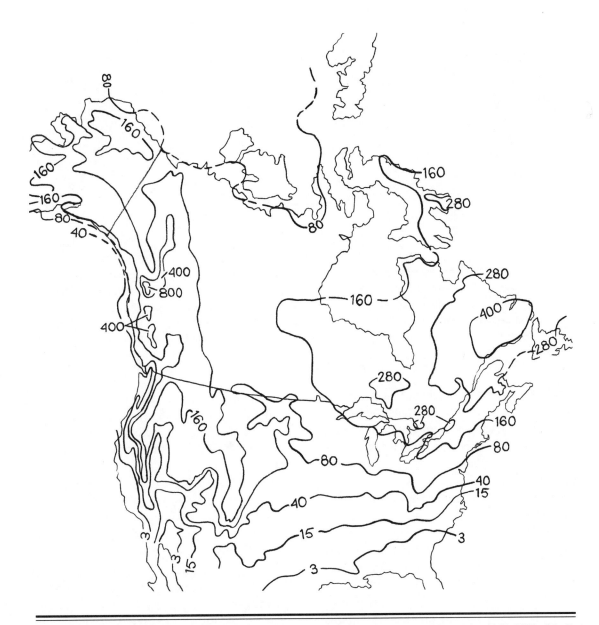

Figure 2. Average annual snowfall (in centimeters) over Canada and the United States for 1941–1970. (Modified from *Handbook of Snow: Principles, Processes, Management, and Use*, by D. M. Gray and D. M. Male, eds., New York: Pergamon Press, 1981, p. 150. Adapted with permission.)

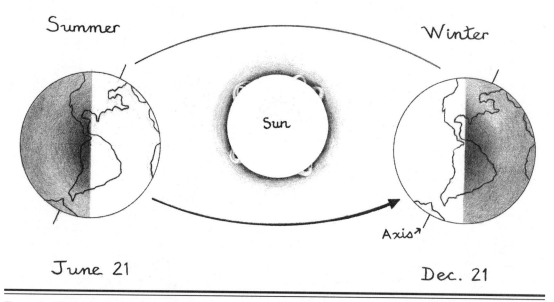

Summer

Winter

Sun

Axis

June 21

Dec. 21

Figure 3. Winter in the Northern Hemisphere. In winter, Earth reaches a position in its orbit around the sun whereby it is tilted on its axis away from the sun; the sun's rays are now slanted and diffused. Winter begins about December 21. In summer, beginning about June 21, Earth's position is opposite to that in winter and the sun's rays are direct. Winter and summer in the Southern Hemisphere are reversed from those seasons in the Northern Hemisphere.

Winter, viewed ecologically, is a time of challenge for animals and plants. Some animals avoid the struggle by migrating to warmer places. Others tough it out by growing warmer coats, napping occasionally, or by hibernating. Plants may die back to their roots, shed leaves, or cut back on their growth, as in the case of evergreen trees. Whatever the stay-at-home tactic, winter for organisms is a time of slower biologic activity, dormancy, or even death. It is a time when an energy deficit occurs—more is expended than is replenished.

Before leaving the question "What is winter?" I feel compelled to point out a human-centered perception of winter. Comparing the stages in a human's lifespan to the seasons, winter is a time of old age culminating irrevocably in death. You may have heard someone say, "I am approaching my winter years"—a time of decline, decay, and adversity. Spring, in this context, is, contrarily, a time of youth accompanied by resurgence and urgency.

Understanding the attributes of winter, let's now delve into its cause. In a word, tilt. That's right, a tilting of Earth on its axis (an imaginary line passing through Earth and the North and South Poles—about 23½ degrees from straight up and down. More correctly, winter ensues not only from Earth's tilting but also from its relative position to the sun as it revolves about that body. (If Earth's axis were at right angles to the plane of its orbit around the sun, we would not experience winter—or spring, summer, or autumn for that matter—anywhere on the Earth.) In winter, then, Earth has reached a position at which the North Pole is tilted away from the sun (Figure 3). (Paradoxically, Earth is closer to the sun in winter than in summer, so the cooling effect of tilt overrides any warming effect of a shorter Earth-sun distance.) The sun's rays reach Earth at a slant or are less focused; consequently, Earth receives less solar energy, or *insolation*, and winter results. Less solar energy is received, too, because of fewer daylight hours. During Northern Hemispheric winter the South Pole is tilted toward the sun, enabling solar energy to be focused on the Southern Hemisphere, which now welcomes summer. A comparison of solar radiation received in the United States during the height of winter (January) and summer (July) is depicted in Figure 4.

Summer, of course, permeates into the North Hemisphere under opposite conditions: Earth attains a position in its path about the sun such that the North Pole is tilted toward this luminous body, whose rays are now direct and received fully. But the Southern Hemisphere, positioned oppositely, receives less direct solar energy and adjusts to the winter season.

Learning to Like Winter

Any of you enthralled by ice skating, skiing, snowshoeing, or snowboarding are already winter world converts. You have accepted the challenge of cold air and snow and readily meet its demands. You put up with a little discomfort for the thrill of a winter sport. Others of you can have fun in the cold season, too, without participating in a winter sport. This book guides you through several non-sport activities that you can enjoy in winter. For winter enjoyment, though, it helps to learn to *like* winter. Let me show you how.

Right off, prepare yourself mentally. Keep an open mind about the cold. Instead of asking "How cold is it?" ask "How warm is it?" If you analyze this perspective further you'll become aware that there is no such thing as cold, only the absence of heat. That is, heat is measurable but cold is not. Realize that discomfort and inconvenience should be expected at times — not only in winter, but equally so during hot summers. The wintry environment will not always be entertaining you. You must mentally meet it part way.

Mental preparedness also includes self-interest. With it, you enter the winter world without hesitation. Self-interest begins with natural curiosity and is cultivated by learning to observe natural features in winter carefully and critically.

Your mind, clicked into a positive mode, must be coupled with suitable clothing for meaningful winter excursions. Cold face, icy fingers, and aching toes cause us to lose interest in our surroundings. We'll examine proper cold-weather attire in the appendix.

Maybe an experiment will help you appreciate how your mind works when your body is stressed, such as from the cold. I'll explain one I've done many times. It deals with kinds of awareness.

J. O. Stevens, in his book *Awareness: Exploring, Experimenting, Experiencing*, recognized three kinds of awareness: awareness of the outside world, awareness of the inside world, and awareness of fantasy. Awareness of the outside world (AO) involves sensory contact with objects and events outside of your body — what you can see, hear, smell, taste, and touch. Awareness of the inside world (AI) deals with sensations inside your body, such as itches, muscular tension and movement, and inner discomfort. Both of these awarenesses take place at the present and are part of reality. Awareness of fantasy (AF) is any mental activity beyond present awarenesses and includes explaining, imagining, interpreting, guessing, thinking, comparing, planning, remembering, and anticipating. Fantasy activity, bear in mind, involves the past or future but not the present. The more you fantasize, the less you fully live the moment.

Now for the experiment. To be meaningful, it must be done alone. And for a good test, allow one to two hours for it. Select a place where you are unlikely to encounter any human for the duration of the experiment. Wildlife refuges and remote sections of parks are good places. If you arrive at a likely spot with a companion, each of you head in opposite directions. It is impractical to take notes while on the trek because of having frequently to remove gloves or mittens and grope for a notebook and pencil. Besides, these interruptions will detract from your assimilating the awarenesses as they come to you. You must, then, concentrate on *remembering* the awarenesses as they appear. Immediately upon your return, list all the awarenesses you've accumulated within three columns in your notebook: AO, AI, and AF.

Let's imagine how an awareness experiment might work. Upon setting out, you notice fox tracks crossing your intended path. Mentally chalk this observation in the AO column. Shortly thereafter, you perceive an ache in your stomach, an item for the AI column. You think, Why did I eat that spicy pizza for lunch? This clearly belongs in the AF column. And on it goes.

As the awareness experiment comes to a close, you might discover that while occupied with one awareness it is difficult or impossible to concentrate on another. If dressed inadequately, preoccupation with cold nose, fingers, and toes markedly hinders your attention for natural features around you. Similarly, devoting much time to fantasizing about the past or future limits your process of observing the real world at the present.

What values lie within these awareness experiments? They aid you in truly *experiencing* objects and events, rather than *imagining* them, and they help you to distinguish between *observation* and *interpretation*. Upon flushing a small bird, you might imagine it to be a chickadee, even though you did not clearly see its distinguishing characters. The honest way to record it is "chickadee?" Later, as the same bird affords you a second look, you might realize it is, in fact, a junco. Analyzing your field notes, you might discover that awareness of fantasy dominates all others. Although fantasizing is useful and healthy, most of us can benefit from increasing our contact with reality and downplaying our commitment to fantasy. For instance, consider the time and mental energy spent in our lives worrying and anguishing about events and situations that never happen. Let's focus more on the *now* and the *real*!

Overall, then, awareness experiments sharpen our senses and elevate our powers of observation through educated use of these senses. Thereby, we gain keen benefits from our winter excursions. And, as an added bonus, we might learn something about ourselves.

Close behind and associated with mental preparedness is physical preparedness. Some kind of regular physical conditioning, accompanied by weight control, is necessary to participate actively in excursions without breathing heavily or perspiring unduly. Whether fit or not, though, be aware not to overexert yourself when on winter excursions, and don't expend more energy than really necessary. Always save some energy in reserve in case you might need it later. Emulate the fox: He tends to

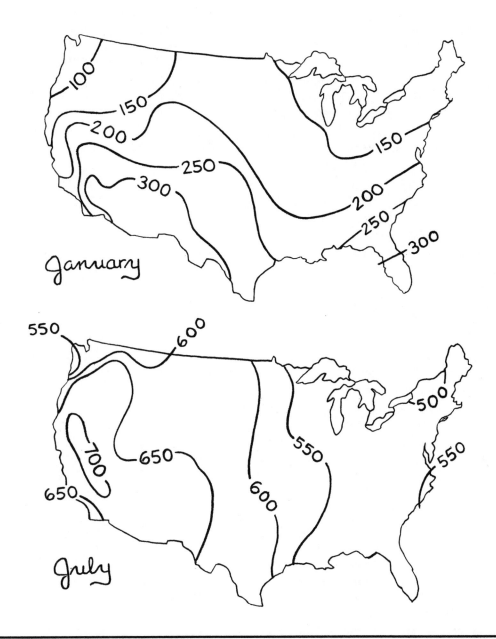

Figure 4. Average solar radiation received in the coterminous United States during January and July. Information for these maps is based on varying periods up to forty-six years in length ending in 1962. (Values are in langleys, or gram calories per centimeter squared.) (Modified from *The National Atlas of the United States of America*, by the United States Geological Survey, Washington, D.C., 1970, p. 93. Adapted with permission.)

move in a straight line—conserving energy, not wandering foolishly about like a dog who can depend on a human for food.

In spite of the cold and snow, winter has something special to offer us. A clean, white snowy blanket is special—a mantle that cloaks everything on which it settles. Unsightly rubbish, ravaged land, and messy yards become equally concealed. Familiar objects assume interesting, subtle forms. The world of white seems to produce an antiseptic state.

On clear days winter provides us a marked crispness and clarity of colors. White-rimed tree branches and twigs stand in marked contrast against blue sky. Reddish fruits, such as those of hawthorns, mountain ash, and roses (rose hips), are beautifully set off against a backdrop of blue or white. Green-needled, snow-shrouded evergreen trees provide a picturesque Christmasy effect. The colorful attire of skiers seems even brighter when placed in direct proximity to snow.

Winter allows us to "walk on water." Now, we can ski or snowshoe freely across streams, lakes, ponds, and marshes. We, literally, can proceed cross-country. Such freedom is incomparable in summer. Those fishing through the ice do so from a stable platform and can ignore the vagaries of a bobbing or drifting boat.

In winter, have you noticed the absence of insect pests? A silly question, perhaps. You need not slap, twitch, scratch, or take on frantic, dancelike behavior provoked by humming or buzzing mosquitoes, flies, and the like. And, even wood ticks can't plague you. Such relief should not be accepted lightly.

And another specialness of winter—it gives you a time to buckle down with a favorite project or study. You can now become fully absorbed with an activity that you've put off too long. The distractions of summer—vacation traveling, grass cutting, house painting—can't bother you. You can concentrate on learning to play the banjo, crocheting an afghan, mastering a new computer program, or whatever pleases and amuses you. Winter allows you the opportunity to expand and rejuvenate your mind.

T W O

Winter Weather and Forecasting It

The blizzard that impressed me the most struck our farm the spring after I had begun elementary school. I was at an impressionable age, to be sure, but I soon realized that this blizzard was impressionable in its own right. This winter fury had all the traits of a full-fledged blizzard—strong winds and cold temperatures accompanied by blowing and drifting snow.

It descended on a Saturday evening—March 15, 1941. This is not an unusual month for blizzards—some of the nastiest winter storms can invade the Northern Plains during March, a time, realistically, of winter-to-spring transition.

This March blizzard was notably devastating. Seventy-two people died from the storm—thirty-eight in North Dakota, twenty-eight in Minnesota, and six in Saskatchewan and Manitoba. Many perished because of poor visibility from the blowing snow. A hired farmhand lost his way while going from the barn to the farmhouse. His body was discovered a mile from the farmstead. A farmer was found standing upright next to a telephone pole—a mere fifty feet from his home. Two teenage girls lost their way in the storm's fury. One of the girls' bodies was draped across a train engine's cowcatcher when it arrived at a railway station. One woman left a stranded car, in which her husband and three children remained, in an attempt to reach a stalled car directly in front of them. Disoriented by the storm, she wandered off-course some three and a half miles—and died within a hundred yards of a farmstead.

At home, I recall the cold, violent, stinging winds and the snowdrifts piling up ten feet or more high. (Reports for this blizzard in the Northern Plains include up to thirty-foot snowdrifts shaped by winds gusting to more than one hundred miles an hour.) A winter storm often is followed by clear skies and plummeting temperatures. This one adhered to the general pattern. And people, after having been isolated by a winter storm, feel a driving desire to

9

resume normal activity in spite of the incapac-
itating cold accompanied by roads and streets
blocked with tightly packed snow.

Especially impressed in my mind is an incident after the blizzard's end.

On Monday morning, I strained for sight of
my "school bus" coming down the snow-
choked county road, about half a mile away
where I would first normally see it. But why
bother, I thought, it surely couldn't fight its
way through all the drifted snow. I must explain that this "school bus" was not of the or-
dinary type—but highly effective, nevertheless.
Devised from sheer need by an ingenious
neighbor, it was, in effect, a heated cabin on
sleigh runners pulled by a team of horses. Inside, we kids were treated to a toasty trip to
school. A small coal burner radiated warmth,
while smoke, vented by a metal chimney, es-
caped through the roof. The driver, inside with
us in solid comfort, held the reins as he
guided the plodding horses while peeping
through a window.

Although the "school bus" was late that
morning, I watched, astonished, as it slowly
appeared. Shortly after its appearance, though,
the "bus" stopped abruptly. I could imagine
the driver attempting to goad his team forward
as they strained vainly to progress a few yards
farther. Finally, it was of no use. The snowdrifts rose up to and beyond the bellies of the
horses. Dejectedly, the driver unhitched the
team, hopped on one horse, guided the other,
and headed home—leaving the "school bus"
in the middle of the road.

Winter weather may be treacherous and
must be approached with caution and respect.
Knowledge of winter weather patterns and
forecasting can be most useful, particularly
during excursions.

Weather Patterns

Main Air Masses

Weather in North America, winter or summer, results from the interplay of three main
moving air masses (Figure 5): cool, moist,
eastward-moving Pacific air; cold, dry, south-
ward-moving Arctic air; and warm, moist,
northward-moving Atlantic air. The Pacific air
becomes warm and dry after it crosses the
Rocky Mountains and loses much of its moisture. Air masses carry with them the temperature and moisture of their place of origin but
are modified by the surfaces over which they
move.

The stability of the air masses affects their
behavior. Those moving over surfaces colder
than themselves are generally stable and result
in steady winds and little precipitation. Conversely, air masses moving over surfaces
warmer than themselves are generally unstable; turbulent, gusty winds ensue, with considerable precipitation.

The three air masses, although clearly iden-
tifiable year-round, behave somewhat differently with the seasons. In winter, the Pacific
air mass extends farther eastward more frequently. This air mass clearly divides into a
northern and a southern part. The less stable
northern part creates cool and wet conditions
along the coasts of northern British Columbia
and southern Alaska throughout the year, but
it is most prominent in winter. The more stable
southern part, on the other hand, produces
warm, dry conditions along the coasts of
southern California and northern Mexico during the year, but it is most prominent in summer. The Arctic air mass in winter is extremely
cold, extends farther southward, and induces

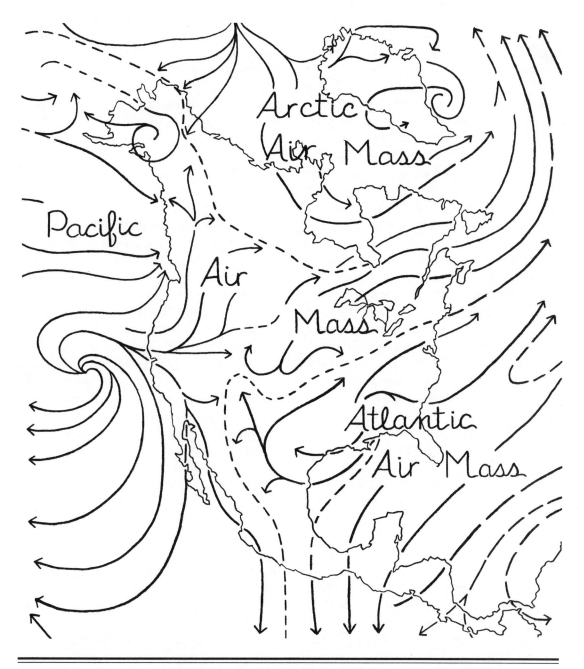

Figure 5. Main air masses in North America and generalized flow lines of surface winds in January. (Modified from *Climates of North America*, Reid A. Bryson and F. Kenneth Hare, eds., Amsterdam: Elsevier Scientific Publishing Company, 1974, p. 8. Adapted with permission.)

stronger air circulation. The Atlantic air mass may bring precipitation when it rises over cold air in winter but, perhaps more important, it brings high humidity and oppressive heat in summer.

Jet streams—high-altitude, meandering belts of high-speed winds exceeding 250 miles per hour—significantly affect winter storm activity in the United States and Canada. Constituting the core of the westerlies, they develop where cold Arctic and warm Gulf air masses converge. New storms tend to originate in the vicinity of jet streams, and old ones are driven eastward by them; jet streams, then, effectively govern storm tracks.

In winter, two jet streams affect the weather in the United States and Canada; they shift their courses not only seasonally but sometimes even daily. In December, the main jet passes from Oregon eastward to Virginia; another, southern jet sweeps from Baja California to central Texas to the Carolinas. In January, the northern jet snakes from southwestern British Columbia to the Great Lakes and the Ohio River Valley; here, it is often joined by a southern jet derived from Mexico and Texas, and the two curve up toward the New Jersey coast. In February, the two jets join similarly in the vicinity of Tennessee, before leaving Virginia in a wake of storms along the Atlantic Coast.

Highs and Lows

General air movements result from air rising or descending. Air rises where heated in regions of low pressure, or *lows*, and descends where cooled in regions of high pressure, or *highs*. Near the equator, a region of low pressure, heated air rises and then slowly drifts toward the poles. At about 30 degrees north the air piles up and creates a high.

Earth's rotation causes any descending airflow to shift to the right in the Northern Hemisphere (but to the left in the Southern Hemisphere); the sinking, northerly airflow twists clockwise to form the westerly winds, whereas that plummeting southerly forms the northeast trade winds. Some of the air piled up at 30 degrees north continues northward, cools, becomes heavier, and settles down near the North Pole to form another high. Upon descending, this air shifts to the right to form the polar easterlies that encounter the opposing westerlies at about 60 degrees latitude.

In the Northern Hemisphere, highs develop mostly over land in winter because land is then colder than water. In North America, highs originate mainly in northwestern Canada and the southwestern United States, and, secondarily, in west-central Quebec and the southern states. In the path of the westerlies, they track toward the east and southeast (Figure 6). Because descending air from highs twists clockwise (in the Northern Hemisphere), northerly winds give way to southerly winds as a high passes eastward. Whether cold region-derived or warm region-derived, highs generally bring fair weather with few or no clouds and little precipitation.

Lows develop mostly over water in the Northern Hemisphere in winter because water is then warmer than the land. In North America, winter lows approach the West Coast and tend to stagnate over the Gulf of Alaska or off Vancouver Island. Other lows materialize, especially east of the Rockies, particularly in Alberta, Colorado, Texas, and along the Gulf Coast, as well as along the Atlantic Coast and west of the Appalachians. Lows migrate easterly, northeasterly, and southeasterly, shoved by highs (Figure 7). Circulation about a low is counterclockwise (Northern Hemisphere), so an eastward-passing low causes southerly

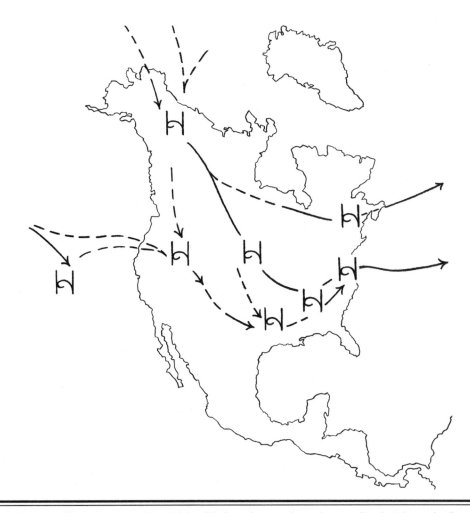

Figure 6. Areas in North America where highs (H) form frequently, and generalized main tracks (heavy lines) of highs. Dashed tracks are relatively unimportant. (Modified from *Climates of North America*, Reid A. Bryson and F. Kenneth Hare, eds., Amsterdam: Elsevier Scientific Publishing Company, 1974, p. 33. Adapted with permission.)

winds to give way to those from the north. Lows bring winter storms, accompanied by rain, freezing rain, or snow, depending on the temperature.

Fronts are the boundaries between two colliding highs of differing temperature. A cold front forms where a cold high displaces a warm high. Where a warm high pushes and climbs over a cold high, a warm front results.

A major front is the Arctic front, formed where warm, Pacific air of the westerlies confronts cold, Arctic air of the polar easterlies. This front, as others, is ever-changing, and may bulge to Florida and beyond in winter. Since lows are sandwiched between highs, a front generally occurs along a low-pressure trough. Fronts are presaged by gathering clouds and stormy and unsettled weather.

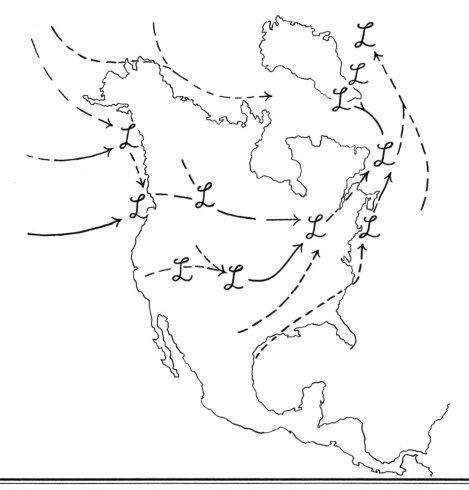

Figure 7. Areas in North America where lows (L) form frequently, and generalized main tracks (heavy lines) of lows. Dashed tracks are relatively unimportant. (Modified from *Climates of North America*, Reid A. Bryson and F. Kenneth Hare, eds., Amsterdam: Elsevier Scientific Publishing Company, 1974, p. 32. Adapted with permission.)

Regional or temporary cold fronts are shown on weather maps as heavy lines with barbs pointing in the direction of movement. They usually orient northeast-southwest and travel southward and eastward at about twenty-five miles per hour. Warm fronts, moving slower at about fifteen miles per hour, are depicted on weather maps by heavy lines with rounded lobes pointing in the direction of their movement. They usually orient north-west-southeast and slip along northward and eastward. When fronts cease moving, they are known as *stationary fronts*. An *occluded front* forms where a cold front overtakes a warm front.

How do you tell when a front is passing through? Perhaps foremost, you will notice that surface winds shift in a clockwise direction, say, from southeast to northwest. Air pressure will drop, followed by a rise, as an eastward-migrating frontal low is followed by a high. Cloudy skies will gradually clear. Finally, a cold front will bring cooler temperatures and a warm front warmer temperatures.

Regional Highlights in the United States

Before delving into regional highlights of winter weather in the United States, you might wish to acquire a quick, overall sense of winter in the nation. To do this, glance back at Figures 1 and 2; gain further perception from a list of lowest recorded temperatures (Table 1).

Pacific Coast Region

The Pacific Coast Region of the United States includes the western parts of Washington, Oregon, and California—the major mountains of the coast ranges with associated broad basins and valleys.

This is the domain of dominantly the Pacific air mass, primarily maritime (ocean-derived) polar air, but some maritime tropical air at the south end. Intrusions of continental (land-derived) polar and tropical air rarely enter this region.

In January, the Pacific subtropical high, a controller of airflow traffic, persists off Baja California. It guides storms, reshaped by a persistent low off the Aleutian Islands, that regularly batter the northern California, Washington, and Oregon coasts. Fronts bring frequent winter rains as far south as Los Angeles—and some induce the notorious mudslides.

Fog accompanies the rain and overcast skies for much of the winter. More important than sea fog in winter, perhaps, is radiation fog, particularly in inland areas of California adjacent to swamps, ponds, and streams. Winter rains produce high humidity; the land, radiating heat at night, chills the moist air to the *dew point*—the temperature at which air is saturated with water vapor or has a relative humidity of 100 percent—and condenses it to a low-lying cloud or fog.

Besides occasional snow, occurring usually at high elevations, periods of freezing temperatures or freezes are not uncommon in the Pacific Coast region. These are especially brought about by easterly winds bearing continental polar air. In November 1955, an early freeze plummeted temperatures to zero degrees Fahrenheit in western Washington and damaged millions of dollars' worth of fruit trees and shrubs. January freezes during 1937 and 1969 devastated truck produce and seriously damaged citrus fruits in Southern California.

Mountain Region

This is the region extending from the Cascade and Sierra Nevada mountains to the eastern front of the Rockies. Mountain peaks exceed 14,000 feet in elevation.

Mountains fix their own special effects upon airflow and weather. Air pushed up the side of a mountain range expands and cools, generally about 5½ degrees Fahrenheit for each 1,000 feet of altitude. When air is cooled to its dew point, clouds form and rain or snow may fall from them. Air that descends on the lee side of a mountain range, on the other hand, is compressed and heated, again at a rate of about 5½ degrees per 1,000 feet; it, therefore,

TABLE 1 Lowest Recorded Temperatures by State Through 1989

State	Temp. (F)	Date	Station	Elevation (Feet)
AL	− 27	01-30-1966	New Market	760
AK	− 80	01-23-1971	Prospect Creek Camp	1,100
AZ	− 40	01-07-1971	Hawley Lake	8,180
AR	− 29	02-13-1905	Pond	1,250
CA	− 45	01-20-1937	Boca	5,532
CO	− 61	02-01-1985	Maybell	5,920
CT	− 32	02-16-1943	Falls Village	585
DE	− 17	01-17-1893	Millsboro	20
DC	− 15	02-11-1899	Washington	112
FL	− 02	02-13-1899	Tallahassee	193
GA	− 17	01-27-1940	CCC Camp F-16	1,000
HI	12	05-17-1979	Mauna Kea	13,770
ID	− 60	01-18-1943	Island Park Dam	6,285
IL	− 35	01-22-1930	Mount Carroll	817
IN	− 35	02-02-1951	Greensburg	954
IA	− 47	01-12-1912	Washta	1,157
KS	− 40	02-13-1905	Lebanon	1,812
KY	− 34	01-28-1963	Cynthiana	684
LA	− 16	02-13-1899	Minden	194
ME	− 48	01-19-1925	Van Buren	510
MD	− 40	01-13-1912	Oakland	2,461
MA	− 35	01-12-1981	Chester	640
MI	− 51	02-09-1934	Vanderbilt	785
MN	− 59	02-16-1903*	Pokegama Dam	1,280
MS	− 19	01-30-1966	Corinth	420
MO	− 40	02-13-1905	Warsaw	700
MT	− 70	01-20-1954	Rogers Pass	5,470
NE	− 47	02-12-1899	Camp Clarke	3,700
NV	− 50	01-08-1937	San Jacinto	5,200
NH	− 46	01-28-1925	Pittsburg	1,575
NJ	− 34	01-05-1904	River Vale	70
NM	− 50	02-01-1951	Gavilan	7,350
NY	− 52	02-18-1979	Old Forge	1,720
NC	− 34	01-21-1985	Mt. Mitchell	6,525
ND	− 60	02-15-1936	Parshall	1,929
OH	− 39	02-10-1899	Milligan	800
OK	− 27	01-18-1930	Watts	958
OR	− 54	02-10-1933	Seneca	4,700
PA	− 42	01-05-1904	Smethport	1,469
RI	− 23	01-11-1942	Kingston	100
SC	− 19	01-21-1985	Caesar's Head	3,100

State	Temp. (F)	Date	Station	Elevation (Feet)
SD	−58	02-17-1936	McIntosh	2,277
TN	−32	12-30-1917	Mountain City	2,471
TX	−23	02-08-1933	Seminole	3,275
UT	−69	02-01-1985	Peter's Sink	8,092
VT	−50	12-30-1933	Bloomfield	915
VA	−30	01-22-1985	Mtn. Lake Bio. Stn.	3,870
WA	−48	12-30-1968	Mazama	2,120
WV	−37	12-30-1917	Lewisburg	2,200
WI	−54	01-24-1922	Danbury	908
WY	−63	02-09-1933	Moran	6,700

*Also on earlier dates at the same or other places in the state.

Source: Adapted from *The World Almanac and Book of Facts 1991*, Mark S. Hoffman, ed., New York: Pharos Book, 1990.

becomes warm and dry. Mountain air may remain on the high plateaus and become cooler or warmer depending on the temperatures there. Protruding mountains also may obstruct the air circulation of highs and lows.

Pacific maritime polar air—dried and warmed after passing over the Cascades or Sierra Nevadas—predominates in the mountainous region. Some continental polar air from the Great Plains and some continental tropical air from central Mexico intermingle; maritime tropical air from the Gulf of California rarely enters the region.

Storms follow two main tracks through the region. The more common northern one enters through the Pacific Northwest and crosses the Rockies through Idaho and Montana. The southern track—less common because the westerlies seldom extend this far south—penetrates Southern California and passes through Arizona and New Mexico and moves on to the Texas Panhandle.

A warm, downslope wind or *chinook* (shuh-NOOK) frequently bathes the region just east of the Rockies—and some intermontane basins—in warmth that is particularly welcome in winter. Chinook, named after a group of Native Americans in Oregon, is the American term for *foehn* (FERN), any warm wind, found worldwide, blowing down the side of a mountain. Well known from Alberta and Montana to eastern Wyoming, Colorado, and northeastern New Mexico, chinooks fringe the Rockies in a belt about 200 to 250 miles wide.

As implied earlier, chinooks, usually blowing from the west or southwest, gain their heat as descending air is compressed. But they also acquire heat when they rise on windward mountain slopes, moisture condenses, and rain or snow falls. Condensing water vapor releases heat to the air—the heat absorbed earlier when water evaporated to form water vapor.

A thirsty chinook, lasting an hour to several days, offers real respite from winter's cold and gobbles up the snow. Temperatures may leap 20 to 40 degrees in ten to fifteen minutes; a record jump of 49 degrees in two minutes took place in Spearfish, South Dakota.

But because of their high speeds chinooks

may do damage as well as provide benefits and may reach velocities of fifty miles an hour or more. In January 1969, a violent chinook struck Boulder, Colorado, at speeds of more than a hundred miles an hour.

Great Plains Region

The Great Plains region extends from the eastern edge of the Rockies to the states bordering the Great Lakes and Gulf of Mexico. It's a relatively flat surface that gradually slopes eastward, from more than 5,000 feet in elevation on the west to about 1,000 feet on the east. Although a region of relatively little relief—few high hills and no mountain ranges—it can generate local storms more severe and more complex than anywhere in the world.

This is a region of several interacting air masses. Modified maritime polar and continental tropical air enters from the mountain region. Continental polar air flows in from Canada, and maritime tropical air sweeps in from the Gulf of Mexico.

Four basic weather situations are possible. The stormiest happens when polar air confronts tropical air. Another results when tropical air rushes north and east, bringing with it rain or snow. If tropical air originates over dry Mexico, little precipitation results. Last, drier Pacific air challenging polar air produces little or no precipitation. More rain or snow falls in the southern plains because the region is closer to moist Gulf air.

Major storm tracks in the Great Plains are essentially extensions of the northern and southern tracks of the mountain region. Intensifying as they loom east from the Rockies, storms pull tropical Gulf air northerly in front of them and polar Arctic air southerly behind them. This region is, of course, a breeding ground for vicious blizzards, the most dramatic and perilous of winter storms.

The National Weather Service issues a blizzard warning when wind speeds of at least thirty-five miles per hour combine with notable falling, blowing, or drifting snow and persistent temperatures of 20 degrees Fahrenheit or lower. A blizzard warning upgrades to a severe blizzard warning when all conditions intensify, especially if wind speeds increase to forty-five miles per hour or more and temperatures drop to 10 degrees or lower. Blizzards generally materialize when cold Arctic air encroaches to the south and east, and warm, tropical Gulf air is forced upward by the cold front between the two air masses.

I began this chapter with a personal account of a Great Plains blizzard. Here are two more examples. The January 11 to 13, 1888, blizzard was the most disastrous known in Montana, the Dakotas, and Minnesota but also brought grief to Wyoming, Nebraska, Kansas, Oklahoma, and Texas. A piercing cold front, originating in Canada, leapt from the Dakotas to Texas in twenty-four hours. Hundreds of pioneers died and thousands of cattle perished; some ranchers lost 90 percent of their stock. Songwriter William Vincent, in his creation "Thirteen Were Saved," immortalized schoolteacher Minnie Freeman, who rescued thirteen schoolchildren during the blizzard. The early season Armistice Day Blizzard of November 11 to 12, 1940, plied a devastating swath from the Dakotas and Nebraska to the Great Lakes. As an Arctic front crept in, winds picked up at fifty miles per hour with gusts to seventy miles per hour or more. One hundred forty-four persons died; more than seventy of that number succumbed as two large grain-carrying ships sank on gale-swept Lake Michigan. Property damage exceeded six million dollars.

Great Lakes Region

The Great Lakes region generally includes the states abutting the Great Lakes. Toward the east and south, this region merges with the Eastern Seaboard and Gulf region.

During much of the year, continental polar (Arctic) air and maritime tropical (Gulf) air vie for control over the Great Lakes; in winter, though, the polar air wins hands down, as if met by an inadequate challenger. Mild, maritime polar (Pacific) air occasionally intervenes between the two competing air masses, but only when high-altitude westerlies blow due east.

Storm tracks tend to converge upon the Great Lakes from the west. Only those tracks directly affecting the Gulf area and the Eastern Seaboard detour this region. The Great Lakes tend to encourage storms in the winter and fall and stifle them—with the development of highs—in the summer and spring.

All the Great Lakes except Lake Erie remain partly open or free of ice during winter, so they exert an influence upon the regional weather. Here's how the process works.

Water retains heat and cold longer than the land, so it is more sluggish in its response to temperature changes. The Great Lakes, therefore, tend to retain summer's warmth in winter (and winter's cold in summer). As winter wears on, the Great Lakes release summer's heat to the air. The warm, moist, unstable air—carried eastward by cold, polar air—strikes the eastern lake shores, rises because of hills, and dumps large amounts of snow. The "lake effect" causes the characteristic snowbelts on the eastern sides of the Great Lakes (see Figure 2), in accumulations of more than ten feet here annually—and three or four times more than that received elsewhere in the region.

Gulf Region

The Gulf region includes those states, or parts of them, that fringe the Gulf of Mexico or are near it.

As might be expected, maritime tropical air from the Gulf—part of the major Atlantic air mass—dominates this region. Less frequent continental polar air drives in from the Arctic and may make the tundra-to-bayou trip in a few days. South of the warm-air-mass–cold-air-mass front, conditions are mild and showery; north of the front, fog, drizzle, ice pellets, and snow are all possible. Occasionally, Pacific maritime and continental tropical air enters the Gulf region. Interaction with the other air masses already there may cause severe thunderstorms and tornadoes in late winter and early spring.

For much of the year major storm tracks pass northward of the Gulf region. In late fall, winter, and early spring, though, storm tracks proceed along or near the coastline and continue their journey northeasterly toward the Atlantic Coast or the Great Lakes.

Ice storms pose an insidious winter hazard when temperatures hover at or near freezing. They result when substantial amounts of *freezing rain* fall upon the ground; water droplets from an overlying, above-freezing air layer strike a below-freezing air layer at the ground surface. Upon impact or just after, everything becomes coated with an ice glaze: roads, streets, sidewalks, power lines and poles, buildings, trees, crops, and livestock. Most often the ice glaze is thin to about an inch thick; but ice coatings up to eight inches in diameter stuck to wires in northern Idaho in January 1961. Slick surfaces bring about human and livestock injuries and deaths, and the heavy ice coatings—especially when accompanied by stiff winds—cause trees and power lines to snap. Frozen raindrops or ice pellets may also fall during ice storms.

Most ice storms prevail in a broad band from the southern Great Plains to the Great Lakes and east to the Middle Atlantic and New England states. But ice storms are particularly damaging in the Gulf region, where life and man-made constructions are unadapted to withstand them. The most damaging in the United States took place from January 28 to February 1, 1951, within a large area from Texas to Alabama to West Virginia, but effects were most severe in the northern parts of the Gulf states and across Tennessee. Ice, up to four inches thick, coated objects, and about four inches of snow covered the ice. Damage costs approached a hundred million dollars. At least twenty-five people died from the storm and hundreds were injured.

Snow, of course, falls in the Gulf region but is a relative rarity. The unusual snowstorm of February 14 to 15, 1895, dropped about fifteen inches on Galveston, Texas, and twenty inches on Houston. This same storm left twenty-four inches at Rayne Parish in western Louisiana, more than eight inches at New Orleans, and three inches at Pensacola in extreme northwestern Florida. The greatest snowstorm in Florida, on February 12 to 13, 1899, brought measurable snow as far south as Tampa on the west coast. But the snowfall of January 18 to 19, 1977, delivered a trace of snow clear to Homestead—at the southern tip of the Florida peninsula.

Freezes have been damaging to the Gulf region, particularly in Florida. One enshrouded essentially the entire peninsula during the January snowfall of 1977. Two others, in December of 1957 and 1962, destroyed millions of dollars' worth of Florida's citrus and other crops.

Eastern Seaboard

The Eastern Seaboard, as delineated here, reaches from the crest of the Appalachian Mountains eastward to the Atlantic Coast. It merges with the Great Lakes and Gulf regions to the west and south.

Three main air masses concoct the weather of the Eastern Seaboard. Maritime tropical air approaches from the southeast or southwest. When from the southeast—the same that primarily affects the Gulf region—some of the rainiest or snowiest weather ensues; the warm, moist air releases its moisture as it journeys over cool air at the surface. Continental polar air arrives along two routes—that blowing above Quebec is colder, drier, more stable, and brings clear skies; that over the Great Lakes is warmer, moister, more unstable, and produces cloudy skies. Atlantic maritime air has traits similar to that from the Great Lakes: cool and damp. It originates from the cold water and ice floes of the North Atlantic and largely contributes to the northeasterly derived storms that pound the Eastern Seaboard, notably in winter. It, too, usually brings gray skies and rain for most of the year. Besides the three main air masses, highly modified Pacific maritime air occasionally drifts into the region.

Two main storm tracks dominate the Eastern Seaboard, both moving northeasterly: one along the St. Lawrence Valley moving from the Great Lakes region, the other passing along the Atlantic Coast. In winter, storms from the St. Lawrence and Atlantic tracks may alternate, and Atlantic snow may thaw from a St. Lawrence-produced melt. The St. Lawrence track may, itself, bring alternating thaws and cold spells as maritime tropical air and continental polar air jockey for dominance. Such alternating freezing and thawing makes it difficult, especially, for plants to adjust and cope with wintry cold.

The Appalachian Mountains, although only some 2,000 to 6,000 feet high, constitute a barrier to the flow of air. They, consequently, inhibit the encroachment of cold, continental polar air, and spare areas to the east and south of the mountains of some of the worst winter weather. But the mountains also retard the eastward flow of some warm air that bathes the Midwest in the spring. In the New England area, mountains prompt the release of rain and snow as Atlantic maritime air penetrating from the northeast rises toward them.

Ice storms, heavy snowfalls, and blizzards are all part of Eastern Seaboard winters. A singular blizzard, that of March 11 to 14, 1888, will illustrate the extent of winter's severity in this region. (Recall that a severe blizzard lashed the Great Plains in January of the same year.)

On March 10, temperatures were surprisingly warm. Long Island farmers were planting potatoes. Fair weather was predicted throughout the Atlantic states.

A low-pressure trough, though, was surging toward the Eastern Seaboard at 600 miles a day. It jettisoned snow in Kentucky and Tennessee on its way and brought near-freezing temperatures to Georgia. But weather people didn't believe a serious storm would threaten the Atlantic Coast.

The wintry onslaught, however, quickly arrived, and many of its effects were recorded in New York City. Freezing rain pelleted the city on Sunday, March 11, causing slick streets and the downing of telegraph and telephone lines laden with ice. Ten inches of snow fell by Monday morning, accompanied by strong, gusty winds, some of which actually blew trolleys over. Electric power eventually failed and traffic stopped.

More severe weather, in fact, struck elsewhere than in New York City. New Haven, Con-necticut, registered a record snowfall of 44.7 inches, more than twice that in Manhattan. Similar high snowfalls were common over New England. The highest snowdrift—fifty-two feet—formed at the southwest tip of Long Island at Gravesend. Southwest of New Bedford, Massachusetts, gales whipped coastal waters and wrecked some 200 ships; many glaze-coated mariners slipped down with their ships.

In the aftermath of the eastern 1888 blizzard, an exact tally of the persons who died was not possible. But it may have been about 400.

Before leaving the Eastern Seaboard, I must mention a winter weather-related observance that involves an animal and folklore. I'll give you a hint: It happens in February. You probably guessed it—Groundhog Day, February 2. Its roots trace to the practice of Germans in Europe relying on the behavior of a hibernating badger or bear in predicting the remainder of winter. Upon their arrival to America, they relied on the groundhog or woodchuck, which is really a kind of marmot, to enlighten them of the severity of winter's final weeks. Tradition follows that if the day dawns clear and the groundhog sees its shadow, six more weeks of winter will ensue; if not, an early spring can be expected. One town in west-central Pennsylvania, Punxsutawney (PUNGK-suh-taw-knee), has capitalized on the local event, publicized by the town's chamber of commerce and the news media.

Forecasting

From Winds

Remembering that highs bring fair weather and lows convey stormy weather, it helps to know where they are in order to begin the process of weather forecasting. You can determine this from wind direction. Directing your back to the wind, the high should be to your right and an associated low to your left—in the Northern Hemisphere. But air whirling around highs and lows is hindered somewhat by friction with the ground surface. You must, therefore, correct for this. Stretch your arms outward at right angles to your body and rotate about 45 degrees to the right. Now, your right and left arms will closely point toward a high and low in the vicinity. This method can be applied only to regional winds. Don't be fooled by variably directed daily and nightly mountain valley breezes, onshore and offshore winds, or winds deflected by hills or mountains.

Once you know the location of a high or low, you are on your way to basic weather forecasting by recalling one fact: Highs and lows generally move easterly, driven by high-altitude westerlies. So, expect any highs or lows to the west to pass over you, whereas ignore those to the east, since they have already gone by. If you infer a low to the south, though, watch out; it may migrate northeast—and skirt close to you—rather than straight east and away.

Finely tune the use of wind direction—and its changing behavior—and forecasting becomes more reliable. Easterly winds—from the southeast, east, and northeast—tend to convey cloudy skies and likely rain or snow, especially when they systematically shift counterclockwise and are known as backing winds. (A meaningful shift in wind direction would be 45 degrees in six hours.) Such a pattern in wind behavior would result from an eastward-moving low, drawing moist, Atlantic air from the south in advance of itself. Westerly winds—southwest, west, and northwest—gen-

erally bear clear, dry weather, particularly if they shift clockwise as veering winds about a passing high. Such winds transport cool to warm, dry, Pacific air (if well inland from the West Coast) or cold, dry, Arctic air. If winds remain steady or the air is calm, assume that the same weather you have been experiencing will continue. Winds directly from the north or south usually bear little or no rain or snow.

From Clouds

Clouds are simply suspensions of water droplets or ice crystals. Those at or near the ground are known as fog. Generally, the darker the cloud, the more moisture it will carry.

Meteorologists recognize four basic cloud types: cumulus, stratus, cirrus, and nimbus, all with descriptive Latin names. *Cumulus* (meaning heap) are puffy clouds with flat bases that form from rising currents of unstable air. *Stratus* (literally, cover or layer) clouds are sheetlike, formed of stable air that rises little or not at all. *Cirrus* (meaning curl or tuft) are thin, wispy clouds. *Nimbus* (meaning rain cloud or storm) are the main rain-producing clouds.

Clouds are further classified by altitude. High clouds have their bases at about 20,000 to 40,000 feet (at latitudes of 30 to 60 degrees). They are made up of ice crystals and include cirrus, cirrocumulus, and cirrostratus clouds. The rare cirrocumulus often form wavelike or rippled masses or occur as small puffs. Cirrostratus clouds appear as gauzelike veils that develop halos as the sun or moon shines through.

A particularly fascinating halo occasionally seen in winter about the sun is the *sundog, mock sun,* or technically, *parhelion* (par-HEE-lee-uhn) (from the Greek *para-,* "beside," plus *helios,* "sun"). Sundogs (Figure 8) are actually

Figure 8. Sun and sundogs, bright arcs flanking the sun, cast long shadows from a lath snow fence in late winter.

TABLE 2 Basic Weather Forecasting for the Winter Traveler (North America)

Forecast	Weather Clues	Explanation
Snow (or rain)	1. Wind from east, southeast, or northeast and/or shifts counterclockwise. 2. Clouds thicken and bases lower. 3. Earth odors pronounced. 4. Lack of frost in morning.	1. Advancing low draws warm, moist air that condenses. 2. Approaching low or front. 3. Approaching low or within it. 4. Evening front-associated clouds hold heat and prevent condensation.
Dry	1. Wind from southwest, west, or northwest, or shifts clockwise. 2. Clear or scattered clouds or clouds break and bases rise. 3. Earth odors not pronounced. 4. Frost in morning.	1. Passing high or front. 2. Passing high or front. 3. Approaching high or within it. 4. Relatively clear evening sky allows air to rise and moisture to condense.
Colder	1. Wind shift to north or northwest. 2. Passage of cold front.	1. Northerly air generally colder. 2. Air behind cold front colder.
Warmer	1. Wind shift to west, southwest, or south. 2. Passage of warm front.	1. Westerly or southerly air generally warmer. 2. Air behind warm front warmer.

bright spots or arcs to the left and right of the sun, whitish or with colors of the spectrum, ranging from reddish closest to the sun to bluish farther away. They form as the sun's rays bend about 22 degrees as they pass through ice crystals; the bending produces vertically oriented, 22-degree sundog arcs that result because most of the ice crystals are oriented vertically. The sundogs intersect the parhelic circle, a white, horizontal band that passes through the sun.

Middle clouds have their bases at about 6,000 to 20,000 feet and, being lower, are composed mostly of water droplets. Altostratus clouds appear as dense veils, resembling frosted glass, but do not produce halos as do cirrostratus clouds. Altocumulus are larger than cirrocumulus clouds.

Low clouds, with bases below about 6,000 feet and made up of water droplets, include cumulus, stratus, and nimbus types and their combinations. Most rain or snow ensues from these. Nimbostratus produce the most precipitation, followed by cumulonimbus (showery) and stratus (drizzly) clouds.

Clouds assemble along fronts—remember, the boundaries between air masses of differing temperature. A cold front, where cold, unstable air forces warm, unstable air upward and outward, is evidenced by cumulus-type clouds; they grade from higher to lower and gradually concentrate as the front approaches. So, generally expect a progression of cirrocumulus, altocumulus, cumulus, and possibly cumulonimbus clouds. Any precipitation tends to be showery and intermittent.

With a warm front, warm air glides up over cold air. If the warm air is stable, expect the front to be preceded, hundreds of miles in advance, by this progression of high-to-low clouds: cirrus, cirrostratus, altostratus, and stratus or nimbostratus. With the thickening and lowering of clouds, precipitation may occur and tends to be continuous, not intermittent as with a cold front. If rather unstable air advances, some cumulus-type clouds may replace stratus-type clouds and intermingle with them. Intermittent precipitation then tends to alternate with continuous precipitation.

By Combining Winds, Clouds, and Anything Else

Now, let's put it all together, remembering that we are attempting forecasts in North America within latitudes of 30 to 60 degrees. Our four forecasting choices will be snow (or rain), dry, cooler, and warmer (Table 2).

Expect snow (or rain) with easterly winds, especially when associated with clouds that gradually amass, descend, and—especially—darken. Winds from the east, southeast, or northeast would place a low to the southwest, west, or south, and it would pass near or over you, pushed by the westerlies. The passing low would be confirmed by a counterclockwise shifting of the winds. Air pressure would drop with the oncoming low, possibly evidenced, in part, also by earth odors becoming more pronounced.

Dry weather identifies with westerly winds, especially if accompanied by clear skies or only scattered clouds. Winds shifting clockwise announce a passing front, with any clouds dissipating, and drier conditions. Cumulus clouds indicate dry weather unless they develop into cumulonimbus clouds. Cirrus clouds also relate to dryness; but if they thicken and lead a progression of lowering and amassing dark clouds, watch out. Morning frost, the winter equivalent of dew, suggests a dry day if other weather signs agree. Northerly and southerly winds tend also to bring dry weather or, at the worst, insignificant precipitation unless associated with nimbostratus clouds.

Cooler or warmer weather results from the type or source of the incoming air. Northerly winds bring the coldest weather because they haul in cold, Arctic air. Except for the extreme West, the coldest winds actually hail from the northwest. Southerly and westerly winds convey warm air from the Atlantic air mass and relatively warm air from the Pacific air mass, particularly if you are east of the mountain region. Recall that air descending from mountain crests becomes warmer, particularly that sinking along the eastern front of the Rockies. Look for the telltale cloud progressions that portend approaching cold or warm fronts. And expect temperatures to drop or fall as cold or warm fronts pass through. Remember, too, that a clockwise wind shift indicates a passing front.

You now have enough knowledge to make some meaningful weather predictions while on winter excursions. Sharpen your forecasting skills by checking your predictions against daily television and newspaper weather predictor maps and the actual weather outcomes; a barometer will better enable you to do this. At times, you may need to rely heavily on your own predictions.

THREE

Ice and Snow

Many of us tend to perceive ice and snow, the tangible stuff of winter, as a nemesis. We slip on ice, scrape it, break it. Snow, we shovel (or blow with a snowblower), and drive and trudge through it. At times, we might curse both. Many of us, however, appreciate ice and snow as wonderful materials on which to skate, ski, snowshoe, or snowboard. Besides a source of recreation, these solid forms of water serve as fascinating natural materials to learn about in their own right.

This chapter examines the kinds of ice and snow, their traits, and how they may change with time. But first, what is the difference between the two?

Ice Versus Snow

Ice, or frozen water, can be viewed as a mineral or a rock. As a mineral, made up of the elements hydrogen and oxygen, it is an oxide of hydrogen or a hydride of oxygen. Pure ice may be colorless, white, or pale blue when found in large masses. It is, of course, crystalline, as are most minerals, crystallizing with a sixfold or hexagonal system of symmetry. The word *crystal*, by the way, is derived from the Greek *krystallos*, meaning "clear ice." The Greeks believed that clear crystals of the mineral quartz were, in fact, petrified ice. Ice, of course, is less dense than water and so floats in it. When ice forms, it expands about 9 percent in volume and exerts an outward pressure of about 138 tons per square foot.

Rocks are made up of minerals, and so ice can be regarded as a rock as well, consisting of the single mineral ice. The rock, ice, may contain several impurities in the form of dust, various salts, and inclusions of liquid or gases. The ice of glaciers is impure and breaks or bends like many rocks, depending on the pressure imposed on it. Glacial ice breaks along *crevasses* near a glacier's surface where it is under little or no pressure, and bends and flows at depths closer to a glacier's base where high pressure exists.

Snow relates directly to ice in that it is made up of ice crystals. It is, in reality, a porous form of ice, with much pore space filled with air, but this lessens as the snow ages. Snow results from the direct freezing of water vapor in the air—not by the freezing of liquid water.

Kinds of Ice and How They Form

We can place the kinds of ice within three groups: water-body ice, land-derived ice, and air-derived ice. Water-body ice includes sea ice, lake ice, and stream ice, formed by water freezing in each of these water bodies. *Candle ice* results from the disintegrating or "rotting" of sea, lake, or stream ice. It's made up of large ice crystals oriented at right angles to the ice cover; these crystals separate and tinkle as the ice cover breaks up as it melts. The crystals may be equal in length to the thickness of the ice cover before its deterioration. *Fast ice* is the name given to ice, broken or not, that is attached to the shore, beached, stranded in shallow water, or anchored to the bottom of a water body. *Pack ice* or an *ice floe* (FLOW) is any sheet of floating ice other than fast ice; it may be amassed of pieces driven together by wind and currents. Icebergs are large, floating masses of ice in the sea or in lakes with an appreciable vertical dimension, usually about two-thirds to nine-tenths of which is below the water's surface. Icebergs form as ice breaks off, or calves, from glaciers entering the sea.

Dominant among land-derived ice is glacial ice. *Glaciers* (from the Latin *glacies*, meaning "ice") are thick masses of ice moving now or having moved in the past. Some are confined to and move down mountain valleys, others are unconfined and move radially outward from a regionally thickened mass. Glacial ice forms in places where more snow accumulates than melts each year. In time, pressure from the weight of accumulated snow and recrystallization convert snow into glacial ice. Points of snow crystals melt from the pressure and water freezes and recrystallizes in intervening spaces subjected to less pressure. Gradually, snowflakes transform into tiny grains that make up granular ice called *firn* (FERN) or *neve* (nay-VAY) (from the Latin *nix* for "snow"), another kind of land-derived ice. (Firn is also found in old snowbanks remaining during late winter or earliest spring.) Additional pressure and recrystallization produce dense, glacial ice made up of interlocking ice crystals with nonconnecting pores. The transformed product is essentially a metamorphic rock. ("Metamorphic" is a term borrowed from geology that means "changed form." A metamorphic rock has been created from some other rock by an increase in heat and pressure.) Such a transformation, from snow to glacial ice, may take a year to tens of years, depending on the climate.

Glacial ice behaves as a brittle material in the upper 100 to 200 feet of a glacier where crevasses form. But deeper, glacial ice is a yielding, plastic material and flows—like an extremely thick, heavy fluid. Flowage is evident by flow lines of rock debris, easily seen on aerial photographs, and by bends or folds in the ice, obvious at the snouts of glaciers.

Icicles, hanging spikes of ice, are another form of land-derived ice. Created by the freezing of dripping water, ice crystals radiate about their long axes.

Air-derived ice, falling from the sky, occurs as several types. *Glaze* (from the Middle English *glas*, meaning "glass") is usually a coating of clear, slick ice on the ground or on objects on the ground; it may also sheet flying aircraft. I mentioned in chapter 2 that accumulations up to eight inches in diameter have been seen layering wires. Glaze results when drops of freezing rain or drizzle, supercooled to below 32 degrees Fahrenheit, freeze upon impact with any cold object. A temperature inversion, with warm, moist air overlying a thin, colder air layer below, provides the right conditions for glaze formation.

Rime is a white, usually opaque (but sometimes clear) coating of grainy ice particles collecting on the windward sides of objects on the ground as well as on flying aircraft. It may appear tufty or feathery. Rime's opacity results from trapped air. Similarly formed as glaze, rime originates as tiny water droplets impact a cold object. Rime differs from glaze by being usually white, less dense, and by forming only on the windward side of objects. Sometimes, rime and glaze may form together or at least during the same ice-coating event.

Some people confuse sleet with glaze. Sleet, in the purest sense, consists of generally clear ice pellets, usually of frozen raindrops; the raindrops fall through a thick, below-freezing layer of air near the ground surface. It can form, too, by the refreezing of melted snowflakes. The British consider sleet to be a mixture of snow and rain dropped at the same time.

Both glaze and sleet may form during ice storms, mentioned in chapter 2; in fact, both may occur at different times during the same ice storm. Some call an ice storm a "silver thaw."

Hail refers to balls or irregular lumps of ice, also called hailstones. They are layered in ringlike fashion internally, sometimes with an onionlike layering of alternating layers of clear and white, air-trapped ice. Hailstones form mainly as ice pellets (frozen raindrops) are forced upward by strong, vertical air currents. They grow as supercooled water vapor is condensed around them, in the middle and upper parts of thunderclouds, or what technically are called cumulonimbus clouds.

Hailstones may be pea- to grapefruit-sized. Presumably the largest, recorded at Coffeyville in southeastern Kansas in September 1970, measured seventeen inches in circumference and weighed 1.67 pounds. Large or small, hailstones may injure or kill humans and animals and seriously damage crops.

Two hailstorms stand out in my mind. One struck when, as a young man, I drove a large tractor pulling a cultivator in a field several miles from home. With no protective cover in sight, my only recourse was to seek shelter beneath the large tractor. Marble-sized hailstones pinged off the metal parts, but I later emerged unscathed, except for a few stings from the tiny ricocheting missiles. Another hailstorm caught me while hiking in rough terrain with my young son. I noticed the light gray, massive, possibly hail-bearing cloud for some time and mentally noted likely hail shelters. Just before the storm's tumult, we slipped into a shallow cavity in limestone where we found adequate protection. After the storm's passage, we felt the marble-sized hailstones crunch on the trail under our boots. Later that day, my wife and I discovered piles or drifts of hailstones against buildings and in road ditches. In need of ice, we gratefully stuffed our ice chest with the conveniently sized ice pellets delivered to us from the sky.

Hailstorms usually develop during the warmer months, but, in some places, they may occur in winter. "Hail Alley" or the "Hail Belt," the region of most hailstorms, stretches along the High Plains east of the Rockies, from Alberta to New Mexico and Texas.

Frost, hoar, or *hoarfrost* is a thin covering of ice crystals on objects and on the ground, and is the winter equivalent of dew. (People often confuse frost with rime.) But it is not frozen dew. Objects and the ground radiate heat at night and may become cooler than the air, particularly on clear nights. If the night air is humid and its temperature falls below the dew point, the water vapor will condense as dew on all cold surfaces. (The "sweat" on the glass of a cold drink in summer is dew, produced as water vapor in the warm air condenses on the cold glass's surface.) Frost forms like dew, usually during clear nights, at below-freezing temperatures. When frost forms, water vapor changes directly to ice without condensing into water drops first.

Frost is of two main types: columnar frost and tabular frost. *Columnar frost* consists of hollow, roughly six-sided columns that are layered or stepped. It often appears as tiny columns jutting out at right angles from blades of grass or twigs. Columnar frost tends to form relatively rapidly at temperatures not much below freezing when the air holds ample moisture. Frosts of spring and autumn are usually of this type. *Tabular frost* is of flat, six-sided plates or flakelike crystals. It forms rather slowly, at temperatures of about 15 degrees and below and when little moisture exists in the air. Tabular frost generally appears during midwinter. Look especially for clusters of tabular, fernlike frost crystals adorning the ice of frozen streams and ponds.

Some other frost types, or variations of the two basic ones, form frequently enough to snatch our attention. On windowpanes we see the intricate artistry of Jack Frost, patterns resembling feathers, ferns, seaweeds, flowers, stars, and the like. Such variety results from swirling air currents, irregularities in the glass, dust particles, and the melting and refreezing

(recrystallization) of ice crystals. At or near the base of thin snowpacks in cold climates is *depth hoar,* often of cuplike or columnar crystals. Its lubricating effect tends to be a major cause of avalanches. As a parallel term, frost at the surface is sometimes called *surface hoar.* Frost lining crevasses on glaciers may be called *crevasse hoar.*

One last point about frost. You've no doubt heard of a "killing frost." It refers not to a type of frost, of course, but to a drop in temperature cold enough to kill all but the hardiest plants.

Snow Occurrences and Their Formation

Accumulations of snow are made up of millions of snow crystals. (Near the beginning of this chapter I said snow is made up of ice crystals; this is not necessarily contradictory. Snow, porous ice, can be said to consist of snow crystals as well as ice crystals.) Before looking at the accumulations, though, let's examine the crystals—the basic units: how they're classified and how they form.

A simple classification of falling snow crystals, the International Classification for Snow (Figure 9), includes eight main categories, excluding ice pellets and hail that we already considered as kinds of air-derived ice. These are plates, stellar crystals, columns, needles, spatial dendrites, capped columns, irregular crystals, and graupel. Before elaborating on them, recall that familiar snow crystals bear shapes that reflect a six-sided or hexagonal symmetry. In the basic plane of symmetry, each of three crystal axes is separated by an angle of 60 degrees from the next. Keep in mind how this symmetry is reflected in each of the snow crystal types.

Plates are flat, six-sided crystals—rarely three-sided—with no obvious projections. Although uncommon, they are usually well formed and readily reflect light off of their flat surfaces.

Stellar (starlike) *crystals*, of usually six—but also three or twelve—projecting rays, arms, or branches extending from the center, bring to mind those crystals we usually perceive as most typical. In actuality, they make up only a small percentage of crystals in a snowstorm. Stellar crystals occur frequently with plates.

Columns are six-sided columns, solid or hollow, with flat or pointed ends. They have grown more along a fourth crystal axis that is at right angles to the basic plane of symmetry. Columns, too, are found infrequently.

Needles can be thought of as skinny columns that may end in sharp points. These crystals are extremely common and make up the bulk of the crystals in a snowstorm. Snow predominantly of needles tends to avalanche easily.

Spatial dendrites represent a variation of stellar crystals. *Dendrite* means "branch" and *spatial* means "pertaining to space"; so fernlike branches or arms of spatial dendrites extend into various directions in space rather than along a single plane.

Capped columns are easy to recognize. They are simply columns terminated by plates at either end or at intermediate places.

Irregular crystals exhibit little or no six-part symmetry. They tend to be common in snowfalls. You assign crystals to this type when others don't fit, essentially a miscellaneous catchall type.

Graupel (GROU—as in ouch—puhl) refers to snow crystals, usually plates or stellar crystals, completely covered by rime. They appear as grainy snow pellets that display little or no trace of the original crystal. Graupel bounces upon impacting hard objects but not as obviously as sleet does. Some call graupel "soft hail." Graupel fall tends to be showery and short-lived.

Size varies considerably among the crystal groups. Stellar crystals, up to about one-half inch across, tend to attain the largest size, followed roughly by plates, spatial dendrites, capped columns, needles, columns, irregular crystals, and graupel.

Numerous variations of the eight types of snow crystals occur. Should you become really serious about snow crystals, you may require a much more elaborate classification, such as the one published by C. Magono and C. Lee in 1966 (see Selected Readings for a complete reference). It recognizes eighty types or variations of snow crystals.

How do snow crystals form? First, basic conditions must usually be met: supersaturated air at a temperature below freezing, containing dust particles or minute crystals of sea salt. Clouds form as water vapor in the supersaturated air condenses. The dust or minute salt crystals serve as nuclei about which water vapor crystallizes to create snow. At a cloud temperature of about 23 degrees Fahrenheit the nuclei begin to form tiny ice crystals; they will continue to grow if within air supersaturated with water vapor. When large enough, they succumb to gravity and fall to the earth.

The temperature at which a crystal grows governs its basic shape, and the degree to which air is supersaturated affects a crystal's rate of growth and its secondary features. In general, crystals grow larger and faster under conditions of higher temperatures and a good supply of water vapor and grow smaller and slower where lower temperatures and little water vapor exist. Here are some examples of how crystal types relate to temperature: Thin plates predominate at temperatures of 32 to 25

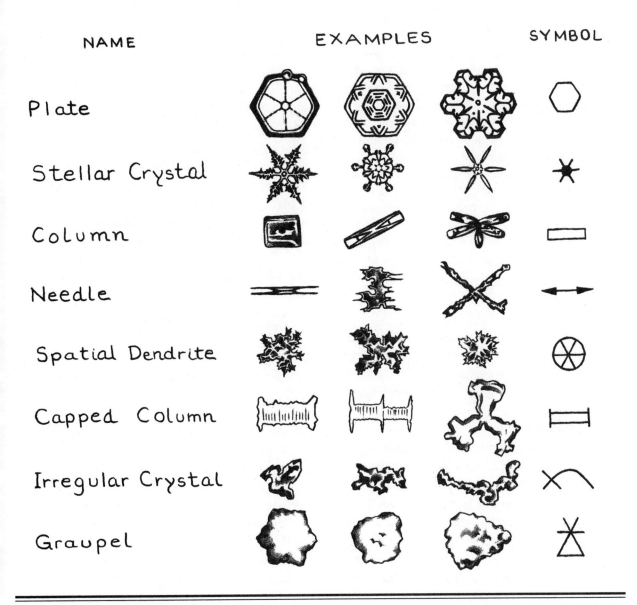

NAME	EXAMPLES			SYMBOL

Figure 9. A simple classification of falling snow crystals. (Modified from National Research Council of Canada Technical Memorandum No. 31, 1954.)

degrees Fahrenheit; columns and needles at 25 to 14 degrees; thick plates and stellar crystals at 14 to −4 degrees; and hollow needles and hollow columns at −4 to −31 degrees.

Crystals may modify considerably as they fall through clouds. Sometimes they become variably covered with rime. This happens when they fall through a cloud of supercooled water droplets. Coated with thin veneers of rime, snow crystals usually can still be readily recognized; totally covered with rime, they convert to graupel. Fewer rimed crystals tend to form within cold, continental climates. As snow crystals fall and collide they tend to gather into clusters or snowflakes—of two to several hundred crystals—up to about two inches across; the largest form at temperatures near 32 degrees Fahrenheit. Stellar crystals

cluster more readily than other types as their branches interlock. As stellar crystals, particularly, fall, turbulent air currents may break off their delicate branches. These branches, however, may continue to grow on their own or collect rime. Another kind of modification allows crystals to change from one type to another with changes in temperature and water saturation. A column may transform to a thick plate or a stellar crystal, for example, as the temperature of a cloud drops and water vapor content expands. Such transformations are more likely if crystals become snagged in updrafts and travel several times through a cloud before reaching the ground. Finally, crystals may encounter above-freezing air and simply melt to oblivion.

BOX 1   Studying and Preserving Snow Crystals

If you become fascinated by snow crystals, begin their study by seeking out as many illustrations of them as you can. Check out E. R. LaChapelle's Field Guide to Snow Crystals. *His book includes Magono and Lee's snow crystal classification and numerous photographs taken by himself. LaChapelle has also described how you can photograph snow crystals. And for a real treat, peruse a copy of* Snow Crystals *by W. A. Bentley and W. J. Humphreys, published originally in 1931 (later reprinted in 1962); this book contains more than 2,000 snow crystal photographs, admittedly mostly of stellar crystals and plates, selected because of their regularity and beauty. Affectionately known by such names as Snowflake Bentley and the Snowflake Man of Jericho, Wilson Bentley produced nearly 6,000 snow crystal photographs in an unheated shack on a farm*

near Jericho, Vermont, prior to his death in 1931.

Once you can confidently identify snow crystals, collect them on a blackboard, black cardboard, or perhaps black felt or velvet stretched on a board. With a hand lens hanging from your neck—a 10-power one works fine—you can readily observe details of the crystals. Take care not to breathe unduly on them.

Now you are ready to evaluate how snow crystals vary with changing conditions. As a snowfall settles on your neighborhood, sample it hourly or every half hour if it seems particularly changeable. Record which crystal type predominates as well as the range of crystal types. Take notes also on air temperature—even though you know that the temperature of the cloud in which the crystals form is the crit-

ical factor—and wind direction and speed. Look for any trends and generalizations as the snowfall wears on. Check for signs of riming. Speculate on the upper-air conditions that gave rise to the crystals that you observe.

You may desire to try your hand at preserving snow crystals to observe them carefully later, possibly with a microscope, in comfort. The air temperature and any equipment you use must be below freezing. Place microscope slides, generally one by three inches, on a board or cardboard. Spray the slides with a clear, plastic spray such as Krylon spray coating or something similar commonly used to preserve artwork. Experiment with more than one type of spray. Caution: *Such plastic sprays tend to contain vapors harmful to your health and may also be highly flammable. Spray in well-ventilated places away from possible* sparks or flames. Allow snow crystals to land on the spray-covered slides. Bring the slides indoors where the plastic coating can dry. if everything goes well, you should have replicas of well-preserved snow crystals that remain clear. Try the spray method under different air temperatures and with different crystal types.

Another method of snow crystal preservation uses a plastic casting material, polyvinyl formal resin dissolved in ethylene dichloride. (You might ask a chemist friend where to obtain these materials or try a scientific supply firm such as Ward's Natural Science Establishment, Inc.) A thin film of the diluted solution may be smeared on a glass slide, upon which a crystal is placed, or a drop of the solution may be dropped onto a crystal. In either case, as the crystal evaporates, a replica of its shape remains preserved in the resin.

Falling snow reaching the ground is often caught up by the wind. Blowing snow, as perceived by the National Weather Service, is lifted to a height of six feet or more, seriously restricting visibility. Drifting snow is carried to a height of less than six feet but accumulates into significant snowdrifts.

Snowdrifts, conspicuous accumulations of wind-blown snow, form in the lee of obstructions or are heaped up by wind eddies or swirls. Some persons and agencies erect barriers or snow fences (see Figure 8), frequently of boards or slats but also of metal, to control the location of snowdrifts. Placed primarily on the windward side of roads, railroad tracks, houses, and barns, snow fences interrupt the wind flow and cause drifting snow to accumulate on their lee sides, well upwind of that which requires protection.

Drifting snow is analogous to drifting sand, so snowdrifts resemble sand dunes, and many dune types can be recognized in snow. I'll mention a few. *Transverse drifts* are long and narrow and orient at right angles or transverse to wind flow; they tend to form when snow is plentiful and wind speed is low to moderate. Fascinating because of their shape, *barchans* (bar-CAHNZ) are crescent-shaped drifts with the points of the crescent pointing downwind. Look for barchans when moderate to high winds have been blowing about only a limited amount of snow. *Longitudinal drifts*, long and narrow, align with the direction of wind flow; they develop under conditions of high-speed winds and limited amounts of snow.

Cornices (CORE-nuh-suhz) are overhanging accumulations of wind-blown snow, typically developed on the lee edges of ridges or cliff faces in the mountains. But look also for smaller versions of them in less conspicuous places, such as on the leeward side of stream cutbanks and low ridges out of the mountains. Use extreme care when approaching cornices; they may collapse and slide under your weight.

Drifted snow may be secondarily sculpted into sharp ridges and grooves usually oriented parallel with the wind. It is then called *sastrugi* (suh-STROO-gee) after a modified Russian word for wind-made furrows. On such scoured snow you can often discern truncated snow layers. On a few occasions I've seen "snow tongues" developed on sastrugi, pointing upwind. In time, the tongues begin to droop. Well-developed sastrugi is difficult to traverse.

The Inuit (Eskimos) and subarctic Indians, the wisest about living among snow, have devised precise words for various aspects of snow. Table 3 lists a selection of Inuit words and their approximate pronunciations.

Properties of Snow

Snow has some interesting properties. To get to know it better, let's examine four of them: low density, good insulator, both reflects and absorbs the sun's energy, and transmits at least some light.

Density refers to the quantity of a substance in relation to a certain volume. Accumulated snow generally has a low density because it usually consists mostly of air. In fact, the air in light, fluffy, freshly fallen snow in protected woods may far exceed the volume of ice (as crystals). As snow piles up, though, that in the lower layers becomes more dense from the squeezing or pressure of the weight of the upper layers. Density also increases with time as snowdrifts age. As snow transforms to firn and

firn to glacial ice, the density becomes greater. Glacial ice is denser than snow because it consists of mostly water and very little air, the opposite of snow. You can ascertain the density of a snow layer—and readily compare it with that of another layer—by weighing a predetermined volume of snow collected with a small metal cup or, perhaps better, a small can open at both ends. Density is usually measured in grams per cubic centimeter but could be done in ounces per cubic inch.

Because snow generally contains much trapped air, it is a good insulator; that is, it tends to retain heat released by the ground beneath it. Dry, fluffy snow insulates better than wet, more dense snow because dry, fluffy snow contains more air. Snow's insulative value can be related to that of clothing. Apparel with the most air space insulates the best. You may want to experiment with how good an insulator snow really is (Box 2).

BOX 2   How to Measure the Insulative Value of Snow

To measure how well snow insulates, or how temperature varies with the amount of snow cover, dig an east-west-trending snow pit in several feet of snow down to ground level. Cut the north-facing side vertically and scrape it evenly and smoothly. Mark the tops of obvious snow layers, which generally represent separate snowstorms, with anything convenient such as Popsicle sticks. Measure the distance from the ground to the middle of each layer and mark each point with a Popsicle stick. Now, as quickly as possible so the air temperature does not appreciably change the snow temperature, insert a thermometer into the midpoints of all snow layers and record the values. Record also the air temperature when you are finished. You should find a gradient in temperature—warmest values near the bottom of the pit and coldest values near the top—and snow temperatures warmer than the air temperature, unless the air temperature is unusually high.

Vary your approach to learn more about snow's insulative value. Compare temperatures of snow pits in different places. You might try recording temperatures hourly for a period of time to determine daily and nightly effects. For this approach you might better use several long thermometers, one for each midpoint, and cover them to lessen the effects of air temperature. If you have access to a thermocouple or a thermistor—ask an electronics expert about each and its use—fasten either to the bottom end of a long pole and push the pole vertically into the snowpack. By means of connecting wires leading to the surface you can record temperatures quickly and conveniently at selected depths without having to dig a snow pit.

One more thing—back in the snow pit. If you wish to find out how density varies within the snowpack and how it affects snow temperature, collect standard-sized snow samples from the midpoints of the layers where you measured the temperatures and place them in marked plastic bags. Later, weigh the snow samples and compare the density with the temperature at the middle of each snow layer.

It's one thing to understand how insulative a snow cover can be, it's another truly to perceive this effect. To experience it ideally, construct a snow shelter and spend the night—or longer—in it. In this way, also, you will gain some sense as to how small animals are able to survive a winter beneath a protective snow blanket. You might even become addicted to uncrowded, insect-free winter camping and prefer overnighting in a warm, quiet snow shelter rather than in a cold, noisy (wind-flapping) tent!

BOX 3   How to Build a Snow Shelter and Sleep Comfortably in It

Two types of snow shelters provide comfortable winter quarters: the piled-snow type and the igloo. They differ in the kind of snow, time, and skill necessary for their construction.

The piled-snow shelter goes by the Athapaskan Indian name, quin-zhee. It is the simpler of the two shelters to build.

Look for an area of loose snow to build a quin-zhee; even if the snow is only several inches thick, you may proceed. Stomp through any crust that may exist on the snow cover. If you don't do this, your snow pile may settle unevenly to your consternation later on. Now, pile the snow into a mound. An aluminum grain shovel represents the ideal tool for this job: It is lightweight and useful for moving much snow in a short time. You might wish to produce a conical mound; if so, one about six feet high and ten feet wide at the base works well. A shelter of this size can house at least three persons comfortably. When sleeping alone, I prefer a mound with traditional pup tentlike proportions (Figure 10), about five feet high, nine feet long, and six feet wide at the base. Don't pile excessive snow on the central point or ridge, depending on the type of shelter; otherwise the roof may later collapse from the added weight. With the mound completed, let the snow set for at least an hour. This settling time allows the ice crystals to coalesce or bond into a relatively strong and stable mass.

Now, for the hollowing. Foremost, you must avoid getting wet, from either kneeling or sitting in the snow or from perspiring because of overexertion or wearing too much clothing. If wet, your body will chill once you stop working in the cold. It helps to wear rain pants when kneeling on the floor of the shelter to excavate. Don't overexert, and wear just the right amount of clothing so you feel slightly cool while working. I find it necessary to have an extra pair of mittens; one pair invariably becomes soaked during the hollowing-out process.

Begin the tunneling with an entrance on the lee side, about two and a half feet wide and high. Carefully sculpt the inside, maintaining the walls and ceiling at about a foot thick. To verify the thickness, place several foot-long sticks into the snow pile before you begin sculpting. Another forethought that aids in hollowing out the conical mound is sustaining a pole vertically in its center during snow piling. It's helpful to know exactly where the center of the mound is when enlarging the inside. Excavate down to the ground; that way you can benefit from the heat escaping from the soil. Shave the inside of the walls and ceiling smooth; this inhibits any dripping should the interior temperature become unduly warm. Poke a two-inch-wide vent hole through the ceiling at about a 60-degree angle from the ground.

You might find the two-and-a-half-foot-high entrance too restrictive while excavating, especially if snow from the ceiling continually drops on you. If so, cut an excavation opening of convenient height on the windward side. When finished with the inside, place poles over the excavation opening and cover it with loose snow or snow blocks. Incise a shorter, final entrance on the lee side.

Figure 10. Snow shelters or quin-zhees constructed for winter camping.

Building an igloo or snow-block shelter requires considerable skill. Be prepared to expend much time in this effort, especially if you haven't watched another builder constructing one.

A prime requirement is completely suitable snow. Although any soft qali is okay for quin-zhees, you specifically need wind-beaten snow or upsik (Table 3) for igloos. Locate a long snowdrift two feet or more deep; the snow should carry your weight and barely show your footprints. It should be uniformly firm throughout without variably softer and harder layers.

Especially shun the weak snow mixed with wind-blown dirt.

Cut snow blocks vertically across your long snowdrift. A long-bladed snow knife or combination snow knife and saw is the ideal tool. If you have neither, I have found that roughing out the blocks with the aluminum grain shovel and trimming them with a machete works reasonably well. Conveniently sized blocks measure about three feet long, one and a half feet high, and a half foot or slightly more wide. After cutting about fifteen blocks, you are ready for the foundation.

TABLE 3   Inuit (Eskimo) Terms for Selected Aspects of Snow

English	Inuit Kobuk Valley, Alaska
Snow that collects on trees	Qali (KAH-lih)
Snow on the ground	Api (AH-pih)
Wind-beaten snow	Upsik (OOP-sick)
Wind-eroded snow (sastrugi)	Kaioglaq (KYE-oh-glahk)
Drifting (smoking) snow	Siqoq (sih-COKE)
Snowdrift	Kimoaqruk (kihm-oh-AHK-rook)

The foundation (Figure 11), a crucial step, begins with tracing a circle in the snow. It should be about eight feet across for an inside diameter of an igloo that can house two persons. Place your blocks around the circle and join them with well-placed cuts of your machete or snow knife. Projections of block joints should all converge toward the center of the floor. The blocks may lean slightly toward the center or their tops may be beveled so as to slope toward the center. Either approach allows succeeding blocks to create a domed igloo. Blocks not only dome upward but also spiral upward. To set the spiral, cut the first four or five blocks diagonally to create a kind of inclined ramp.

With the foundation established, you concentrate on carefully fitting the successive blocks. Each later block overlaps the joint of those two it rests upon. To lock each block in place, it must lean on the directly previous one. To accomplish this, you cut the end joints at a slight angle so the latest block just slightly overlaps the one before it. Also trim the base of each new block so that it conforms with the blocks just beneath it. Try to maintain a sym-

metrical curve to the walls and strive for a relatively low dome. Pointed igloos sleep colder than low-domed ones.

As your igloo nears completion (Figure 12), cut a low entrance on the lee side. A friend can now aid you with placing the last blocks from the inside. The final or key block is cut with downward-tapering sides.

Now, for a few finishing touches. For a warmer igloo, chink the joints between blocks with snow. As for the quin-zhee, trim off any irregularities on the inside to prevent possible dripping, and bore a vent hole. You might also consider building a short snow wall on either side of the entrance for wind protection.

And now, the ultimate test: sleeping comfortably in a quin-zhee or igloo. Temperatures inside will be relatively warm, 25 degrees or higher than outside temperatures. Partially cover the entrance with a snow block, or better, a skin flap or a small tarp. Leave a small space at the bottom for air to enter; it circulates out through the vent hole. You must insulate your sleeping bag from the ground. I prefer a poncho directly on the ground over which I place a thinner, closed-cell foam pad followed by a thicker, open-cell foam pad. To lessen heat loss from your head, sleep wearing a knit cap or balaclava.

If you wish to add a cheery touch—and a little warmth as well—light your snow shelter with a candle. Drip-stick the candle to the bowl of a long-handled spoon and push the handle into the wall of the shelter. By this light you might even want to do a bit of reading "in bed" before turning in!

During the night you will likely be im-pressed by the quiet, even if you know it is blowing outside. No flapping of tents here. Imagine the ever-present quiet experienced by small mammals beneath the snow cover.

In the morning, you can arise feeling warm. First, melt snow and heat water for hot cereal and a hot drink on a backpacking stove while in your sleeping bag—and eat breakfast where you are. Second, dress, except for boots, while also still in your sleeping bag—in which you warmed your clothes during the night.

Figure 11. Foundation for an igloo. Additional snow blocks will spiral and dome upward.

Figure 12. A nearly completed igloo. The person inside will aid in placing the final snow blocks.

Snow both reflects and absorbs the sun's energy. When fresh, snow may reflect up to 95 percent of the sun's short-wave radiation. It may reflect only half of this or less as it ages or grows dirtier.

Though this may seem paradoxical, snow is a nearly perfect absorber of the sun's long-wave radiation or energy, as well as a good reflector. It does this indirectly. Objects on the ground receive short-wave energy from the sun and emit that energy in the long-wave form, which snow absorbs. One evidence of snow absorbing this energy is the bowl-shaped depression that develops around a tree trunk, called *qamaniq* (KAHM-uhn-ick) by the Inuit, as the snow wastes away. Knowing this, you would be warmer in an emergency by remaining below a forest canopy where long-wave energy is redirected downward toward the snow's surface. Snow also radiates energy back to objects, especially at night when it loses more energy than it gains.

Although we might expect snow to transmit little light, some—even of use to plants—gets through. For example, spring beauties develop leaves and flower parts beneath the snow, and the flowers of snow buttercups may open within the snow. Such plants can function under at least twenty inches of snow. Light at the blue end of the light spectrum will penetrate more deeply than light at the red end. Snow transmits light better where snow grains are smaller and at lower and higher densities than at middle densities.

The Changing Snowpack

As soon as falling snow reaches the ground it begins to change. Most obvious is the formation of wind or sun crusts on a snowpack's surface. A wind crust or slab consists of snow crystals—broken by the action of the wind—whose fragments have frozen together; the crystals may change to rounded, high-density grains. A sun crust—*siqoqtoaq* (sih-COKE-toe-ahk) in Inuit—veneering a snowpack results from snow at the surface alternately melting and freezing. Snow algae may live beneath a thin, clear, sun crust.

Beneath the surface of a snowpack less obvious, but nevertheless profound, changes are taking place. One kind of change is called *destructive metamorphism*. Destructive metamorphism alludes to snow crystals having their original shapes destroyed. In snowpacks with nearly a uniform temperature throughout, snow crystals change drastically. Stellar crystals, for example, gradually deteriorate: the branches reduce to tiny ice grains and the central parts to larger grains. Crystals change shape as water molecules move from one part of a crystal to another. Because the space occupied by each crystal is reduced, the entire snowpack settles. This settling of the snowpack—not by melting—is an obvious sign that metamorphism is going on.

Destructive metamorphism takes place by changes in temperature and pressure. It happens faster when temperatures are near freezing and lessens as temperatures drop. Higher pressures, from the weight of thicker snow, intensify the changes, one of which is greater mechanical strength of the snow. Destructive metamorphism occurs when you build a quinzhee: Ice grains bond more tightly as they pack together.

Ultimate destructive metamorphism leads to firn, and eventually to glacial ice. In the early stages of the formation of firn, in temperate climates, the ice grains are bonded by meltwater refreezing. Later, as the firn is buried under more snow, both pressure and refreezing bond the grains as they become denser to form glacial ice. In polar climates, firn and glacial ice form solely by pressure as snow compacts.

In *constructive metamorphism* crystal shapes are not destroyed but new ones are created. This happens because of a difference in temperature, or temperature gradient, between the bottom of a snowpack and its top. Heat released from the ground usually causes a snowpack to be warmer at its base and cooler at its surface. Because of this arrangement, metamorphism occurs faster at the bottom of the snowpack.

Crystals grow as water vapor flows from warmer snow (at the bottom under higher air pressure) to colder snow (at the top under lower pressure). Water molecules are variably added or removed as they ride with the water vapor upward. Remember depth hoar? Although we earlier called it a kind of frost, depth hoar—or *pukak* (POO-kahk) in Inuit—also refers to the ice crystals created by constructive metamorphism. The crystals frequently assume a cuplike or columnar shape and characteristically display a layered structure of steps or ribs on the crystal faces. The formation of depth hoar may be carried to the point where snow is completely eroded by evaporation and hollow spaces develop at the base of a snowpack.

Depth hoar translates to brittle ice crystals that do not bond well; the resultant snow, consequently, is structurally weak. Not only is depth hoar prone to cause avalanches, it hinders the compaction of roads, runways, and ski runs.

Depth hoar forms mostly in cold, continental climates that induce strong temperature gradients in snowpacks. Expect to see it more often early in the winter when the snowpack is still relatively thin; thicker snowpacks set up less well-defined temperature gradients.

Keep in mind that the kind of change within a snowpack varies with the weather and as the winter wears on. A period of warmer temperatures may allow destructive metamorphism to proceed with good crystal bonding and good snow strength. Later, temperatures may drop for a period; constructive metamorphism ensues and, in time, structurally weakens the snow. These variations may be repeated many times. Finally, in the spring, firn may form, followed by meltwater permeating the snowpack. Eventually, the snowpack is destroyed by complete melting.

F O U R

Winter Travel

Before concerning yourself about how to travel in winter, it is crucial to know *when* to venture out. Many people find their comfort or even lives threatened when they set out on winter trips at inopportune times—when they should have stayed at home. They tend to ignore weather forecasts, shrug their shoulders, and say something like "It's not that bad." Such people may luckily complete a trip under marginal weather conditions, but they might also shudder through a long night in a frigid, snow-stalled car. Don't take chances by moving about during questionable weather unless an emergency warrants it. Be conservative when planning winter trips. Play it safe; put off an excursion when the weather is borderline. Why suffer rather than relish a winter journey?

In this chapter we will explore basic preparations and techniques for winter rambling by automobile, walking, snowshoeing, or skiing, as well as some procedures for navigating with confidence. For tips on dressing warmly, coping with winter hazards while traveling, and

suggestions on how to assemble survival kits, see the appendix.

Traveling by Automobile

Vehicles, like humans, are vulnerable to cold. We must prepare them, with preventive maintenance, for the wintry season so they convey us reliably. Here's a checklist to follow to ensure your vehicle's cold-weather dependability:

(1) *Engine.* Is it time for a tune-up? A well-tuned engine starts better under cold-weather stress than a poorly tuned one. Most mechanics advise a tune-up every 12,000 to 18,000 miles under normal driving conditions and when not pulling a camper or trailer. Some vehicles, therefore, may require a tune-up at fewer miles. Check the conditions of all drive belts; imagine the consequence of snapping a frayed drive belt at 20 degrees below zero. And

keep your gas tank full; this lessens the chances of water-contaminated fuel reaching your engine and freezing your fuel line.

(2) *Battery*. For a battery to withstand the brunt of cold temperatures it must be fully charged. Even a properly charged battery operates at only 65 percent efficiency at temperatures below freezing. Low-speed, short-trip city driving may not allow for full charging. You may wish to invest in a battery charger to maintain a healthy battery at full strength. An incompletely charged battery may also result from a faulty charging system. Inspect the battery terminals for good contact with the connecting cables; they may need cleaning. Sometimes a vehicle won't start simply because of poor contact at battery terminals.

(3) *Cooling system*. Every fall check the strength of the antifreeze in your vehicle's radiator to accommodate the coldest temperatures you expect. About every two years drain and flush the cooling system, especially if the coolant is discolored; replace the old coolant with fresh antifreeze. While you're at it, inspect the hoses for leaks and determine if the pressure cap on the radiator and the thermostat are operating as they should.

(4) *Heating system*. Well before cold temperatures enshroud your region, try out the heater and defroster. You must *know* that the heating system is okay before setting out on a winter trip.

(5) *Oil change and filter*. Although changing oil and the oil filter is a mandatory part of normal vehicle maintenance, it becomes especially important prior to winter. An engine with dirty oil will not turn over as readily in the cold. And, of course, use a lower weight oil (one of lower viscosity) for winter driving. A lower weight oil allows the engine to turn over more easily.

(6) *Brakes*. Give your brakes a good test be-

fore winter arrives. You certainly want the best chances of safe, smooth stopping while driving on ice and snow.

(7) *Tires*. Like shoes on human feet, tires need to be continually maintained for good service. If you have snow tires, check the tread depth, which should be at least one-eighth of an inch for reasonable gripping. And, of course, keep all your tires inflated at the right pressure and properly aligned and balanced for even wear. For frequent driving on ice and packed snow you may wish to buy studded snow tires—if you live in a state that allows them—or chains. Chains may be really necessary while driving on mountain roads.

(8) *Windshield wiper system*. Replace worn wiper blades or those that don't wipe evenly. Keep the windshield washer container full of windshield washer fluid. Have handy a windshield scraper with an attached snow brush.

(9) *Lights*. Test all lights, including flashers and turning lights. Good front and rear lights are especially crucial when driving in fog or a snowstorm so you don't strike a slower or parked vehicle from the rear or encounter the same experience from a motorist following you.

(10) *Inside the trunk or back of a pickup*. Necessary items to take along include: spare tire, jack, jack handle, tire wrench, selected tools (such as pliers, screwdrivers, and an adjustable wrench), sand, snow shovel, tow rope or chain, jumper cables, extra antifreeze, and a deicer for the gas. Although seemingly obvious, make sure the spare tire is properly inflated. Imagine changing a tire in the snow, and you might wish to add a piece of carpet to lie or kneel on. A wooden block to place in front of the tire diagonally opposite the raised tire would also be useful to safeguard the vehicle from falling off the jack. Sprinkling sand directly in front of the tires driving the vehicle

usually extricates you from icy spots. Regarding jumper cables: Know exactly how to connect them on the running and stranded vehicles and *never connect them to a frozen battery.* Hydrogen gas may be trapped in the battery; attaching a jumper cable may create a spark and cause the gas (and battery) to explode.

(11) *Door locks.* Before cold weather sets in, check the ease with which a vehicle key enters the door locks. If the lock offers some resistance, you might apply a little very light-weight lubricant.

More important is knowing how to handle a frozen lock. First, try this. Heat the key with a match or cigarette lighter, then quickly insert it into the lock. If the heated key doesn't thaw out the lock, spray an aerosol lock defroster into it. It's a good idea to carry a can of this spray in a spare coat pocket—you can't store it in your vehicle.

You can cut down on locks freezing by not washing your vehicle on a below-freezing day. Jets of water at car washes may penetrate the locks, causing freezing as you drive away.

Besides readying your vehicle for cold-weather travel, you need to develop skills when driving on snow and ice. Let's begin with starting and stopping.

On loose snow you need to apply more power to start rolling because of the snow's resistance. On slick roads and streets offering little traction, accelerate very slowly and gradually to lessen spinning the wheels. Front-wheel drive vehicles tend to begin rolling more readily than those driven from the rear. Pickups are notoriously bad for starting on packed snow and ice because of little weight in the rear. To increase traction in the rear, haul bags of sand or a load of wood in the box.

Safe stopping on slick surfaces ranks as one of the important defensive driving skills. Slam-

ming on the brakes is a no-no and usually causes the rear end to slip to one side or the other. Instead, gently depress the brake pedal until you just begin to feel the brakes grab; then release pressure on the brake pedal. Repeat as needed, which amounts to a kind of quick pumping action. Gradually your vehicle slows to a stop.

How do you cope with wheels losing their traction while turning, especially when going into a curve? If the rear wheels lose their grip, your vehicle could start spinning. Resist the natural impulse to hit the brake pedal. Rather, steer slightly in the direction your vehicle is skidding and accelerate a little without spinning the wheels. Your tires should grip the road once again, and you steer gradually back on course.

If the front wheels lose their grip in a turn, your vehicle will not spin but will surge straight ahead. Again, don't brake. Remove your foot from the accelerator and turn the wheels slightly until they regain their grip. Now, resume the original turn.

Traveling on Foot

Traveling on foot has several general points in common. Let's examine these before entering the specifics of walking in snow, snowshoeing, or skiing.

Before attempting any foot travel you must ask yourself if you are physically fit. If not, work out a basic physical conditioning program for yourself. First, if you have any medical problems, get an okay from your personal physician. A conditioning program needs to be neither elaborate nor that demanding. But include a good walking regimen. You might begin with twenty minutes three times a week and gradually work up to more time and frequency until you reach that higher level that is comfortable and sustaining. Climbing hills or stairs will strengthen your legs, expand your breathing, and increase your stamina. Swimming will complement this activity.

It's a good idea to begin and end each walking exercise—as well as any on-foot excursions—with a series of stretching exercises. Preliminary stretching allows muscles to "warm up" and prepares them for the demands that will be placed upon them without their being shocked or surprised. After-walk stretching prevents blood from pooling in the extremities, which may place additional strain on the heart.

Feet must obviously be well cared for, since the body's weight continually stresses them. Wear well-fitted—and well-broken-in—footgear, the lightest possible while still giving good support. Wear also well-fitted socks; a wrinkle in a too-large sock can produce an irritated or blistered toe in record time. Keep your feet clean to prevent their irritation. In like manner, tend periodically to trim the toenails. Besides cutting holes in socks that can irritate toes, a too-long nail of one toe can painfully jab a neighboring toe. For long treks, gradually condition your feet. Don't plan on a ten-mile trek if your conditioning walks have only stretched to two or three miles.

Backpackers frequently take a hiking staff to steady themselves in rough terrain or periodically to lean on for a brief rest. A hiking staff (or two) is equally appropriate for a snow walker, snowshoer, or ski tourer. The cross-country skier is, of course, habitually equipped with two staffs, the ski poles, to aid in propulsion as well as balance. A good hiking staff for a snow walker or snowshoer is

also a ski pole, preferably one with a large basket to prevent the pole from sinking deeply in snow. For a comfortable length, the top of the pole should just fit under an armpit when its point is on the floor. Fiberglass or metal poles are stronger than those of bamboo but they may be heavier. Get poles with adjustable straps that can be changed with the gloves or mittens you are using at the time.

You might extract at least two other uses from the staff (pole). Mark known intervals on it with tape and it becomes a snow ruler; invert the staff for snow measurement. Affix a camera mounting screw at its top and the staff doubles as a monopod to keep your camera semi-steady.

Use gaiters to prevent snow from overtopping your footgear, regardless of the kind of foot travel. Usually opt for the knee-length type over the ankle-length type because you frequently end up in snow deeper than you intend. Although convenient, I stay away from zippered gaiters because they tend to jam when filled with snow or ice. Laced gaiters, or those closed with Velcro or a similar fastener, are usually more reliable.

One cardinal rule for on-foot winter travel is: Conserve your energy. You never know when you must tap a much-needed reserve, maybe in a survival situation. Save your strength and don't overexert. Maintain a steady pace broken by occasional, brief resting periods. Avoid, as some do, charging at full speed followed by resting for long spells. This approach tires you unduly and may stiffen your muscles.

Think of ways to traverse so as to cut down on your body's strain. Avoid going up and down ridges and valleys or canyons. Instead, maintain your elevation as much as possible by following ridges and paralleling valleys or canyons. When confronted with steep slopes, don't bull your way straight up. Take a clue from the larger animals and zigzag your way up; it's longer this way, but much less tiring.

A second cardinal rule is: Don't take unnecessary chances. Condition your mind to think that you simply cannot afford accidents—especially confronted with winter's cold—and strive in every way to avoid them. Be particularly wary of falling. Always attempt to control your center of gravity, so that if you fall it will be in a safer sitting position.

A third cardinal rule is: Avoid perspiring. Perspiration is followed by body-chilling cold once you stop moving. The appendix gives some tips on how to avoid perspiring when traveling.

Walking

Walking is the most basic and natural way to travel, on or off snow. It allows you the freedom to range freely, subject, of course, to any violation of trespass and the capability of your legs to transport you. Walking requires no equipment. Protective clothing for your body is the only necessity (see the appendix).

Footgear preference for walking in snow varies widely. A simple, lightweight, inexpensive choice is rugged, low-cut walking or running shoes encased in flexible, rubber overboots, usually closed with a zipper. Some prefer moccasins with high uppers. (I dislike moccasins because they lack an arch support.) A heavier, but more durable option is rubber-bottomed boots with leather uppers, called pacs or pac boots; they are fitted with liners, removable or attached, that both insulate and absorb perspiration. A similar alternative is rubber-bottomed boots with nylon uppers as used in snowmobiling. Should you lack liners for rubber boots, at least fit the bottoms with innersoles of felt or some other insulative material. Leather hiking boots are a poor choice because they tend to produce cold feet.

Whatever the outer footgear, wear good insulative socks, preferably more than a single pair. The choice of material is up to you. I favor socks mostly of wool, a lighter inner pair and a heavier outer pair.

When ascending slopes, walk with the soles flat on the ground. Walking on the balls sets up additional strain on the feet and is more tiring. On the steeper slopes, pause slightly at the end of each step for a brief "rest"; this tactic allows you to proceed up a slope for some time without undue fatigue. On the steepest slopes, try a side-step—as if climbing a stairway sideways.

When descending slopes, go straight down unless you fear slipping; zigzagging is usually unnecessary. Keep your back straight and your knees bent for good stability and balance. On the steepest slopes, if slipping or if you dread descending too rapidly, resort to the side-step approach.

Don't climb on snow-covered fallen trees, rocks, or similar obstacles. This sets you up for a twisted ankle or some other foot or leg injury. Further, don't step on anything you can step over and don't step over anything you can step around. Finally, avoid running, especially down a slope over deep snow that seems supportive. Should you abruptly sink in deeply you could injure yourself seriously, maybe even sustain a broken bone.

Snowshoeing

I'm always excited by the magical experience of viewing fat, exclamation point-like

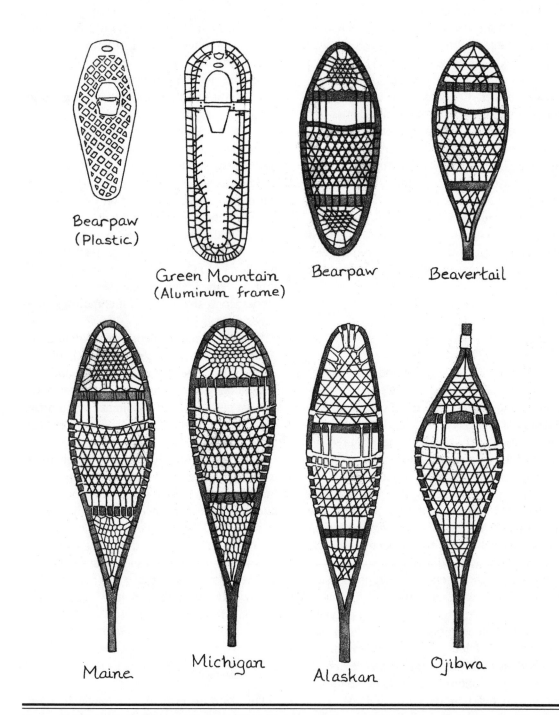

Bearpaw
(Plastic)

Green Mountain
(Aluminum frame)

Bearpaw

Beavertail

Maine

Michigan

Alaskan

Ojibwa

Figure 13. Types of snowshoes. All, except the plastic bearpaw and the aluminum-framed Green Mountain, are made of wood.

tracks of classic snowshoe tracks—either my own or someone else's—in newly fallen snow! Neither human footprints nor ski tracks thrill me in the same way. Why? Maybe it's because of the snowshoe track's unique shape or the intricate pattern of the webbing. Then, maybe, it's knowing that snowshoe tracks can go literally *anywhere*, giving them that special mystical or spiritual quality.

Snowshoes allow you truly to traverse cross-country in soft, deep snow. Walking becomes nearly impossible under these conditions, and skis sink in awkwardly. Although not swift, snowshoes are dependable and safer when carrying heavy loads over long distances.

Several kinds of traditional snowshoes have evolved since humans first devised them, maybe nearly 6,000 years ago. Each type was designed for a specific mode of travel.

The oval bearpaw type (Figure 13) works best in heavy woods or where frequent turning is necessary. It is turned up only slightly at the front. The Beavertail or Westover retains the oval shape and upturn of the bearpaw but terminates in a stubby tail. Longer and narrower with more front upturn, the Green Mountain or Otter resembles a stretched-out bearpaw.

For trails and open terrain, the Maine and Michigan types are preferred choices. Either conjures the classic snowshoe with a teardrop shape and a long, narrow tail, which produces the exclamation points in snow I mentioned earlier. As each foot is raised, the tail drops and acts like a rudder—to help keep the snowshoe aligned with the foot. The two types are closely similar: the Maine with a bluntly pointed toe and more upturn, the Michigan with a rounded toe and less upturn.

Two snowshoe types have been developed for deep snow and open terrain. The Alaskan type—also called Trail, Yukon, and Pickerel—resembles a long, narrow Maine or Michigan snowshoe with a markedly upturned toe that lessens the chances of catching it in deep snow or under a snow crust. The Ojibwa is long and narrow like the Alaskan but pointed at the front because the frame is of two pieces joined at the front and tail, not bent at the front from a single piece, as for all the other traditional snowshoes. The pointed, elevated front slices through deep snow and doesn't load up with it.

Materials for making snowshoes have changed considerably. Traditionally the frame was of wood, usually ash, and the webbing of rawhide, laced while wet so it would shrink and tighten securely on the frame after drying. You can still buy snowshoes of these materials. But available also are snowshoes with frames of lightweight aluminum or magnesium alloy. The most common synthetic webbing material is neoprene, a rubber reinforced with nylon. Neoprene is better than rawhide in being stronger, it doesn't stretch when wet, snow doesn't cling to it, and it requires no maintenance. Some modern snowshoes lack a true webbing but are fitted instead with decking, like a miniature trampoline, within the frame. The decking is usually of neoprene or possibly polyurethane. Another variation is a snowshoe constructed entirely of a single piece of plastic, molded so that the frame and "webbing" are one. Most snowshoes of strictly synthetic materials tend to follow the bearpaw or Green Mountain designs.

Which type of snowshoe is the best for you? First, select the lightest snowshoes that will readily support you. Don't load your feet more than is absolutely necessary. Further, gauge your choice of snowshoe against the snow and terrain conditions you intend to traverse most often.

To increase your chances of being ultimately satisfied, try out several types of snowshoes

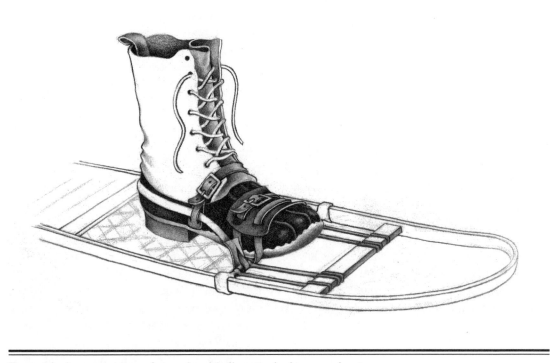

Figure 14. A common type of snowshoe binding attached to a pac boot.

before buying any. If your friends don't have them, rent several sets before making the final choice.

Whether to opt for snowshoes of traditional or synthetic materials is a matter of aesthetics as well as utility. Handmade wooden snowshoes with rawhide webbing reflect a natural warmth and offer a link to our heritage. And they look great hanging on a wall of rough-cut lumber or logs! I own a pair of Alaskan snowshoes and two pairs of Maines—all of wood and rawhide. (I usually select one of the Maines for a trip because they're lighter.) But I might also eventually defect to using machine-made snowshoes of lighter synthetic materials that don't require periodic varnishing of both the wood and rawhide.

Bindings (Figure 14), for attaching footgear to snowshoes, vary as widely as the snowshoes themselves. A widely used type, though, consists of a toepiece that receives the toe of your boot, a heel strap, and a cross strap that fits over the instep. It is called an H binding; the cross strap forms an H as it connects to the two parts of the heel strap. Adjust the toepiece first, then the heel strap. Bindings, usually of leather or neoprene, are attached to the master cord—or a cross or pivot rod in the synthetic snowshoes—at the rear end of the toe hole in the snowshoe. The ball of the foot should position where the bindings attach, and the toe of your boot should move freely within the toe hole.

For snowshoes, use any type of footgear

suitable for walking. William Osgood and Leslie Hurley, in the *The Snowshoe Book*, have suggested even using *no* shoes at all—the lightest of footgear! They have snowshoed with only three pairs of woolen socks in soft, dry snow at temperatures ranging from −15 to −20 degrees Fahrenheit.

Snowshoeing is easily learned by walking with a normal gait and taking two precautions. First, as you move one snowshoe forward make certain that it doesn't land on the stationary one. One must be clearly forward and slightly to the side before moving the other. Second, avoid walking spread-legged, which is unnecessary and results in developing sore hips.

Begin under ideal conditions: warm temperatures, compacted snow, and level terrain. If you bought your snowshoes early, you might try them under really ideal conditions—on a late autumn lawn.

At the onset, snowshoe with two ski poles. (Later you may resort to using only one pole as most do.) They help you maintain balance and ease arising should you fall. To upright yourself, either use the poles as vertical props or lay them horizontally as you press down on them.

Before embarking on slopes, try a couple of turns. The *step turn* is easiest. You simply take one or more short, arcing steps in the direction you wish to turn, first one foot and then the other, until you have assumed your new line of travel. With the *kick turn* you lift or kick one snowshoe, turn it 180 degrees, and set it down. Follow this with the other snowshoe, and you totally reverse your direction in two movements. The turns are easier with ski poles but try them first without; otherwise you may depend on them too heavily. At first, too, the poles may seem to get in your way.

If you find yourself snug against a tree, bush, rock or some other obstacle, turning may not be feasible. Instead, try this maneuver. With your ski poles, press down on the toe of each snowshoe, which raises each tail. Now, you can readily back out of your awkward position.

Try two techniques when climbing short, moderately steep slopes. With the *herringbone* technique, toe out each snowshoe at a slight angle as you proceed directly up the slope; your snowshoes will trace a herringbone or V pattern in the snow. Likely you will find this approach tiring. The other, easier technique involves *side-stepping* up a slope, just as in walking. Maintain the snowshoes as horizontally as possible, at right angles to the slope. This involves "edging" the snowshoes, stamping so that the uphill edge receives more pressure. On steeper slopes you effectively develop temporary terraces beneath the snowshoes.

Traversing long, steep slopes works best in a zigzag course. Your diagonal tracks follow a longer distance but a path that is less steep and less tiring. Employ a step turn or a kick turn when changing direction. Be conscious of edging your snowshoes.

When descending gentler slopes, simply lean back and place more weight on the tails as you proceed.

You have at least two options when descending steeper slopes. On short slopes, if steep enough for sliding, place one shoe ahead of the other, sit on the rear one, and slide down. You might drag the poles in the snow as a brake or rudder. On long slopes, for greatest safety, descend as you ascended: by following a zigzag course.

When climbing slopes you may need to increase traction. Temporary measures include winding rope around the snowshoe frame, inserting tree branches through the lacing, or lashing a trimmed tree branch across the shoe on the underside. Permanent traction devices, called *crampons* —detachable or built-in—are of metal wedges, angled plates, teeth, studs, or spikes.

Cross-Country Skiing

Winter sport enthusiasts indulge in four main kinds of cross-country skiing: racing, light touring, standard touring, and mountain skiing. Both racing and light touring depend on prepared trails and imply crowds or at least groups of people. Standard or deep-snow touring happens away from prepared trails, and practitioners use heavier and sturdier equipment than is needed for racing or light touring; it is best suited for exploring nature in winter away from concentrations of people. Mountain skiing is an extension in rugged terrain of standard touring and depends on the heaviest and sturdiest equipment.

Before delving into cross-country skiing techniques, let's briefly consider the equipment. I'll touch on boots, bindings, and skis, in that order.

Footgear ranks as the most important piece of equipment in skiing, as it does for snow walking and snowshoeing. A rather wide range of ski boots is available. For standard touring a boot with higher leather uppers, above the ankle, is probably best. A higher upper provides a warmer boot, and leather breathes whereas vinyl does not, thereby allowing less buildup of perspiration. Wear two pairs of socks; you might also add insulative innersoles for added warmth.

Fit the boots snugly but not tightly, with the socks you intend to wear skiing. The heels shouldn't ride up and down as you move your foot. Allow about a finger's width in front of the toes.

Bindings must be totally compatible with your boots. In fact, select the bindings first to ensure a good match. Pin bindings, in which pins engage in sockets at the boot toes, are standard for racing and light touring skis. But cable bindings, in which a cable wraps around the boot's heels, are better for standard touring off prepared trails in deep snow. You may, however, find it difficult acquiring quality cable bindings. A boot to be used with a cable binding should have a stiff sole and a stout well-grooved heel to receive the binding. If you've searched long for a boot-binding combination to your liking, buy an extra set at the outset to ensure being well equipped for years.

Skis vary in weight and width according to their intended use. Racing skis are the lightest and less than fifty millimeters at their widest just back of the tips; mountain skis are the heaviest and widest, more than sixty millimeters wide. Standard touring skis are heavier and wider than racing and light touring skis, generally about fifty to sixty millimeters.

How long should your skis be? As a general rule, stand upright with a hand exending vertically. The tip of the ski should reach to about your wrist. If you are a little light for your height, pick a slightly shorter ski; if a little heavy for your height, select a slightly longer ski.

Besides appropriate length, skis must have the correct flexibility or yield to your weight when you stand on them. Skis have a built-in arch or bend; when you stand on them you flatten this arch. Good flexibility means that you get a firm grip on the snow with one ski— in its middle—as you push off with the other. You tend to slip more with skis that are too stiff. Skis too flexible may not glide well.

One way roughly to gauge the right flexibility is by the paper test. Place a sheet of paper under the skis where you place your feet, and stand on them. If the paper can be withdrawn with only slight resistance, the flexibility is about right. Too much flexibility and the paper cannot be withdrawn, too little and it slips out easily.

Waxable or waxless skis, which are better? The answer depends on your preference and how you will use the skis. Waxable skis are generally faster and tend to be more efficient when climbing. Waxing, however, is a bother for some, and not always easily learned. One type of waxless ski may be waxed if desired. The second type, never waxed, has a machined pattern, such as a fish scale, for gripping. For nature study, many prefer the slower waxless skis.

As for snowshoes, it's a good idea to try out several skis before buying any. Try various lengths, weights, and flexibilities; waxables and waxless; and skis of different materials— varying combinations of wood, fiberglass, and plastic.

You might fancy more than one type of ski, depending on the trekking you wish to do. And don't be afraid to experiment. I have one set of conventional, narrow, light-touring waxable skis 200 centimeters (6.6 feet) long for swift going on trails. My other, heretic, set is wide— a whopping 85 millimeters, waxless, and unbelievably short—150 centimeters (4.9 feet). I stray farther from the orthodox with the waxless skis by using cable bindings with an over-the-toe strap and felt-lined pacs with them. Admittedly my short, waxless skis are slow, but they take me nearly anywhere that my snowshoes will. In fact, they are essentially *sliding* snowshoes!

Although learning to cross-country ski is probably best done by taking a course from a qualified instructor, you can acquire considerable technique on your own with a little help. Here are several tips to get you started.

Begin on level terrain on a thin layer of snow or snow that has been packed. First, simply get the feel of your skis. Test how much effort it takes to maneuver them.

Practice two basic turns, since you often find yourself confronted by obstacles or other skiers. These are the step and kick turns already described for snowshoes. You will likely find the kick turn more difficult with the longer skis.

Now try the *diagonal stride,* the basic mile-eating technique for cross-country skiing. Think of it as accentuated or exaggerated walking with a glide. An opposite leg and arm move in unison. If you lead off with your left leg, as in marching, your right arm should strike forward simultaneously. Then follow with your right leg and left arm. After planting either foot, glide momentarily. This technique is called the diagonal stride because diagonal lines can be mentally drawn from arm to arm or leg to leg as you traverse the snow.

Incorporate *double poling* with the diagonal stride when you desire to accelerate, either on the level or when going down gentle hills; it offers a good change of pace. You push off with both poles in unison instead of alternately, as in the diagonal stride. Plant both poles vertically forward, bend your body, and try to gain forward thrust primarily from your body weight against the poles. Push off with your arms when your body has passed the planted poles. You might include a leg kick with your double poling maneuver.

Climb gentler hills straight up with a diagonal stride if you have sufficient momentum. On longer, steeper hills you will more likely traverse in zigzag fashion and incorporate step or kick turns, as you would if you were ascending hills on snowshoes. For short, steep hills, try

Figure 15. The telemark position, for greater stability when skiing down slopes.

the side-step and herringbone techniques. If all else fails, don't be too proud to remove your skis and *walk* up!

Assume one of three positions when descending slopes straight down. In the simplest, bend your knees and place one ski forward. For greater stability, use the *telemark* position (Figure 15). With your skis about seven inches apart and your upper body erect, bend your forward leg at the knee at a right angle; your shin should be at right angles to the ski. With your other ski well backward, your rear leg below the knee is about parallel to the snow's surface. Keep your arms low and extend them outward. In the *tuck* position, you assume a crouch with most of your weight on your heels. Your poles are stowed under your arms with points trailing.

You may descend diagonally and make turns in the process. The step turn is the same as for ascending slopes but must be done quickly and nimbly. The *telemark turn,* which works best in soft snow, requires more practice and concentration. While in a telemark position, tilt or slightly twist your forward ski in the direction of turn. Lean slightly into the turn, as if you were riding a bicycle. For a right turn, the left ski must be forward, and for a left turn the right ski must be forward. On very steep slopes, your center of gravity should be very low, so your trailing knee may drag in the snow.

At times you may need to slow your speed while descending. One efficient braking method is the *snowplow,* so named because the skis form a V, with the V pointing downhill. Bend your knees and ankles and press your heels outward so your ski tips form the apex of a V. Maintain pressure on the inner edges of your skis. Direct your poles backward. Don't attempt the snowplow on steep slopes until you have tested it on gentle slopes. The snowplow works best on soft snow. Another way to check speed while skiing downhill is by the *ski glissade* (gliss-ODD)—using your ski poles as a brake. With your body low, grasp both ski poles together firmly near the baskets and at the grips, and plow the points into the snow to one side of your body.

Practice falling and arising, since both might happen frequently during your first skiing attempts. If you sense you are losing your balance while descending, squat low, relax, and simply sit down. Or, you might try to fall to one side or the other. But avoid, at all times,

a face-first landing. In both prepared falls, try to keep your skis and feet between your upper body and any trees or other obstacles. To get up, place your skis on the downhill side and directed across the slope. Draw your skis directly beneath you and swing your body over them. Push up with your hands, either directly against the snow or against your poles lying on the snow. If unsuccessful, remove your skis and then get up.

Staying Found

When traveling in winter, particularly on foot, it is crucial that you know your location at all times. Losing your way in summer may mean an uncomfortable day or night but in winter such an experience can be a matter of survival.

To stay found, instill in yourself a need to locate yourself continually, and be receptive to any locating sign. Don't let anything distract you from this quest.

Always travel in relation to some reference; among the obvious are a mountain peak, a prominent hill or butte, or a lake. Strive to keep it in view and check it frequently.

If the sun is unobscured, welcome its guidance as you trek in relation to it. Continually monitor its changing position with the time of day. Realize that it arcs more southerly in winter than in summer; that is, it rises in the southeast and sets in the southwest.

Wind direction may be good reference as you travel. Although wind direction may change abruptly, at times it remains essentially constant for hours or even days. If other guides are lacking, don't hesitate to rely on wind direction. I've maintained my orientation many times by placing my left or right cheek into the wind as I traveled on foot. One time I snowshoed across a lake at night this way.

Linear features are particularly useful references. Among them are ranges of hills, streams, trails, and roads that may serve as baselines. Before you leave a major trail or road, ascertain whether it has a name or number and its nearest intersection. This information may prove useful should you attempt to return by a different route.

To see how a road serves as a baseline, imagine that you parked your vehicle on a turnoff of a north-south road. You struck out easterly on snowshoes through wooded terrain with intervening meadows and marshes for two hours. Since the day was pleasant you decided to return by another route and headed west-northwest for more than two hours before reaching the road. You couldn't see your vehicle but you knew you had to head south (left) to reach it—and after a time you did. You made a purposeful route adjustment with a linear feature to take the guesswork out of locating your vehicle.

Notice in the above example that travel time was monitored. This is always a good idea and is an added means of keeping yourself located.

You may be able to retrace a route by following your tracks, but don't count on it. The wind may fill in your tracks and obscure them. Be prepared with a backup tactic if this happens.

Following a course by compass is a reliable method, provided you are thoroughly familiar with how to use a compass. Select a compass that is versatile and easy to use. I prefer one where the 360 degrees around the dial are easy to read, any designated bearing can be set in, and the compass can be adjusted for *declination,* the value in degrees between magnetic

north and true north. (When adjusted for declination, you read true bearings because they are in relation to true north.) To follow a chosen bearing, sight along your compass toward an easily recognizable object, such as a prominent tree or cliff, and keep it in sight as you move toward it. When you reach the object, if you intend to follow the same course, sight on another object with the same bearing and proceed toward the new object as before. When you change course, read a new bearing. Learn to rely on a compass. Its needle almost always points correctly except if near a mineral ore body or a metallic object such as an axe, hammer, or steel belt buckle.

Navigating by topographic map and compass is much better than by compass alone. Frequently orient the map with your compass. Look first for two arrows on the map that indicate magnetic north and true north, as well as the intervening degrees of declination. If you haven't adjusted your compass for declination, place the compass on the map and rotate both until the magnetic north arrow on the map and the arrow of your compass—pointing toward magnetic north—are parallel. Your map is now correctly oriented.

If after orienting the map you cannot locate yourself on it, your compass can help further. Choose two features on the map that are well separated in your field of view. They may be prominent peaks or hilltops or islands in a lake. Determine their bearings, and from each draw lines on the map representing the reverse bearings. Your location should be where the lines cross. A compass mounted on a straight edge makes the drawing of the reverse bearings easier.

If you lack a compass or a map, resort to two other approaches. Maintain a reasonably straight course by lining up two or three ob-

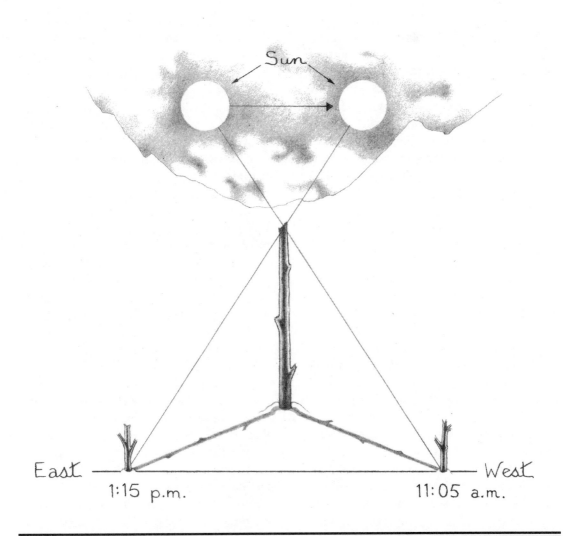

Figure 16. The stick and shadow method for determining direction. A line connecting the tips of shadows from a stick or ski pole, spaced fifteen minutes or more apart, trends about east-west.

jects as you travel. Here you are not so concerned with the specific direction of travel as you are in following a consistent course. Sketch a rough map as you go. Although admittedly inaccurate, it provides a means to record much detail that you likely would soon forget. Even travel times are well worth jotting down directly on the map between sketched-in features.

Direction Finding Without a Compass

On occasion, you may wish to know a direction for travel, but you are caught without a compass. Here are a few methods to establish direction.

I've already mentioned maintaining a course

with reference to the sun and aided by your watch. For direction finding, though, realize that the sun rises *exactly* in the east and sets *exactly* in the west only two times each year: on March 21 and September 23, during the spring and autumn equinoxes. During the winter it rises generally southeasterly and sets generally southwesterly. Reversed in summer, it rises north of east and sets north of west.

The stick and shadow method (Figure 16) is an easy and more accurate method of direction finding utilizing the sun. It works even when the sun is not visible as long as obvious shadows are discernible. Push a straight stick or a ski pole vertically in the snow. Mark the shadow's tip with a short stick. Wait fifteen minutes or more and mark the second position of the shadow's tip with another short stick. A line connecting the two short sticks trends about east-west. Such a line is most accurate near the middle of the day, and when it is formed by widely spaced control points, which represent more time separating them. If formed in the morning, the line trends a little south of west; created in the afternoon, it trends a little north of west.

If you have time, straddle midday and mark the shadow's tip several times. You will witness the shadows beginning to shorten and later lengthen once again. The shortest shadow will trend north-south and represents the sun's position at local noon time. If you are anywhere north of 23.4 degrees north, the sun will always be directly south of you at local noon.

Having a watch with hands, you can quickly determine direction with the sun's help. Place a matchstick or a straight twig vertically on your watch—held flat—at the tip of the hour hand. Rotate your body until the shadow formed by the matchstick or twig aligns perfectly with the hour hand. South is midway between the hour hand and twelve o'clock on the watch, as determined along the shorter arc of the watch's face. You can also reverse this process to *set* your watch to within a few minutes of local standard time.

At night you can readily tell direction from the North Star (Box 5) or from the constellation Orion (Box 6).

Finally, several natural features can aid you in direction finding. Recall that snowdrifts form on the lee side of objects and rime forms on the windward side. If you know from what direction the wind was blowing when either the snowdrifts or rime formed, then you can directly read direction from either of them. (Aligned drifts also aid you in maintaining a straight cross-country course.) General southerly or northerly directions can be extrapolated from trees. Growth rings of trees are generally widest on the south sides of trunks, and coniferous trees tend to be bushiest on their southern sides. Look at several stumps or living trees for either indicator, especially those that are well apart from one another. The bark of aspen and poplar trees tends to be lighter on the south side because of bleaching by the sun. Lastly, moss and frequently lichens predominate on the north sides of tree trunks.

If even after practicing all your staying found and direction finding skills you become lost, what should you do? Tell yourself not to panic, and use common sense for all your actions. Apply the winter survivalist techniques covered in the appendix.

FIVE

Winter Botany: Recognizing Plants

Plants can be arranged into two main groups: woody and nonwoody. Woody plants include mainly trees and shrubs; vines may be considered separately or as shrubs. Nonwoody plants, annual, biennial, or perennial, lack any woody parts and die back to the ground at the end of a growing season.

In this chapter I have selected several of the most common trees, shrubs, and nonwoody plants that project well above the snow and that you are likely to see. For each, I shall provide you with one or more diagnostic features that are readily apparent in winter. After becoming acquainted with the plants I characterize here, you may be motivated to learn several of the common species in your region.

After you take the time to *identify* a plant by diagnostic details, you will later happily *recognize* it as you would an old friend. You then *know* it without having to mull over specific characters once again. Once you truly know your friend Dean, let's say, you need not continually check his blue eyes and brown hair. The same is true for a plant.

Trees

Trees are woody perennial plants with usually a single stem or trunk just above ground. Fully grown trees are taller than shrubs, about fifteen feet or more. Trees are conveniently grouped as conifers or cone-bearing types—which retain their leaves—and the deciduous trees that periodically shed them (and usually lack cones). Conifers (KAHN-uh-furz or CONE-uh-furz) generally bear narrow or needlelike leaves and deciduous trees produce relatively broad leaves.

We can recognize conifers or "evergreen" trees as vividly in winter as in summer. *Pines* bear needlelike leaves in bundles, usually two, three, or five to a bundle, depending on the species. Widespread examples include the eastern white pine (mostly northeastern United States and southeastern Canada), jack pine (Great Lakes region and much of southern and central Canada), lodgepole pine (western United States and western Canada), and ponderosa pine (western United States and southwestern Canada).

The cones of some pines, notably those of jack pine and lodgepole pine, remain on the trees for years. Heat from forest fires opens them to release the seeds.

Pines can be significant food sources. Birds and small mammals eat the seeds, and large mammals, such as deer, porcupines, and rabbits, feed on the foliage and bark.

You can brew a tasty cup of tea from pine needles (see the appendix).

Pines continually fill the senses. Few would dispute the delectability of "whispering pines" as wind softly rustles through their needles, combined with the aroma of resin exuding from sun-warmed trunks.

Some confuse spruces with pines. *Spruces*, however, grow needlelike leaves singly that are squarish in cross profile and sharply pointed. As a test, roll a needle between a thumb and forefinger to feel the squarish configuration, then try pricking your skin with the sharp point. The needles bristle around twigs like a bottle brush or curve toward the upper sides.

Most widespread of the spruces are the white and black spruces (both in the northeastern United States and most of Canada to Alaska) and Engelmann spruce (much of the Rocky Mountains in the United States and Canada).

Because of their dense, stiff foliage, spruces hold much snow and provide a buffer from harsh, winter winds. Many mammals, consequently, linger near spruces for warmth and to move beneath them with relative ease in the shallow snow cover. Small birds and such small mammals as squirrels feed on spruce seeds. Although occurring singly as for the

spruces, the needlelike leaves of *hemlocks* are mostly flat, with generally two white lines on their undersides, and are attached by short stems to twigs. The cones are small, less than an inch long, and hang from the tips of branches, not behind the tips as in the pines and spruces.

Two widespread hemlocks are the eastern hemlock (northeastern United States and southeastern Canada) and the western hemlock (westernmost United States and Canada to Alaska and northern Rockies).

Such animals as rabbits and deer feed on spruce foliage (and buds), and porcupines gnaw the bark.

Although flat like those of hemlocks, the needlelike leaves of firs are attached directly to twigs and, therefore, lack short stems. Fir cones are upright, and disintegrate upon maturing, so that eventually only a central spike remains.

Two widespread firs include the balsam fir (northeastern United States and much of eastern and southern Canada) and the subalpine fir (much of the Rocky Mountain region in the United States and Canada). Both of these firs exhibit swellings, called resin blisters, on young trunks. When bruised, balsam fir leaves release a pleasant aroma that reminds me of crushed orange peel. Several birds and small mammals eat fir seeds.

Douglas firs are not true firs. They possess flat needlelike leaves, as do true firs, but their cones hang from branches; three-pointed "bracts" (modified leaves) project from between the cone scales.

The most common Douglas fir grows naturally in the western United States and southwestern Canada and has been planted extensively in the eastern United States. It reaches more than 300 feet high within the moist Pacific Coast region.

Cedars, also known as arbor vitae, have scalelike leaves arranged in flattened branchlets. Their woody cones are upright or hang from branches. Cedar bark, fibrous and shredded, serves as a good tinder for starting campfires. (Be conservative in peeling only a little at one time from the outermost layers.) Cedar wood is aromatic and strongly resistant to decay; its use in canoe frames is well known.

The most widespread cedar is the northern white cedar, occupying the northeastern United States and southeastern Canada.

Deer habitually browse the leaves and twigs of cedars. Birds, especially finches, eat the seeds.

Junipers resemble cedars but their leaves may be prickly or scalelike and dispose in rounded or angled branchlets. Cones of junipers resemble pea-sized blue or reddish-brown berries and taste like resin. Juniper bark and wood is similar to that of cedars.

The most widespread tree-sized junipers are the eastern red cedar (eastern United States) and the Rocky Mountain juniper (Rockies of the United States and southwestern Canada). (Notice that the eastern "red cedar" is considered a "juniper." "Cedar" and "juniper" tend to be used rather inconsistently. To make matters worse, true cedars are not native to North America!) Common juniper (mostly northern United States and southern Canada to Alaska), largely a sprawling shrub often four feet or less high, is closely related to red cedar; it, however, has three-sided twigs, whereas the red cedar has four-sided twigs.

Birds and small mammals eat the berrylike cones of junipers. The cedar waxwing received its name because of its fondness for juniper ("cedar") "berries." Because the seeds pass through their bodies unharmed, both birds and mammals are significant in dispersing junipers.

Larches, or tamaracks, are deciduous evergreens—a seeming contradiction—and an appropriate group to end this section on conifers. In autumn, similar to deciduous, broad-leaved trees, their brushlike clusters of needle-like leaves turn golden yellow and drop off. So, in winter, you only see spurlike nubbins on branches where leaves once were, usually along with upright cones.

The most widespread larch is called tamarack or eastern larch (northeastern United States, much of southern and central Canada, and to Alaska). In the southern part of its range, tamarack grows in wet places. Tamarack wood, somewhat oily, is highly resistant to decay.

Because deciduous trees in temperate climates nearly always lack leaves in winter, they are more difficult to identify than conifers. Lacking knowledge of their growth form or bark, you must resort especially to twigs and seeds as identifiers, and, perhaps, any adhering dried leaves. With twigs, you first pay attention to the side buds, whether they are arranged oppositely to one another or alternately (Figure 17). Then you might check the size, shape, and color of both the end and side buds. Later, you might scrutinize other details: the number of scales covering the buds, the leaf scars where autumn leaves detach, and other features seen with a hand lens. If you become engrossed in these details, you might eventually consult winter keys that base identifications on those characteristics. (Some keys are given in George A. Petrides's book listed in the Selected Readings.)

Three groups of deciduous trees display an

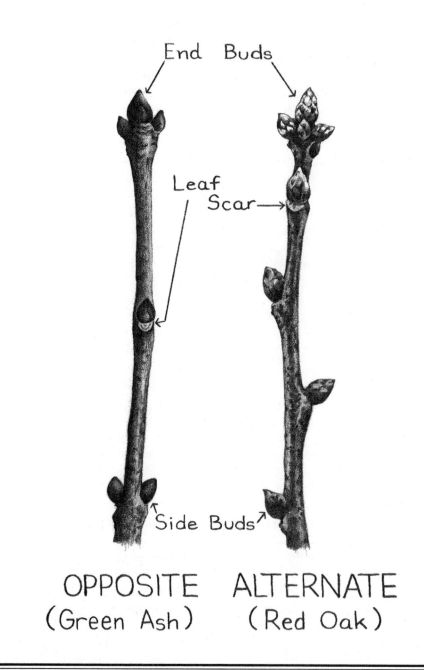

End Buds

Leaf Scar→

Side Buds

OPPOSITE   ALTERNATE
(Green Ash) (Red Oak)

Figure 17. Two basic kinds of winter twigs of deciduous trees and shrubs, with oppositely or alternately arranged side buds and leaf scars. Leaf scars are places where leaf stalks of a previous season's leaves were attached.

opposite arrangement of their twigs, buds, and leaf scars: the maples, ashes, and buckeyes. First check for the opposite twigs as you look up into the branches.

Twigs of *maples* are slender and numerous with larger end buds than side buds. Search for any adhering seeds or leaves; the seeds are paired and winged, and the leaves have pointed lobes. Most widespread are the sugar maple (northeastern United States and southeastern Canada), red maple, and silver maple (both eastern United States and southeastern Canada).

The sap of all maples contains sugar.

Wildlife feeds on maples. Such mammals as beavers and porcupines eat the bark; rabbits, hares, and deer are among the animals that consume the twigs and buds; and various birds and mammals devour the seeds.

The end buds of *ashes* are larger than the side buds—as for maples, but the twigs are stouter and fewer. Ash seeds, although similarly winged as in the maples, differ, too, in being single (not paired) and resemble short-handled canoe paddles. The most widespread ashes are the white ash (eastern half of United States and southeastern Canada) and the green ash (eastern and central United States and south-central and southeastern Canada).

Among other uses, ash wood has been used in making traditional snowshoes because it is relatively light and very strong.

Various birds eat ash seeds; such animals as beavers and porcupines consume the bark; and deer and rabbits are among the animals that browse on the twigs of ash saplings.

The stout twigs of *buckeyes* sport very large end buds. During a spring thaw you might find the seed capsules on the ground. Smooth or prickly, the seed capsules release one or two inedible chestnut brown seeds. A light spot on each seed reminded some of a "buck's eye"—coining the tree's name. The most widespread of the group is the Ohio buckeye (east-central United States). A common introduced species is the horse chestnut, native to Asia and Europe.

Buckeye seeds are generally inedible for humans, and all parts of the horse chestnut—containing a dangerous substance, a glycoside—are poisonous. Wildlife rarely eats the buckeyes, probably sensing the presence of a toxin.

The remaining deciduous trees I've selected—because they are commonplace—all share one feature: an alternate arrangement of their twigs, buds, and leaf scars. These include the birches, poplars, willows, oaks, elms, basswoods, sycamores, hickories, walnuts, apples, plums, cherries, locusts, and sassafras.

Immediately noticeable about *birches* is a bark with cross lines or streaks that often peels on young trunks. The cross lines are actually breathing slits that allow air to reach the inner growing layer of the wood. Two kinds of oblong structures hang from the twigs: the slimmer catkins and the stouter catkinlike cones. In spring, larger catkins (said by some to resemble a cat's tail) open and enlarge to scatter pollen on smaller catkins that become fertilized to develop into catkinlike cones that produce seed. These catkinlike cones disintegrate in autumn and winter as they release the tiny, winged seeds and protective, three-lobed scales. Search for both scattered on the snow. Any still-attached leaves usually show doubly-toothed margins.

Two widespread birches are the paper or white birch (northernmost United States and much of Canada to Alaska) and yellow birch (northeastern United States and southeastern

Canada). Indians, of course, covered their canoes with bark from the paper birch, and some artisans still continue this tradition.

Consider birches as a food source. Tap their trunks in spring for sweet sap, as you would maples. Both the yellow birch (yellowish bark) and the sweet or black birch (nearly black bark) grow twigs with a wintergreen flavor that you can quickly verify by chewing. Boil the twigs to make tea.

Deer and rabbits are among the animals that browse birch twigs. Many birds eat the buds and seeds.

Although *poplars* include what are separately known as poplars, aspens, and cottonwoods, botanists place them all in a single group or genus: *Populus*. The bark of the general group of poplars is generally smooth and whitish on young trunks, but deeply furrowed and dark on old trunks. Often tracing a zigzag pattern, the twigs bear pointed end and side buds, both types of about the same size. For an added, distinctive characteristic, cut through a twig crosswise. The pith or central wood will appear star-shaped.

Most widespread of the poplar species are the quaking aspen (young bark white or greenish-white; northeastern and western United States and much of Canada to Alaska), balsam poplar (young bark greenish or brownish; buds sticky; parts of northern United States and much of Canada and Alaska), and the eastern cottonwood (yellowish green young bark; eastern United States and southeastern Canada). A well-known poplar introduced from Europe, the Lombardy, exhibits a steeple-like form with sharply rising branches.

Various birds and mammals consume the seeds, buds, and twigs of poplars. Beavers, especially, relish the bark.

Occurring mostly as shrubs, *willows* are closely related to poplars. Often arising as several trunks, you can also recognize willows by their colorful twigs, frequently bright yellow, orange, red, or olive green. Buds usually hug twigs and are covered by a single scale. Another way to identify willows is by galls—deformities generated by insects—on the twigs, some of which resemble pine cones (illustrated at the beginning of this chapter.) Expanding flower buds in the late winter or early spring become the fuzzy, pollen-bearing flowers known as pussies. Willows grow mostly along streams and on other wet ground.

The most widespread of the tree willows are: the peachleaf willow (much of United States and part of southern Canada)—especially common along prairie streams; pussy willow (northern United States, and southern and southeastern Canada); and black willow (eastern United States and southeastern Canada).

American Indians used willows for a variety of ailments. The bark of several willows (and poplars) contains salicin (SAL-uh-suhn) (the genus of willows is *Salix*), a substance used in the manufacture of aspirin.

Many birds and mammals eat willow buds and twigs, including grouse, deer, hares, and beavers.

End buds of *oaks* occur in clusters, and twigs, when cut across, show a star-shaped pith, as do poplars. Oaks, of course, also bear acorns, which you may see scattered on the ground during a winter thaw. Look for leaves frequently attached in winter; they most commonly feature rounded or pointed lobes. Many insects induce galls on oak leaves, twigs and branches, roots, and buds.

Most widespread of the oaks are the bur oak, northern red oak (both eastern United States and southeastern Canada), and white oak (eastern United States).

Several oaks are rich in tannin, a substance used in curing leather. Tannin makes some acorns bitter and must be removed with boiling water before the acorns can be eaten.

Many birds and mammals, including grouse, wood ducks, wild turkeys, squirrels, bears, raccoons, foxes, and deer eat acorns. Deer, rabbits, and hares browse the twigs.

Elms have slender twigs with the side buds positioned off-center from the leaf scars. Elm bark often exhibits flat-topped, intersecting ridges.

Two elms are the most widespread: the American elm (eastern United States and southeastern Canada) and slippery elm (mostly eastern United States). Diagnostic of the American elm is the vase-shaped crown that results from its trunk dividing into several, distinctly rising branches. The fragrant, inner bark of slippery elm is gummy or slippery; it can be used as a survival food or for tea.

Numerous elms, but particularly the American elm, have succumbed to Dutch elm disease. It is caused by a fungus spread by bark beetles.

Beeches display gray bark that, atypically, is smooth even on old trees. Their slender twigs bear pointed buds that angle outward. Still on the tree or beneath the snow you are apt to discover spiny husks that house two or three three-cornered edible nuts. The only North American species is the American beech (eastern United States and southeasternmost Canada).

Beech nuts are eaten by many birds and mammals, such as grouse, wild turkeys, bears, raccoons, squirrels, and deer.

When identifying *basswoods*, also called *lindens*, look for short, usually red buds covered by two scales. The seeds, which may still adhere in winter, occur in clusters of round nutlets about a third of an inch in diameter. These clusters hang beneath leafy wings. The most widespread species is the American basswood (mostly northeastern United States and southeasternmost Canada).

As you trek through the woods, try nibbling on the pleasant, slightly gummy buds. Having the forethought to pick basswood blossoms at their prime in midsummer, you could savor mild basswood blossom tea after your walk.

Among the birds and mammals that eat the buds and nutlets are grouse, quails, squirrels, and chipmunks. Deer and rabbits feed on the twigs.

Recognize *sycamores* first by their mottled bark: the brown outer bark flakes off to reveal a whitish, yellowish, or greenish bark underneath. Pendant, ball-shaped seed heads or "buttonballs," an inch in diameter or more and containing numerous hairy seeds, often last into winter. The buds are covered by a single scale. Look for sycamores on bottomlands along streams and lakes. Most widespread is the American sycamore (most of eastern United States).

Deer and muskrats eat sycamore twigs. Cavities in the rotted wood are used for nesting or shelter by wood ducks, opossums, raccoons, and skunks.

Stout twigs with large leaf scars and end buds characterize *hickories*. Look also for the mostly smooth nut husks, still possibly hanging on the twigs or beneath the snow, which split into four sections to release a single nut; this nut is smooth except for a few ridges. Most conspicuous is the shagbark hickory (eastern United States and southeasternmost Canada) with shaggy bark that separates into long plates; the other most widespread species, primarily in the eastern United States, are the pignut hickory, bitternut hickory, and mockernut hickory. The well-known pecan, of the southeastern United States, is also a hickory.

The nuts of several hickories, especially the shagbark and mockernut hickories and the pecan are eminently edible. Many use the green, unseasoned wood to flavor meat in smoking or barbecuing; the wood also makes a good charcoal.

Walnuts possess stout twigs with large leaf scars and end buds, reminiscent of hickories. Walnut twigs, however, differ notably in their chambered pith. You can observe the tiny chambers by carving a twig lengthwise down to its pith or splitting it with a pocketknife. Another difference is that walnut husks do not split open when ripe and house an edible nut with a rough shell. The most widespread walnuts are the black walnut (eastern United States) and butternut (mostly northeastern United States and southeasternmost Canada). Highly acclaimed for its nut, the introduced English walnut is native to Europe, India, and China.

Many mammals, including squirrels and mice, feed on the nuts. Deer consume the twigs.

Three groups of trees all have edible fruit: the apples, plums, and cherries.

You can usually verify apples in winter by their many short, spurlike twigs and scaly bark. These spurlike twigs, which are roughened by leaf scars and may display thornlike tips, support the several-seeded fruit and leaves in summer. The only apples native to North America are several kinds of crab apples that bear small and usually tart fruit, suitable mostly for jellies and preserves. The several varieties of domestic apples are derived mainly from one species native to Eurasia. Apple fruit, particularly that of crab apples, may hang on the twigs into winter.

Wildlife favors apple fruit. Among the apple consumers are deer, foxes, raccoons, pheasants, and mourning doves.

Plums overlap in their characteristics with some other trees: Their young bark often exhibits cross lines or streaks (as for birches) and they often have spurlike twigs (as for apples). Some possess thorns; such thorns may be simple spikes or actually sharp twigs bearing buds. Finding any fruit will clinch your suspicion of a possible plum; within the fleshy, edible fruit is a single, large, somewhat flattened seed. Most widespread is the American plum (most of eastern and central United States and part of southern Canada).

Many birds and mammals feed on plum fruits. Because the excreted or regurgitated pits remain unharmed, such feeding provides an efficient method for spreading plums.

Cherries, although often displaying spurlike twigs as do plums, always possess cross lines on young bark and always are thornless. The dark, young cross-lined bark of cherries could be confused with that of young birches, but cherries lack catkins. The edible cherry fruits are generally smaller than those of plums and contain a single round seed. (You should not eat fresh cherry seeds because they contain cyanide; cooking the berries, however, destroys it.) Black knot fungus, a black warty mass attached to branches, frequently attacks cherry trees and aids in their identification. It kills plant cells and distorts the branches.

The most widespread cherries include the chokecherry (much of United States and southern Canada), often only of shrub size; the pin cherry (much of northern United States and southern Canada); and the black cherry (mostly eastern United States and southeasternmost Canada).

Many birds and mammals eat cherry fruits and provide a ready means of cherry dispersal, as they do for the plums.

Locusts are readily recognized by their thorns and long seedpods. Thorns occur on the branches only or on both branches and trunks. Seedpods may reach to eighteen inches long. Most widespread are the honey locust and black locust (both in much of eastern United States).

Birds and mammals that eat locust seeds include bobwhites, pheasants, rabbits, hares, deer, and squirrels.

Sassafras can be spotted by its reddish-brown bark and bright green twigs with a lemony flavor when chewed. It ranges over much of the eastern United States.

All parts of sassafras are aromatic. Its roots and bark, however, have been popular in making a tasty, reddish-brown tea. Simply boil the roots and bark.

Rabbits and deer are among the animals that eat sassafras twigs. Several kinds of birds consume the prewinter blue fruits.

Shrubs

Let's begin recognizing some common shrubs by first considering three groups that share oppositely arranged buds, leaf scars, and twigs. These are the dogwoods, the highbush cranberry, and the American mistletoe.

Some *dogwoods* reach tree size. Only the rare exception exhibits alternately arranged buds, leaf scars, and twigs. Similar to the willows, dogwood twigs are often highly colored, usually red, green, or purple but also brown. The buds are covered with only two scales, and the leaf scars are raised. Dogwood berries, largely inedible and white, blue, or red, group in umbrella-shaped clusters and often last into the winter. One of the most widespread is the red-osier dogwood (northern United States, southern and western Canada to Alaska) with red twigs and white fruit.

Among the birds and mammals that feed on dogwood berries are grouse, pheasants, songbirds, deer, and skunks. Rabbits, hares, deer, and elk browse the twigs.

Highbush cranberry sports greenish buds encased within two scales. Red berries, tart, but edible, and often lasting on twigs into winter, occur in clusters and encase flat seeds. This shrub ranges over the northern United States and southern Canada.

Although unrelated to commercial cranberries, highbush cranberry fruit can be prepared and eaten in the same ways.

Birds that eat the berries include various songbirds, grouse, and pheasants.

American mistletoe is the only shrub in colder North America parasitic on broad-leaved trees, infesting trunks or branches. (Another mistletoe, dwarf mistletoe with scalelike leaves, is parasitic on conifers.) It grows broad, leathery evergreen leaves, jointed stems, and whitish, round, single-seeded berries. This shrub ranges over the eastern United States.

Many birds and mammals eat the berries. The birds, however, must be responsible for the extensive spread of mistletoe.

Now, let's turn to several shrubs with alternately arranged buds, leaf scars, and twigs. I've selected Labrador tea, sumacs, roses, hawthorns, hazelnuts, and alders.

A low shrub, up to three feet high, *Labrador tea* (Figure 18) inhabits northern bogs and swamps. Often in tight clusters, its elongate, smooth-margined, leathery, evergreen leaves have rolled-over edges and exude a fragrance when crushed. The leaves display a rusty wool underside, which may also be white in sum-

Figure 18. Labrador tea exposed in a snow-covered bog. Leaves of this plant make an excellent tea all year round.

mer. Labrador tea spreads through the northern United States and much of Canada and Alaska.

Here's one plant you can make a pleasant, mild tea from throughout the year. Dry the best-appearing leaves before steeping them.

The most conspicuous of sumacs flaunt dense, red, spikelike clusters of hairy fruit at the tips of their branches that usually persist into winter. Their stout twigs yield milky sap when broken. Included are staghorn sumac, smooth sumac, and dwarf sumac, which, as a group, stretch across southern Canada and most of the United States. (Avoid the less conspicuous poison sumac, with its loose cluster of white berries; all parts highly irritate the skin.)

Try a refreshing "sumacade." Soak and crush the berries and strain the mixture through a cloth to remove the seeds and hairs. Sweeten the pink fluid to your taste. It's best to gather the red spikes in summer or autumn and save them for a winter drink to remind you of warmer times.

Deer, moose, and rabbits are some of the animals that eat sumac twigs. Birds that feed on the berries include songbirds, grouse, bobwhites, pheasants.

Recognize *roses* in winter by their prickly stems that mostly arch back toward the ground with generally green or red twigs and red buds. Clinching the identification are red fruits called hips, containing many small seeds, that often persist in winter. Tufts characteristically adorn the hips' tips. Hips distinguish the roses from other prickly shrubs such as raspberries and blackberries. The many roses range widely.

If caught in a survival situation, eat the pulpy outside of rose hips, which are rich in vitamin C. Wildlife eats the hips, too, but usually only if more desirable foods are unavailable.

Hawthorns also reach the size of trees. They are equipped with thorns, as their name suggests, mostly more than an inch long. Their small, round, reddish buds usually terminate spurlike twigs. Red or orange fruits, called haws, resemble rose hips or perhaps miniature apples, but are only about half an inch in diameter; they often last into winter. The many hawthorns, like roses, range widely.

You can rely on hawthorns for survival food. As you munch the dry haws, spit out the several nutlets.

Birds and mammals that eat haws include bobwhites, partridges, pheasants, foxes, rabbits, and deer.

Hazelnuts or filberts, some of which attain tree size, customarily form thickets or undergrowths in open woods. Twigs bear catkins, as do those of birches. The bark, however, lacks the cross lines evident on birches. A highly edible nut is enclosed within a leafy husk that occasionally remains attached in winter. The commercial filbert nut is very similar to that of the American hazelnut. Hazelnuts occupy much of the United States and southern Canada.

Among the birds and mammals that consume the nuts are pheasants, grouse, quails, squirrels, chipmunks, and deer.

Attaining also the size of trees, alders might at first be confused with hazelnuts or birches because catkins likewise hang from the twigs. Alders, however, produce cones that do not disintegrate as do those of birches. Further, the buds are reddish-brown and on tiny stalks. Widespread and of many species, alders are found mostly along streams and on wet slopes.

Birds and mammals that consume alder twigs include ptarmigans, grouse, deer, rabbits, moose, and muskrats.

Nonwoody Plants

Great numbers of nonwoody plants die back to their roots with the onset of winter, but their remains often stand erect. I've selected several that usually project above the snow: cattails, reed grass, sedges, beggarticks, docks, common mullein, burdocks, teasels, common tansy, milkweeds, goldenrods, and common evening primrose. All are widespread, but their presence may be spotty. If "winter weeds" fascinate you, go further with such guides as Lauren Brown's *Weeds in Winter* and chapter 1 of Donald W. Stokes's *A Guide to Nature in Winter.*

Cattails, as well as reed grass, sedges, and beggar-ticks, are confined to wet places, in water or along shores. So expect to see some of them projecting above the ice. Cattails sport swordlike leaves and brown, cylindrical spikes, many of which literally explode in autumn to scatter fluffy seeds. But many of the spikes survive into winter. As you walk through cattails, realize that beneath you the wet or frozen ground is riddled with their starchy rootstocks; from them, in spring, new shoots will burst from sprouts to initiate a new crop.

Under "ideal" conditions you could eat cattails in winter. "Ideal" means open water shallow enough to recover quickly rootstocks and sprouts without becoming unduly chilled. If this should occur, wash and peel the rootstocks for their starchy cores. Mash the cores in cold water and separate the fibers from them. You are left with a white flour. The horn-shaped sprouts can be eaten as a raw or cooked vegetable. Other cattails parts edible in the warmer months include the shoots and stalks, green flower spikes, and the yellow pollen. Offering such a wide choice of food, Euell Gibbons, a prolific writer of wild edible plants, called the cattail the "Supermarket of the Swamps"! Muskrats particularly relish cattails, but waterfowl feed on them as well.

Reed grass is a true grass, having hollow, round, jointed stems with narrow leaves in two rows, and is notably tall, reaching thirteen feet high. Its plumelike seed clusters generally persist into winter but become partially destroyed by this time. The tall stems are anchored by stout rootstocks from which sprouts and shoots arise in spring, similarly as for cattails.

Reed grass is a favorite food of muskrats. Plumed reed grass makes an appealing, tall, decorative plant but should be picked in late summer while the leaves are still green and the seed clusters fully intact.

Sedges, although grasslike, differ from true grasses by their solid stems, most of which are triangular in cross profile. Tiny seeds are borne in spikelets that may be single or clustered. Some sedges, called *bulrushes*, have spongy tissue making up their stems, several of which are round in cross profile. Stems of bulrushes are frequently seen protruding above the ice along the margins of lakes (see Figure 39). Perennials, sedges proliferate each year from rootstocks, tubers, or seeds.

Such mammals as muskrats, moose, beavers, and deer feed on the stems, leaves, and rootstocks of sedges, and many birds consume their seeds.

If you return home from a winter trek to discover tiny seeds with usually two or more barbs sticking to your clothing, you have easily just learned another group of plants favoring wet places, including ditches and low meadows: the *beggar-ticks*, also known as stick-tights or bur marigolds. Next time out, see if you can find the plants yielding the strange seeds. If you're lucky, you will see the seeds issuing from seed heads on plants with oppositely arranged branches. Beggar-ticks are annuals, reproducing by their well-dispersed seeds. In summer, yellow flowers, complex like sunflowers, precede the seed heads.

Docks frequently occur in wet places but can be found in rich, drier soils as well. In winter you recognize them as reddish-brown plants with seeds in spiked clusters; the tiny, three-angled seeds are enclosed within three wings. Perennial plants, leaves of docks arise from the base of the stem in early spring and again in the autumn. The leaves, rich in protein and vitamins A and C, can be eaten raw in salads or as a cooked vegetable.

Many birds feed on dock seeds. Such mammals as deer and muskrats browse the stems and leaves.

Jutting impressively above the snow, the stem of *common mullein* towers up to eight feet or more above the ground. From the stem looms a single seed spike or a cluster of a few seed spikes up to three feet high. Rap the seed spike and watch minute seeds, scarcely a thirty-second of an inch across, fleck the snow. Under a hand lens the brown seeds reveal wavy ridges alternating with deep grooves. A closer look at the stem reveals it covered by woolly hairs; if the base of the plant is accessible, you will see a rosette of leaves, woolly as the stem. A biennial, common mullein grows a rosette of leaves the first year and a yellow flowering spike the second. Look for common mullein, naturalized from Eurasia, in any dry, open area, especially where the soils are stony.

Burdocks attach to you as do the beggar-ticks: their round burs with hooked bristles covering the seeds stick to your clothing. Both groups, consequently, spread easily by animals, including you and me. When out again, try to find the plants, which will be easier than locating those bearing beggar-tick seeds. Burdock plants, with alternate branches, stretch up to nine feet high. Their broad, rhubarblike leaves may still remain in winter, although appearing badly shriveled. Burdocks, native to Eurasia, are biennial, producing a rosette of leaves and a taproot the first year; this first-year root can be eaten as a cooked vegetable if first boiled in two or more changes of water. A

flower stalk forms the second year, bedecked with purplish, many-flowered heads. Burdocks flourish on waste ground where the soil is productive but usually not disturbed by cultivation, or where the soil has returned to another state, as neglected farmland.

Particularly indicative of *teasels* are prickly, dense, flower heads resembling egg-shaped pincushions, up to four inches long, on prickly stems up to six feet high. Prickly bracts curve up around the heads from beneath. Minute, four-angled, brownish seeds scatter from the heads. In summer, the prickly heads bear numerous, tiny lilac or white flowers. Teasels, native to Europe, grow along roadsides, in pastures, and in old fields. Biennials, they produce a rosette of wrinkled leaves the first year, followed the next year by a flower stalk with opposite leaves.

Gather flower stalks of teasels in autumn or winter for an attractive floral arrangement complemented by placing it in a tall vase. Teasels have also been used to card or *tease* wool—comb or disentangle it prior to spinning.

Buttonlike seed heads, about one-half inch in diameter or less, in flat clusters distinguish *common tansy*. Derived from yellow flower heads, the seed heads perch on stems up to three feet high; fernlike leaves may still clutch the stems. With a hand lens you can see the five-angled, brownish seeds about one-sixteenth of an inch long. Originally an alien from Europe, common tansy lives along the borders of fields, in pastures, along roadsides, and on other waste ground. Common tansy is a perennial that reproduces from seed and rootstocks.

In summer, you can use the aromatic leaves and flowers as a flavoring like sage; use with caution, however, as both can be poisonous if used in large amounts. In winter, the dried seed heads still emit a slight scent when crushed.

If you see attached seedpods that split along their entire length, suspect milkweeds. Any remaining flat, brown seeds with parachutelike tufts of whitish, silky hairs should corroborate your tentative identification. Further, any discernible attached leaves will be opposite or whorled about the stem. Milkweeds, so named because they exude a milky juice when cut or bruised in summer, reach to about six feet high but frequently are shorter. You find milkweeds mostly on open, dry ground, but expect them on wet ground as well.

Frequently seen on dry ground, common milkweed displays distinctive seedpods: swollen at the bottom, pointed at the tip, and with spiny projections. In spring and summer you can eat the shoots, young leaves, young seedpods, and flower buds as a vegetable by boiling any of them in two or more changes of water to dispel the bitter, milky juice. I particularly like the flower buds, picked when green, which taste somewhat like broccoli to me. You can also nibble on the slightly sweet, purplish, pink, or white flowers. Common milkweed, with opposite leaves, is a perennial that replenishes itself by rootstocks or seeds.

Goldenrods flaunt spikelike-to-flat-topped seed clusters, with several cluster shape variations in between. Any adhering leaves are alternate. Look for round or elongate galls commonly found *on* the stems. Goldenrods, three to six feet high, form raised galls by growing around insect eggs laid on the stems. Larvae may overwinter inside the galls. Expect goldenrods in practically all habitats, open or wooded, but usually not on recently cultivated land. Perennials, goldenrods persist in the same places from rootstocks and seeds; in summer, they display yellowish flowers.

Goldenrods are good honey-producing plants. Many birds, including juncos, finches, and sparrows, eat their seeds.

Characteristic of the common evening primrose in winter is a spike of woody, cylindrical seedpods about an inch long; the tips curl back as the pods split into four sections. Under a hand lens, the brown seeds, about one-sixteenth of an inch long, appear irregularly angular. The stems, up to five feet high but frequently less, stand in open, dry places, such as along roadsides, fields, and waste ground. A biennial, common evening primrose forms a rosette of lance-shaped leaves and a taproot the first year, followed by a flower stalk the next year.

Aptly named, this plant's four-petaled yellow flowers open toward evening and wilt the next day. You can eat the first-year roots in the fall and early spring by boiling them in two or three changes of water.

If you can consistently distinguish these plants protruding above the snow that I've surveyed, you are well on your way to recognizing plants in winter.

SIX

More Winter Botany:
How Plants Adapt and
the Winter Garden

Plants, being immobile, have fewer options than animals in coping with winter in northern regions. They can't migrate. They can't burrow into the ground or snow. And they don't hibernate, unless existing through the wintry period in a dormant state might be considered hibernation.

Strategies that plants use in adapting to winter depend, in large part, on their general type: woody and nonwoody. Let's consider the conspicuous woody types first.

Woody Plants

Woody plants, the trees and shrubs, are continually exposed to wintry conditions. Unless they are very short or the snow is extremely deep, these plants rise above the snow. Their main winter concerns are the cold and drying out.

In the autumn, unless a sudden, unusual cold snap arrives, plants gradually become resistant to lower temperatures. Plants acclimate, acclimatize, or adapt—these words are used somewhat interchangeably—or undergo a kind of "hardening" process: They become tolerant of subfreezing temperatures without experiencing freezing injury. (In scientific writings about animals, *acclimating* usually refers to short-term adjustments, and *acclimatizing* or *adapting* allude to long-term adjustments, seasonally or longer.) This acclimating or hardening process occurs in two, or possibly, three stages.

During the first stage, growth gradually ceases with shorter days, which are perceived through the leaves that respond directly to sunlight. Frequently, during the last days of autumn, plants receive less water, which also affects their growth. Certain chemical changes take place that enable plants to react to lower temperatures. An especially significant one is the plant hormone abscisic (ab-SIZZ-ick) acid, which becomes more concentrated with the shorter days. Abscisic acid retards plant growth and promotes the separation and falling of leaves from twigs in deciduous trees and shrubs.

The second stage of cold hardening is induced by the first autumn frost. Membranes of the plant cells now become chemically altered as the temperatures drop. Proteins and sugars making up the cell membranes undergo chemical changes, and the fats become less saturated, allowing the membranes to remain more flexible. The lesser saturation also means that the fats crystallize at lower temperatures. The presence of more abscisic acid also enables the cell membranes to pass water through them more easily; this trait retards ice crystals forming within the cells.

Finally, a third stage of acclimating may occur after prolonged exposure to frigid temperatures of about -22 to -58 degrees Fahrenheit.

Resistance to freezing in plants varies in a number of ways. Important variables include the time of year and the speed with which freezing occurs. An early, hard frost in autumn doesn't allow the cold hardening process to complete itself. Rapid freezing allows ice to form within the cells where it is more damaging; in contrast, slow freezing first induces less damaging ice to crystallize in pores outside of the cells. A late, hard frost in spring may come at a time when the plants have "dehardened" and their resistance to freezing is reduced.

Different species of trees (Table 4) and other plants vary in their freezing resistance. For some, their resistance temperature is close to the average low temperature at their northern range limit (e.g., live oaks, slash pines). In others, their resistance temperature is far below any low temperature they may experience (e.g., bald cypresses, eastern cottonwoods). To appreciate this second group directly, compare the lowest temperatures recorded for Wisconsin, Minnesota, and Mississippi (Table 2) with those resistance temperatures given in Table 4. Still other trees have the capability of adjusting to the low temperatures of a region in which they grow. Green ashes from southeastern Minnesota, for example, can tolerate lower temperatures than green ashes from west-central Mississippi.

As might be expected, different parts of a plant may have different freeze resistances. Table 4 shows that buds may be more or less resistant to freezing than twigs, and different parts of twigs may vary in their resistance to freezing.

In spite of building up resistance to cold, plants may still freeze. A dramatic way of perceiving this event is by hearing loud, cracking sounds as tree trunks split. On one cold, winter night, I was startled by such sounds while shivering in my sleeping bag. The following morning my thermometer, six feet above the ground, recorded an air temperature of -26 degrees Fahrenheit.

How does freezing injury occur in plants? First, plant tissue is supercooled; that is, it cools below the freezing temperature without ice forming. At lower temperatures, though, ice crystals develop but occur initially within pore spaces *outside* of the cells. Here, the higher concentration of dissolved materials, higher than that within the cells, lowers the freezing point of water. Eventually, at slightly lower temperatures, ice forms *inside* the cells. Cells die because ice crystallizes, and not strictly because of cold temperatures. Death results from dehydration as water in the cells is used up to form ice crystals and from the physical damage by ice crystals as they puncture cell membranes.

Besides freezing, another major problem of woody plants in winter is drying out. These plants cope with desiccation by at least three

TABLE 4 Freezing Resistance of Selected Trees from Three Regions in the United States

Species	Lowest Temperature Without Freezing Injury (Degrees Centigrade)		
	Bud	Twig	Evergreen Leaf
Northern Wisconsin			
Balsam Poplar	− 80	− 80	—
Quaking Aspen	− 80	− 80	—
Paper Birch	− 80	− 80	—
Jack Pine	− 80	− 80	− 80
Tamarack	− 80	− 80	—
Red Pine	− 80	− 80	− 80
Eastern White Pine	− 80	− 80	− 80
Balsam Fir	− 80	− 80	− 80
Black Spruce	− 50	− 80	− 80
White Spruce	− 50	− 80	− 80
Southeastern Minnesota			
Northern White Cedar	− 80	− 80	− 80
Sugar Maple	− 80	− 40 to − 80*	—
American Basswood	− 80	− 80	—
American Elm	− 80	− 40 to − 80*	—
Bur Oak	− 60	− 40 to − 60*	—
Green Ash	− 40	− 40 to − 70*	—
Hackberry	− 40	− 40 to − 80*	—
Black Walnut	− 30	− 30 to − 80*	—
West-Central Mississippi			
Black Willow	− 60	− 80	—
Eastern Cottonwood	− 50	− 80	—
Black Tupelo	− 30	− 30 to − 50*	—
Green Ash	− 30	− 30 to − 40*	—
Red Maple	− 30	− 25 to − 30*	—
Baldcypress	− 30	− 30	—
Sweetgum	− 25	− 25 to − 30*	—
American Sycamore	− 20	− 20 to − 25*	—
Overcup Oak	− 20	− 20	—
Swamp Chestnut Oak	− 20	− 20	—
Southern Magnolia	− 20	− 17	—
Slash Pine	− 20	− 10	—
Live Oak	− 8	− 8	− 8

*Resistant temperatures for two parts of the stem. − 80 degrees Centigrade equals − 112 degrees Fahrenheit.
Source: "Freezing Resistance of Trees in North America with Reference to Tree Regions," A. Sakai, and C. J. Weiser, *Science* 54 (1973):118–126.

significant ways. Deciduous trees and shrubs develop winter buds for both flowers and leaves. The thick, waxy bud scales cover the buds to inhibit water loss. Probably the scales offer little, if any, protection against freezing. Besides bud scales conserving water, leaf scars also play a part; the corky layer at a leaf scar forms an effective seal. In summer, evergreen needles and broad leaves lose water as water vapor passes through tiny openings, the *stomata* (stoe-MAY-tuh), by a process called *transpiration*. During most of the winter, however, the evergreens close their stomata to reduce water loss. The waxy covering of evergreen leaves also retards the escape of water.

Apart from sealing winter buds and stomata, the deciduous or leaf-shedding habit of many trees and shrubs, in itself, dramatically cuts down on water loss. Removing the water-disposing leaves is a more effective water conservation maneuver than closing the stomata. (Realize, too, that the deciduous habit—the removal of cold-sensitive leaves—also raises a tree's or shrub's tolerance to lowered temperatures.)

Drying out in winter is often alleviated by woody plants replenishing their water supply when temperatures rise. Studies using dye solutions show that water movement takes place when root and stem temperatures are above freezing. Water may transfer through interconnected openings in cell walls rather than through the conducting vessels normally followed. Besides periodic water replenishment, it is always desirable for plants to go into winter with stored water reserves. An autumn drought can be disastrous for woody plant survival.

Besides the need for water, do plants require food in winter? Overall, woody plants probably subsist mainly on stored food in win-

ter; some growth may occur, at least in the roots. Evergreens in severe winter climates engage in little or no *photosynthesis*, the process of manufacturing plant food from water and carbon dioxide in the presence of light and chlorophyll, a green pigment. Evergreens in milder winter climates, however, often photosynthesize when temperatures are above freezing. Many trees, most of them deciduous, contain chlorophyll in their bark; aspen and tamarack are among them. Photosynthesis is known to occur in aspen bark, so presumably plant food is produced there and used by the tree.

In spite of their adaptations to the rigors of winter, woody plants are susceptible to several kinds of winter injury other than by freezing and drying out. One is stem bending and breaking resulting from snow loading. (A similar effect results from the thick accumulation of glaze during ice storms.) Stem breaking is most serious, but stem bending may last into the spring and beyond. Wet, heavy snow creates the greatest damage, its effects enhanced by prolonged periods of calm when the snow cannot be removed by wind. In the western mountains, where snow depths may readily reach sixty feet or more, snow loading may exert forces of more than 250 pounds per square foot. The spire form of conifers in northern regions reduces the likelihood of stem deformation by accumulating snow.

Twigs, especially those of conifers, may break by being covered with rime. The weight of the rime, coupled with strong wind, causes twigs to snap with relative ease. This damaging process is evident in spring by a litter of green twigs on the forest floor.

Wind abrasion of bark and foliage is another source of winter injury. Blowing ice particles pit or wear away bark and may remove foliage already damaged by drying or freezing. Removed fresh foliage may compound a tree's plight by contributing to the loss of its water. Especially near timberline, where wind exposure is greatest, trees and shrubs become markedly misshapen by arrested growth on the windward side and relatively normal growth on the leeward side.

Evergreens are often afflicted by winter drying or *winter burn*, which causes a browning and dying of the foliage and buds. Drying occurs by the sun, and possibly wind, in combination with low soil temperatures, which together reduce the ability of roots to absorb moisture and replenish the moisture lost by the foilage.

Winter sunscald generally affects the young bark of trees and shrubs facing south and southwest. The sun's heat dries out the young, thin bark and burns it, much like the skin of a sunburned person. Such scalded bark is then more susceptible to freezing, as is the woody tissue just beneath it. The bark may split and loosen from the underlying wood.

Finally, browsing by mammals causes considerable injury to the twigs and bark of woody plants in winter. Although some animals browse on woody vegetation much of the year, others, such as moose, hares, and rabbits, change their winter diet to mainly woody browse.

Nonwoody Plants

Nonwoody plants include the grasses, sedges, and numerous broad-leaved plants, several of which were characterized in chapter 5. Nonwoody plants generally die back to their roots in the autumn and overwinter as seeds, bulbs, rootstocks, and the like.

Although generally exhibiting little or no growth, some nonwoody plants grow under the snow, particularly those blossoming in early spring. Bulbs of spring-flowering plants generally begin their dormancy in midsummer and become active in midwinter. The necessary conditions for photosynthesis may be present: moisture, relatively warm temperatures, high amounts of carbon dioxide, and useful light—down to at least about thirty inches.

Spring beauties and snowdrops, two of the earliest, native blossoming plants found in much of the Rocky Mountain region, develop flower parts and leaves beneath the snowpack. Emerging through melting snowbanks, both blossom in April and May at low altitudes as the snow recedes. Both spring beauties and snowdrops grow from food-storing tubers, which are eaten by rodents, grizzly bears, and even people.

Even the lowly algae may be viable during winter. Blue-green algae frozen in ice, for example, are known to photosynthesize if exposed to sufficient sunlight. The pink snow algae, too, can carry on photosynthesis at near-freezing conditions.

For added insight into how plants adapt to or cope with winter, you might wish to try your hand at what may be broadly called winter gardening. This may or may not require actual gardening during the winter season.

Winter Gardening

Many people think of gardens in the broadest sense, with which I concur. This includes any plot of ground where vegetables, flowers, fruits, trees, shrubs, herbs, or other plants are cultivated. By this concept, such large tracts known as arboretums are also "gardens." Home owners' yards, too, are gardens with their included lawns, hedges, walks, patios, fences, and walls. If you lack a plot of ground and live in an apartment or condominium, your garden may be simply a window box, tub, half barrell, pail, or pot with plant-nourishing soil.

Excepting that done indoors, the kind of winter gardening you do depends on where you plot on the United States Department of Agriculture Plant Hardiness Map, the zones of which are based on average annual minimum temperatures. Zones 3 and 4 cover essentially the northernmost United States and southernmost Canada but extend considerably farther south in the Rocky Mountain region. Zone 3 signifies average annual minimum temperatures of -40 to -30 degrees Fahrenheit, zone 4 with temperatures of -30 to -20 degrees. Zones 1 and 2, in southern and central Canada, impose, of course, even harsher conditions upon plants than do zones 3 and 4. In these zones plants are essentially dormant all winter; you don't really garden outdoors *in* winter here, but you might garden in summer *for* the enjoyment of your garden in winter. I'll focus on these two zones while giving specific examples of plants that enhance a garden in winter; if you can garden in these zones, you can do it nearly anywhere. Progressively south of zones 3 and 4, considerable gardening actually takes place in winter, much as it would in summer.

For winter enjoyment, a garden's framework must be well planned. A sound framework is more important in winter because the conspicuous summer foliage of deciduous trees and shrubs and flowers is lacking. You must select plants that keep their beauty through winter and organize them in a pleasing blend of

shapes, silhouettes, and textures. Go for an attractive mix of woody evergreens and deciduous plants as well as some vestiges of non-woody perennials that you intentionally leave standing. The deciduous plants, particularly, are set off by their delicate branches, bark patterns, and colorful bark and twigs.

Besides planning for the plants themselves, envision also the beauty of their shadows—especially their patterns—playing on the snow. On clear winter days shadows are particularly crisp and distinct on the snow's surface.

Evergreens tend to form the basis of a broadly conceived garden. They produce a catchy green backdrop, so desirably needed to enhance the appearance of other plants in winter. And they whet your visual appetite in the way they catch and hold snow. You have plenty of shapes and sizes to pick from; in small gardens, consider the dwarf varieties.

Many evergreens can withstand the winter rigor of zones 3 and 4. A favorite among the spruces is the Colorado spruce, whose foliage varies from dark green through blue to almost white; the silver spruce variety possesses silver-white needles. Appealing pines include the red (reddish-brown bark), Scotch (orange-brown young bark), and mugho. Mugho pine, rarely over eight feet tall, is an irregular, spreading shrub usually broader than high. Arbor vitae (cedars) and junipers offer a variety of shapes—conical, oval, vase-shaped, columnlike, globeshaped, and spreading, low to or on the ground. Several dwarf varieties of junipers and arbor vitae are available for cramped gardens. Creeping juniper provides an appealing ground cover. A cold-tolerant fir is the subalpine fir, and the eastern hemlock is a hardy member of its group.

Colorful plants in winter? Although green, gray, and brown dominate the plants of the wintry landscape, other striking colors add zest to gardens in winter. Various shades of green, of course, are displayed mostly by the evergreens. Gray comes forth from the bark of many trees but is especially appealing, I think, in the lighter shades, as in various maples and basswoods. Silver maple comes to mind, as does striped maple, which offers a bonus. One of the so-called snakebark maples, striped maple's gray to green bark is attractively beset with lengthwise, whitish stripes. Some of the gray you see on tree trunks is not from the bark but from lichens. Brown is displayed on many tree barks, such as those of red and Scotch pine, the young branches of white birches, and the seed heads of teasels and coneflowers—left to stand in the flower garden, to name a few.

Vivid colors appear sparingly on plants in winter, with few exceptions. Think of such colors as accents, as a lady might select them creatively in her jewelry or as parts of her clothing.

Yellow appears in such places as the twigs of weeping willows and in the cornstalks you might leave standing in a vegetable garden. Some lichens growing on tree bark are also yellow.

Orange is not a common plant color in winter. Some willow twigs, the bark of some Scotch pines, and the seedpods of bittersweets are among the orange-coloring candidates.

Red flaunts itself in plants, more than you might, at first, expect. The berries of highbush cranberries, roses (hips), hawthorns, crab apples, mountain ashes, and some dogwoods; the twigs of redstem willows and some dogwoods; and the seed clusters of staghorn sumacs all exhibit red hues. Siberian dogwoods display especially bright red stems.

Purple is revealed rather sparingly by cold-hardy plants. Subalpine, and other, firs grow purple cones, and some dogwoods have purple-colored twigs.

Blue seems more notable than purple. Bring to mind the common bluish foliage of Colorado spruces found in many gardens. Other examples include the blue fescue grasses, some lichens and dogwood berries, and the bluish-tinged bark of American hornbeam trees.

With white snow so dramatically displayed, you may miss some of the white that plants offer. But certainly not the white bark of white birch or perhaps weeping birch. Expect white also in the pussy willow catkins (light gray as well) and in the disk-shaped seedpods—called silver dollars or pennies—of the plants known as money plants or lunarias.

Finally, black is present on plants as well as white. Places to look for black include, perhaps strangely, the elongate cross-blotches on white and weeping birches, and the bark of northern red and black oaks.

One last point about color accents in winter gardens: Birds add welcome flashes of color—the cardinal's red, the blue jay's blue, the goldfinch's yellow. And gardens provide fitting places to feed and watch the colorful birds.

In northern gardens some preparations should be made well before winter arrives to ensure that plants receive a better-than-average chance of winter survival.

Beginning in spring, strive for healthy plants, which make it through rigorous winters better than unhealthy ones, because, for one thing, they can store more food and harden more readily. Water and fertilize them well, and treat them for insect pests and disease. Provide the plants with good drainage, which prevents frost heaving and consequent snapping of their roots.

Avoid a few practices after midsummer.

Don't fertilize late in the season because tender growth will then be zapped by the first hard frost. After the first hard frost, though, you can lighly fertilize some still-active roots. Resist late-season pruning. This stimulates tender new growth, subject to killing by frost. Wait until after the first hard frost, when the plants are dormant, to prune, especially the maples, birches, beeches, and others that "bleed" upon spring pruning. Water sparingly in the early fall to restrain growth at this time and lessen frost heaving of the soil.

Mulching before winter's arrival conserves root moisture, inhibits deep freezing, and insulates against alternate thawing and freezing of the soil, which can break shallow roots and expose them to frigid air. Mulching materials include wood and bark chips, compost, peanut shells, straw, hay, and leaves that curl, such as those of oaks, birches, and basswoods. Place mulch at least an inch away from stems to prevent their rotting, and avoid placing mulch on any evergreen leaves.

Attend to the possibility of winter drying, sunscald, and chewing damage from mice and rabbits on woody garden plants. Mulching is one precaution against winter drying. Evergreens can be sprayed with antidesiccants or antitranspirants that form films on foliage to check the transpiration of moisture. Prevent sunscald by planting trees and shrubs against the shaded sides of walls or hedges or wrapping trunks with tape or burlap. You can also shield woody plants from the sun on the south and west with burlap screens attached to stakes. Mice and rabbits, by chewing bark, can girdle stems and kill shrubs and trees. Stem wraps of wire netting or repellents that can be sprayed or painted on the bark deter them. Mice may nest in mulch, so don't place it next to stems, or delay mulching until after the ground is frozen.

Even in northern regions, you can keep your hand directly in winter gardening with a few indoor projects. These are especially appropriate for green-thumb apartment or condominium dwellers lacking garden ground. I've selected three projects: growing sprouts and herbs, establishing a bottle garden, and forcing the twigs of early flowering shrubs and trees to blossom prematurely.

Why grow sprouts? First, they are *natural* additives that contribute toward a healthy diet. Sprouts are seeds of legumes or grains that have germinated; in so doing, fats and starches are converted into vitamins, sugars, and proteins. Sprouted seeds provide a more digestible, less fattening, and more nutritious food than those same seeds before sprouting. Second, growing sprouts is *instant gardening*! Planting, growing, and harvesting occurs within a few days in a small place with little equipment.

Seeds frequently used for sprouting include those of mung beans, soybeans, garbanzo beans, lentils, and alfalfa—all high in protein. Soybeans may contain up to 40 percent protein. Collectively, these five groups of sprouted seeds are used in salads, soups, meatballs, meat loaf, casseroles, breads, cakes, and cookies to name a few foods.

Let's consider a simple way to grow sprouts using mung beans, the main source of bean sprouts. Place one-half cup of fresh and untreated seeds in a wide-mouth glass jar that holds two cups or more. Add four times the amount of water and soak the seeds overnight. Discard the water. Place half of the soaked beans in another jar. Rinse the beans with fresh, cool water and lay the jars, covered with a screen, in a dark place. Remember to rinse the beans two or three times a day. The sprouts should appear on the second day, and be ready to use on the third or fourth day, when they should be one-half to one inch long. One cup of seeds makes four cups of sprouts, which can be kept refrigerated about three days.

For larger quantities of sprouts, you might try plastic trays or screened racks. The basic sprouting process is the same as with glass jars, but after each rinse place a damp paper towel over the drained sprouts. When using plastic trays, rinse the sprouts in a food strainer; with the screened racks, rinse them through the screens. Spread the sprouts well so they get plenty of air and don't ferment or become rancid.

Growing herbs indoors offers an opportunity at true winter gardening, as with various so-called house plants. Few experiences match the satisfaction of pinching off a fresh herb to please your palate in the dead of winter. Herbs that grow well indoors include basil, marjoram, savory, tarragon, thyme, mint, parsley, and chives.

Growth preparations for herbs are relatively simple. Place light, well-drained soil in a large flower pot, pail, or some other container. Attempt to plant cuttings at the end of the summer because herbs generally propagate best this way; you can, however, also begin with seed. Place your herb garden in good natural light or under special fluorescent lights designed for indoor plant growers. Water well, and fertilize frequently, perhaps every couple of weeks or so.

The best time for harvesting most herbs is when flowers begin to appear. Some purists even say collect herb leaves before noon, when the essential oils are most concentrated.

For later use, traditional herbalists dry herbs, hanging them in bunches in a cool, dark, well-ventilated place. Drying is complete when the leaves rustle when shaken—or crumble when crushed—or when the stems snap rather than bend. Store the dried herbs in air-tight containers away from sunlight.

You can also freeze herbs. One method is simply to rinse them and place them in a sealed plastic bag. Periodically snip off what you need from the frozen batch. Others blanch the fresh herbs in boiling water for a few seconds and then dunk them briefly in ice water before freezing.

Planting a garden in a bottle requires almost the dexterity and resourcefulness of inserting a ship in a bottle. But a bottle garden can satisfy a gardener immensely, as well as be a striking conversation piece.

With the plants in place, watered, and the bottle corked or capped, a self-contained, closed atmosphere is created. Watering is unnecessary for months—perhaps up to a year. Such a closed, moist "greenhouse" requires plants that thrive under these conditions. Examples include some begonias, creeping figs, coleuses, African violets, and various ferns such as maidenhair ferns.

Begin with a large bottle—such as a gallon-size apple cider bottle or larger, and wash and dry it thoroughly inside. With a paper funnel pour in a few inches of dry, sandy soil—dry, so it doesn't adhere to the sides. Level out the soil by shaking, or try smoothing with a spoon tied to a slim bamboo cane or other extension.

Doing the planting requires dexterity. Select only small plants that can be handled readily. I've found that a split bamboo cane works to grasp a stem as a plant is carefully lowered into a cavity in the soil. You might cover the roots with the spoon tool and tamp the soil around them with the blunt end of a bamboo cane.

Water the bottle garden with a tube, seal the bottle, and you're set to watch the results. Set the bottle in good light but not direct sunlight.

Forcing twigs of early-blooming shrubs and trees to blossom in late winter can be a pleasurable spring-hastening activity. Forsythias, dogwoods, lilacs, and crab apples are among the possibilities in northern regions.

When to try the force is a matter of guesswork. The timing varies with the weather and the stage in a plant's growth cycle. Under the right conditions, you might coerce a plant to blossom a month or two ahead of its normal time.

Select twigs with many flower buds, which tend to be darker and more rounded than leaf buds. Cut each twig cleanly from a tree or bush at 45 degrees just above a leaf bud.

Indoors, make the final preparations. Split or crush the bases of the twigs or shave off the bark so they absorb more water. Wrap the twigs in newspaper and place them in tepid water in a cool room for several days. When the buds open slightly, remove the newspaper and place the twigs in a well-lit place but not in direct sunlight. The opened flowers last longer if the surrounding air is cool and moist.

These, then, are a few projects to whet your winter gardening appetite. The step up from here, and the casual growing of house plants, might be gardening under special fluorescent lights whereby you carefully control the amount and quality of light. More ambitious, still, is gardening in winter within a greenhouse.

SEVEN

Tracking Winter Wildlife: Recognizing Animal Sign

U nlike plants, which remain fixed in place, an animal's presence is most often realized by its sign. This sign is most evident particularly in winter because the snow acts as a huge recording blanket.

We can place animal sign into two groups: that produced in winter and that created prior to winter's onset. Sign produced in winter includes, of course, the tracks and droppings laid on the snow blanket, as well as chewed twigs, rasped bark, and the like. Animal sign carrying over from summer and autumn include beaver dams and lodges, muskrat lodges, bird nests, and insect galls. I'll focus on the sign developed in winter but consider some of the prewinter sign as well.

Animal sign tells us not only what kinds of animals are active in a region but depicts also their behavior—their range, how they move, and what they eat. Learning both the animals and their behavior from sign offers a real challenge at honest-to-goodness detective work. While doing so, the whole process can be a lot of fun. *Caution*: When following animal sign produced in winter, don't get so close to

the animals that they become alarmed. Their anxiety and conceived need to flee consumes too much of the animals' precious energy—so badly needed to cope with winter's stress.

Mammal Tracks and Associated Sign

B efore considering tracking four-footed mammals, it's useful to comprehend their gaits or how they move. In *walking*, the simplest movement requiring least energy, two feet are always on the ground. Some walk by first moving both limbs on one side, followed by both limbs on the other; this approach makes the animal waddle. Others move a hind leg with an opposite foreleg diagonally, exactly in the manner of the diagonal stride of cross-country skiing. *Trotting*, somewhat like our jogging, resembles a fast diagonal walk, but the whole body is, at times, off the ground. In *loping* or *bounding* the front feet strike out as a pair, followed likewise by the hind feet, which land where the front feet did or just behind them. Weasels and their relatives choicely illustrate this gait. *Jumping*, where all limbs leave the ground simultaneously, is the gait assumed by alarmed mule deer. *Galloping* is similar to loping or bounding, but the hind feet land ahead of the front feet or straddle them. Rabbits, squirrels, and mice characteristically gallop. Other animals gallop when pressed, but such movement consumes much energy, and larger animals rarely resort to it.

To really gain an understanding of the kinds of mammal gaits, try doing them yourself. But be careful when attempting the gallop. Don't strain those muscles when "making like a rabbit"!

Identifying mammal tracks is best done by first zeroing in on track patterns or the telltale arrangements of tracks. Track patterns are visible even when individual tracks are obscured. Relate the track patterns to the general habitat,

associated animal sign, and to the individual footprints where they are discernible. I will review for each track pattern only those tracks commonly seen in winter. Keep an eye on Table 5 for track pattern and footprint measurements. Notice especially the width of the track pattern.

Always follow trails a ways for a good understanding of variations in track patterns. Animals of the dog family, for example, develop a single print when walking but generally a two-print pattern when trotting; and when galloping, theirs is a four-print pattern! Track patterns of other animals may vary as much. Learn the predominant pattern for each animal or group of animals, but become keenly aware of the variations.

Unless you remember to always carry a ruler with you, measure your hand as an aid to footprint sizes. The length of my right hand from the wrist to the tip of the longest finger is about

TABLE 5   **Measurements* of Common Mammal Tracks in Winter Arranged by Most Common Track Pattern**

Mammal or Mammal Group	Width of Track Pattern	Distance Between Tracks or Track Groups	Length × Width of Largest Footprint
Single-Print Track Pattern: Walking or Trotting			
LONG-BODIED MAMMALS: GREATER THAN 8–9 INCHES BETWEEN FOOTPRINTS			
Bison	11–21	14–32	6 × 6
Moose	10–20	18–36	6 × 5
Elk	8–12	16–30	5 × 4
Caribou	9–13	16–30	4.5 × 5
Deer	5–10	10–20	3.5 × 2.5
Mountain Goats	8–12	10–19	3.5 × 3.3
Mountain Sheep	7–13	14–24	3.5 × 2.5
Pronghorns	5–9	8–19	3.5 × 2.5

Mammal or Mammal Group	Width of Track Pattern	Distance Between Tracks or Track Groups	Length × Width of Largest Footprint
Wolves	6–9	13–32	5.5 × 5
Coyotes	4–7	6–20	3.5 × 2.8
Large Foxes	3.5–5	5–16	3.1 × 2.5
Small Foxes	3–3.8	5–12	2 × 1.5
Mountain Lions	8–12	13–28	4.5 × 5
Lynx	6–9	12–28	4.5 × 4.8
Bobcats	5–7	5–16	2.5 × 2.8
SMALL-BODIED MAMMALS: LESS THAN 8–9 INCHES BETWEEN FOOTPRINTS			
Porcupines	5.5–9	1–8	4.5 × 2.5
Skunks	2–5	1.5–4	2.5 × 1.5

Two-Print Track Pattern

EQUAL-SIZED FOOTPRINTS: LOPING OR TROTTING			
Otters	7–9	13–21	5 × 4
Fishers	4.5–7	12–50	4.8 × 3
Minks	2.3–3.5	8–27	2.5 × 1.8
Weasels	0.8–2.8	4–34	1.8 × 1
UNEQUAL-SIZED FOOTPRINTS: WALKING			
Raccoons	3.5–7	5–12	4 × 2.5

Four-Print Track Pattern: Galloping or Jumping

LARGE TRACK GROUPS			
Hares	4.5–8	10–60	6 × 3.5
MEDIUM-SIZED TRACK GROUPS			
Rabbits	3–5	6–22	3.5 × 1.6
Tree Squirrels	3.5–5.3	5–40	2.6 × 1.5
SMALL TRACK GROUPS			
Voles and Lemmings	1.3–2	2–10	1.5 × 0.8
Mice	1.4–1.8	1.5–3.5	1 × 0.5
Shrews	0.9–1.1	1.5–3	0.5 × 0.5

*All measurements are in inches.

Source: Measurements from *Field Guide to Tracking Animals in Snow,* Louise R. Forrest, Harrisburg, PA: Stackpole Books, 1988.

7.5 inches; the distance from the tip of the little finger to the tip of the thumb, with the hand fully outstretched, is about 9.5 inches; the width at the base of the fingers is about 3.5 inches; and the length from the tip of the index finger to the second joint is almost exactly 2.0 inches. When measuring prints, keep in mind that they change with age; those in melting snow become much larger.

You might also be interested in an animal's direction of travel. Establish this easily by toe or claw marks if they register. Snow is more compressed at the front of the track. And use the shape of the print and print placement as aids to decipher travel direction.

The *single-print track pattern* (Figure 19) consists of two parallel rows of footprints, placed alternately when an animal is walking or trotting. Although two-footed, we make this type of pattern. Animals' hind feet may land exactly on the front footprints, or, particularly in shallow snow, slightly behind, ahead, or to one side. Animals that typically form a single-print track pattern include the two-toed hoofed mammals, those of the dog and cat families, and the porcupines and skunks. Hoofed mammals, except moose, tend to congregate in small groups or herds. They devote considerable time to resting or bedding down together in depressions in the snow. Those feeding on ground vegetation dig craters in the snow in pursuit of their food.

Two-toed hoofed mammals leave double grooves in the deeper snow as their toes drag. Dewclaws at the back of the leg make impressions along with the footprints when the snow is a few inches or more thick.

Bison footprints are rounded, similar to those of cattle, but usually larger. The leg slot in deep snow measures about 4.5 to 5.5 inches wide. Associated sign includes droppings similar to cow pies and tufts of woolly hair. Expect bison tracks in grasslands and shrub lands in several western states and Canada where the animals have been secondarily introduced in protected areas; also, look for them on some ranches.

Tracks of *moose* are more oval than those of bison but of about the same size. In deep snow the leg slot is about 4 to 4.5 inches wide. Moose droppings or pellets tend to be elongate and an inch or more long; inside, they resemble compressed sawdust. Look also for long, dark hair. Browsed willow and aspen twigs, and those of other trees, will show ragged tooth cuts. Search for gnawed tree bark, especially on aspens. Expect moose particularly in wet shrub lands where willow, their favored food, is plentiful. Moose range over most of Canada and Alaska and part of the coterminous United States in the northern Rockies and the Great Lakes area.

Elk footprints are smaller than those of moose and less pointed. The leg slot is also narrower, about 2 to 3.5 inches wide. Elk pellets resemble moose's but are smaller, tend to be barrel-shaped, and are more often dimpled at one end. Besides digging in snow for grasses, elk nip twigs with ragged cuts; look also for gnawed tree bark, especially aspen, and bruised, torn bark and broken branches resulting from them rubbing their antlers. Anticipate elk in semiopen forests and mountain meadows but also in mountain valleys in winter in much of the western United States and southwestern Canada.

Tracks of *deer* are smaller than those of elk and more pointed. They characteristically appear as split hearts, but often the two parts of the footprint are splayed or separated. Narrower than that made by elk, the leg slot is about 1 to 2 inches wide. Deer pellets tend toward egg-shaped, are smaller than those of elk, and often pointed at one end. Deer snip

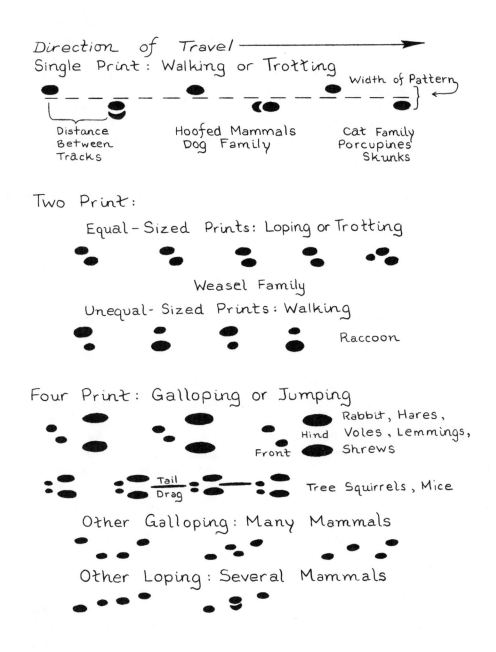

Figure 19. Kinds of mammal track patterns with representative animals that make them.

twigs with ragged cuts, as do moose and elk, but also feed on lichens on trees. They tend to band or "yard up" in deep snow to conserve energy in foot-packed areas. Tracks of white-tailed and mule deer are essentially impossible to distinguish, so keep in mind the preferred habitat and range of the two species to help sort them out. White-tailed deer prefer woods and brush lands, mule deer frequent more open places. Although white-tailed deer inhabit much of the United States and southern Canada, mule deer live primarily west of the Mississippi. When galloping, white-tailed deer place their hind feet far ahead of their front feet. Jumping pogo stick-style with all feet landing together, mule deer, on the other hand, maintain their hind feet to the rear.

Caribou footprints are rounded, somewhat like those of bison but smaller, and noticeably splayed, as are the dewclaws. Caribou release elklike, dimpled pellets. Since caribou feed on lichens and other ground vegetation, look for their pawed craters in the snow; they also feed on tree lichens. Trees show rubbings and bruising from their antlers. Look for caribou in the arctic tundra or in open coniferous woods; they tend to move to more forested areas in winter. Caribou mostly occupy much of Canada and Alaska.

Although deer-sized, *mountain goat* tracks tend toward being distinctively splayed at the tips. Pellets look like those of deer and sheep but are smaller. It's easiest to identify mountain goat sign by an awareness of the animals' habitat and range. Characteristically dwellers of crags, mountain goats frequently shift to wooded areas or slopes with southern exposure in winter. These sure-footed animals range over parts of the Rocky Mountains, western Canada, and southern Alaska. Nibbled twigs or pawed depressions made in snow while searching for grasses also attest to the presence of mountain goats.

Mountain sheep footprints, similar to those of domestic sheep, are squarish and about the same size as deer and goat prints. The tracks of mountain sheep, however, are less pointed than deer prints and less splayed than goat prints. Sheep pellets resemble those of deer and mountain goats. Bighorn sheep slip to the lower mountain valleys in winter, whereas Dall sheep descend to the lower, south-facing slopes. Both types of sheep paw depressions in the snow, searching for plant food. Mountain sheep range over much of the western United States, part of western Canada, and into Alaska.

Footprints of *pronghorns* are similar to deer prints in size and shape but are wider at the rear. As might be expected, pronghorn droppings are deerlike. Pronghorns prefer grasslands and open shrub lands. They inhabit part of the western United States and a small part of southern Canada. Look for sagebrush and other shrubs browsed by pronghorns in winter.

Animals of the dog family leave egg-shaped footprints, longer than wide, that usually terminate in claw marks. Toes commonly incise drag marks in the snow. Look also for streaks of urine as scent markers along trails. The wild, doglike animals move deliberately to conserve energy, thereby producing regular, often straight trails. Domestic dogs, freed of the constant need to hunt their own food, wander freely or even aimlessly and produce complicated or haphazard trails.

Wolf tracks are usually larger than dog tracks; their doglike droppings consist primarily of hair and bone fragments that reflect their prey of mostly two-toed hoofed mammals. Wolves, more social than coyotes, often travel in packs, so expect wolf trails in groups. You can expect wolves wherever their prey might be. They populate Alaska, most of Canada, and parts of the northernmost coterminous United States.

Smaller than wolves, *coyote* footprints overlap in size with dogs' footprints. Droppings, often made up largely of hair and bone fragments, can be confused with those of wolves. Coyotes, however, tend to vary their diet more than wolves and may consume small mammals, young hoofed mammals, carrion, insects, and plant food—such as pine nuts and berries. Don't be surprised to find coyotes in all habitats, but they prefer mostly open places. More wide-ranging than wolves, coyotes inhabit all of the coterminous United States and Alaska and much of Canada.

Fox tracks (Figure 20) are smaller than wolf and coyote tracks and look like those of small dogs. As one would expect, they also excrete droppings reminiscent of those of small dogs. Large foxes include arctic and red foxes, and the gray and swift foxes make up the group of small foxes. Expect foxes in a variety of habitats. They feed mainly on small mammals and carrion and sometimes berries. Foxes cache many of their kills in snow pits covered with snow. The red fox, the most widespread, ranges over most of North America north of Mexico.

Animals of the cat family display rounded tracks—as wide as long, or wider than long—that show no claw marks. Cats tend not to show drag marks in the snow from their toes as dogs commonly do. Cats walk more than dogs, and run infrequently. Although inconsistent, cats tend to cover their droppings with snow. And, as is the habit of dogs, cats leave urine scent markers.

Mountain lions display the largest footprints

Figure 20. Tracks in the snow show that a fox, walking from the upper right, turned and began following a white-footed mouse toward the lower right.

of the North American cats. Their bellies and tails may leave drag marks in deep snow. Droppings from mountain lions resemble those of large dogs and usually contain hair and bone fragments—reflecting their feeding on deer, other hoofed and small mammals, as well as carrion. You may come upon a mountain lion kill cached in snow. You can expect to find mountain lions in mountain forests and semiwooded areas. They range primarily in much of the western United States and southwestern Canada.

Footprints of *lynx* closely approach mountain lion tracks in size but sink less into the snow and group within a narrower track pattern. Hair on the feet tends to obscure the foot pads, which mountain lions usually display distinctly. Ignoring differences in shape and the lack of claw marks, you could still distinguish lynx tracks from the similarly sized wolf and coyote tracks because lynx tracks tend to meander more. These cats prefer snowshoe hares but also prey on hoofed and various small mammals and feed on carrion. Lynx typically inhabit dense northern forests but also enter the tundra. They can be found in much of Canada and Alaska and parts of the northern, coterminous United States.

Bobcat footprints appear about twice the size of house cats'. They differ from similarly sized fox tracks by the rounded shape, lack of claw marks, and their tendency to meander rather than trend relatively straightly. Look for bobcat, and other cat, scratch marks on tree trunks. Droppings reveal bobcats' diet, chiefly of rodents, rabbits, and other small mammals. These cats inhabit both wooded and partly open places throughout much of the United States and parts of southern Canada.

Smaller-bodied mammals that regularly make a single-print track pattern include porcupines and skunks.

Porcupines' waddling gait produces a pigeon-toed, alternating pattern with accompanying quill drag marks, emphasized by the side-to-side swishing of the tail quills. Quill marks resemble whisk broom markings. Droppings look somewhat like those of deer but are rough and irregular; they accumulate at the base of the tree where a porcupine feeds. Telltale porcupine sign is primarily neatly gnawed tree or shrub bark—somewhat like that done by beaver but higher up; these animals, however, also feed on buds and catkins. Their food preferences usually keep them in woods, but they may be found in open places as well. Look for porcupine sign in Alaska, much of Canada, and the western and northeastern coterminous United States.

Don't expect *skunks* regularly in winter; they emerge from their dens only on mild days especially late in the season. Of the two kinds of skunks, striped skunks are larger than spotted skunks. Skunk track patterns are irregular or erratic and tend to meander. Although roughly the size and shape of fox tracks, skunk footprints show five toes and different foot pads, and claws often leave traces. Cylinder-shaped droppings might accompany the prints. Being of the weasel family, skunks might be predicted to feed on small mammals and carrion; they, however, vary their winter diet with fruit, nuts, and seeds. Anticipate skunk sign in most any habitat, including farmlands. They occupy most of the coterminous United States and southern Canada.

Animals imprinting a *two-print track pattern* leave two close footprints separated by a space from the next two. This pattern can be formed by a loping or trotting gait or by walking.

Most animals of the weasel family produce a characteristic two-print pattern of equal-sized prints when they lope. Usually one print is placed slightly behind the other. Hind and front prints tend to occur in the same spot, with some variation. The prints are usually longer than wide and portray five toes and claw marks under the right conditions; the long heel pad on the hind foot may also show.

Largest of the weasel family seen in winter, *otters* display large, webbed hind feet in their track pattern and often a tail drag. Their cylinder-shaped droppings usually contain remains of fish—their primary food, which is supplemented by crayfish and other aquatic animals. Playful otters often create snow slides— troughs in the snow twenty or more feet long. Expect them along shores of lakes and streams; besides other sign, look for their access holes for fishing through the ice. Otters range through much of Canada and Alaska and parts of the coterminous United States.

Fishers make smaller footprints than do otters, and their hind feet are not webbed. Droppings from fishers are cylinder shaped and may contain rabbit or hare fur and porcupine quills, which indicate their significant foods, supplemented by small mammals, birds, and carrion. Fishers, sighted infrequently, are slightly more common than the rare, smaller martens. Fishers prefer woods and are often spotted near water. They can be anticipated over much of southern Canada and in parts of the northern coterminous United States.

Mink footprints are smaller than those of fishers but larger than weasel prints. You find their trails along waterways, and they often slide into the water or even slip under the snow. They may leave troughs by pushing their way through the snow or by sliding down slopes as otters do. Mink droppings resemble fishers' but are smaller. Among mink foods are small mammals, including muskrats, and fish, and crayfish, and birds. Widespread, minks range across much of Canada, Alaska, and the coterminous United States.

Weasels generate footprints that are usually smaller than those made by minks, about the size of human fingerprints or slightly larger. Droppings are also smaller. Weasel trails, straight or zigzagged, often tunnel under the snow as the animals seek prey or warmth. Long-tailed weasels are larger than short-tailed weasels (or ermines), which exceed the smallest or least weasels in size. Weasels prey on small mammals, especially voles and mice; they may cache their kills in dens, burrows, or under roots. These carnivores are found in a variety of wooded or open habitats and occur in Alaska and most of Canada and the coterminous United States.

Raccoons and opossums produce double footprints of unequal size while walking. I'll only characterize raccoon tracks and other raccoon sign because these animals are more widespread.

You find *raccoons* active in winter only during mild periods. Flat-footed, raccoons create five-toed footprints like miniature bear prints (see Figure 42). The larger hind prints place next to the smaller, opposite front prints; so, a right hind print would position to the side of a left front print. This arrangement ensues because raccoons' waddling gait allows both limbs on one side to move before the remaining limbs on the other side ambulate. Cylinder-shaped raccoon droppings are often crumbly. The omnivorous raccoons include such foods as nuts, fruits, carrion, crayfish, clams, and occasionally birds and rodents in their diets. Look for them in brushy or well-wooded places especially near water. Raccoons inhabit all of the coterminous United States and part of southern Canada.

Four footprints are grouped together in the *four-print track pattern*. Hind prints place on the outside of the front prints and ahead of them. Animals make the four-print pattern as they gallop or jump.

Hares and *rabbits* are the largest animals

that habitually form a four-print track pattern. Hares, born with their eyes open and covered with hair, differ from the generally smaller rabbits, which are born blind and without hair. Hares include the snowshoe hare, arctic hare, and jackrabbits; the snowshoe hares grow a white coat for winter. Rabbits are well exemplified by the cottontails. Both hares and rabbits possess hind feet much larger than the front feet. Front footprints of hares and rabbits occur diagonally, or one is slightly behind the other.

Droppings of these animals litter the snow as slightly flattened balls of chewed plant matter about one-half inch in diameter or less. Hares and rabbits chew buds, twigs, and bark of young trees and shrubs; those inhabiting open places also eat dry grass. Twigs cut at a neat, 45-degree angle a foot or two off the ground differ from the rough, straight-across nips of hoofed mammals such as deer. Hares and rabbits generally rest during the day in depressions in the snow and occasionally burrow into it. Both groups of mammals are widespread in North America.

Having prints smaller than those of rabbits, *tree squirrels* present a squarish four-print group within which the front prints position side by side. The tracks, however, may merge to form a two-print pattern when an animal slows down or lopes in deep snow, when also foot drag marks may show. Trails usually go between trees and disappear at them. Some squirrels also make snow tunnels. Look, too, for leafy tree nests. For those squirrels that cache nuts and seeds on the ground in burrows or under tree roots, such as the red squirrels, you might see piles of shells or the scales of pine or spruce cones as additional sign. As a group, tree squirrels are widespread in the woods of North America.

Voles and *lemmings* are mouselike animals with chunky bodies and short tails. Their four-print track pattern includes diagonally placed front prints in the manner of hares and rabbits. Feet drag in deeper snow but tails rarely drag. Trails generally lead under the snow to nests and feeding places; upon snow melt in spring, you can see the grassy nests and runways lined with litter. For voles, the four-print pattern often merges to a two-print pattern. Voles and lemmings, taken together, occupy virtually all habitats, where they feed on grasses, plant roots, and twigs and bark of shrubs and trees. Lemmings range over Alaska, Canada, and the northeastern coterminous United States. The voles extend farther to include most of the coterminous United States.

Mice differ from voles and lemmings in having slender bodies and long tails. Their four-print track pattern is squarish like that of tree squirrels because the front feet usually position side by side. In deeper, soft snow, the four-print pattern merges to a two-print pattern with a tail drag; the distance between track groups for this two-print pattern generally is shorter than it is for the larger voles. Most small rodent tracks in snow are of white-footed mice, also called deer mice, and meadow voles. Mice feed primarily on seeds. They favor grasslands but inhabit a variety of other habitats as well. Mice range throughout the United States and much of Canada.

Pointed snouts and different teeth help distinguish the tiny *shrews* from the larger voles and lemmings and mice. The shrews' four-print track pattern may merge to a two-print or U-shaped track in deeper, soft snow in which tails also drag. Trails may disappear into snow tunnels that are often ridged at the snow's surface. Front prints are often diagonally placed like those of voles and lemmings or hares and rabbits. Primarily insect eaters, shrews feed on insect larvae and pupae in winter but also eat mice and other shrews as well as carrion, nuts, and berries. Shrews live in both wooded and open habitats, and, as might be expected, are very widespread.

Bird Tracks and Associated Sign

The two-footed birds give rise to two basic track patterns. Perching birds, such as sparrows, chickadees, and blue jays that spend much time in trees, hop when on the ground, and so create a two-print or paired pattern reminiscent of some jumping tree squirrels. Those birds expending much time on the ground, such as game birds, waterfowl, shorebirds, and others, leave mostly an alternating, single-print track pattern resembling that of walking mammals. Exceptions, of course, occur. The great horned owl, for example, alternates its tracks on the ground, and the junco may as well.

Bird tracks generally lack the distinctive individuality of many mammal footprints. They, however, usually display three distinct front toes and, occasionally, a rear fourth toe. Some, like the flicker, though, show two front and two rear toes. Aquatic birds, like geese and ducks, tend to exhibit webbed prints that toe in. And another characteristic: Bird prints disappear when their bearers take off! A good way to learn about the individuality of prints of the smaller birds in winter is to look below your bird feeder where seeds have spilled and witness tracks in the making.

Two distinctive bird tracks in snow that arrange within an alternate, single-print pattern are those of crows and grouse. Prints of crows show the inner and middle toes close together; each print is up to three inches long, and about four inches separates them. Look especially for such tracks near carrion, where raven and magpie tracks may also congregate. Grouse prints differ from those of other upland game birds in having wider toes; their prints are about two to three inches long.

As you become familiar with mammal and bird tracks, you may wish to preserve them (Box 4). Preserving footprints makes the learning more definitive but can become an engrossing activity in itself.

BOX 4   Preserving Tracks Formed in Snow

To best preserve tracks formed in snow, select the right conditions. These include below-freezing temperatures and packed, wet snow for better track details.

You will be making plaster of paris facsimiles of the track impressions. Materials needed include strips of flexible cardboard, paper clips or staples, plaster of paris, cold water, a spray bottle, and a lightweight, plastic mixing bowl and spoon.

With the flexible cardboard, fashion a two-

inch-high circular or egg-shaped ring held together with paper clips or staples; a containing barrier for the liquid plaster of paris, this cardboard ring should be large enough to allow ample space around the desired footprint. Carefully press it into the snow.

With the spray bottle, spray a mist of cold water on and around the footprint within the cardboard containing ring, and allow the spray to freeze. This hardens the surface of the track. Add cold water to plaster of paris in the mixing bowl, and mix until the plaster reaches the consistency of slightly thick pancake batter. You might add a teaspoon of salt to the "batter" so it hardens faster. Tap the sides of the bowl to remove any air bubbles. Pour the fluid plaster of paris gently around and on the footprint. Let it set for twenty minutes or more.

If everything goes well—and the plaster of paris was neither too thick nor too fluid and the water cool enough—you now have a mold of the track, or a negative, raised impression. To get a cast, a positive or exact depressed facsimile of the original print, you place the cardboard-containing ring around the mold or casting form. Lightly grease the surface of the mold and pour fluid plaster of paris over it. After hardening, separate your newly formed cast from the mold.

You may also "preserve" tracks by photo-graphing them. Do this only in direct sunlight so shadows can distinctly mold them and bring out revealing characters. Use side light instead of front light or back light. Take close-up shots, snapped straight down to avoid distortion. Chapter 11 tells you how to determine correct exposure in snow.

Photograph not only the tracks but also the track patterns. The track patterns are necessary to show their variation, widths, and the distances between tracks or track groups. Use a ruler for scale—better than a less specific glove, pencil, or lens cap—in only some of the shots to establish size of the track patterns or prints. When you show your best photographs to others, you want them fully to appreciate your record of a track or track pattern, not be distracted by an attention-getting object for scale.

Associated bird sign formed during winter includes droppings, castings or pellets, tail or wing marks, and snow burrows.

Bird droppings are usually covered with a white, limy coating, at least at one end, a feature not seen in mammal droppings. Likewise for mammal droppings, hard droppings result from dry food, and soft droppings from wet food.

Castings or pellets are of undigested materials habitually regurgitated by such birds as owls, hawks, eagles, crows, magpies, ravens, and gulls. They are made up most often of feathers, fur, and bones and are generally free of digestive residue.

Tail and wing marks in snow are fascinating indirect bird sign. Tail marks usually form when a bird lands, and wing marks are recorded upon takeoff. A bird of prey may im-press both tail and wing marks in the snow when seizing its hapless victim.

Ruffled grouse are among those birds that create snow burrows (Figure 21) when the weather is severe. They enter the snow by digging or simply by diving in. Once under the snow they tunnel in a ways. Other evidence of ruffed grouse burrows are cylinder-shaped droppings of plant material about an inch long and often tracks and wing and tail marks registering a landing or takeoff.

Nests, of course, are among those bird sign manufactured before the onset of winter. They stand out conspicuously in deciduous trees in winter because of the lack of foliage. You see only those substantial enough to withstand the forces of wind and rain or those not concealed by the snow. Even those that survive may be

Figure 21. Ruffed grouse roosting burrow and tracks in snow. The bird entered the snow where the tracks end, tunneled in a ways for the night, and left the burrow at the lower right.

considerably altered. Although not easy to identify, I'll briefly characterize a few types constructed by songbirds that are commonly seen in winter. I'm sure you realize that nest identification presents a challenge even in summer when nests are in prime condition; they might contain eggs, and their builders may be nearby.

Let's first look at three types of *larger nests* built by birds about eight to fourteen inches long. One type contains a *layer of mud*. Variations include: (1) a foundation of sticks or weed stalks and lined with grasses (e.g., common grackle); (2) a foundation of leaves and lined with rootlets (e.g., wood thrush); and (3) having no sticks or leaves in the foundation and lined with grasses (e.g., robin).

Another larger nest type lacks mud and has a *foundation* of *twigs and bark strips*. If lined with dark rootlets, likely builders include catbirds, mockingbirds, and brown thrashers. Possible builders if the nest is lined by grasses are cardinals.

A third layer nest type is pendant or hanging from the tips of branches like a pouch and fashioned of such materials as plant fibers, hair, and yarn. Northern orioles make nests of this kind.

Three types of *smaller nests* are crafted by birds about five to seven inches long or less. One type, of a neat, cuplike shape, consists *of grasses* and is placed usually only a few feet off the ground. Several kinds of sparrows make this kind of nest.

Another kind of small nest shows considerable milkweed and thistle down in its construction. This kind of nest breaks down readily when pelted by rain and buffeted by wind. Goldfinches and yellow warblers are among the birds fashioning these nests.

A third type of small nest is *suspended at its rim* by a forked branch. That is, like a hand food strainer, the nest largely hangs below the branch that supports it. This nest is formed largely of plant fibers and spider silk and lined with pine needles and grasses. Vireos make this kind of nest.

Finally, some birds quarry *nest holes in tree trunks.* Such birds as the woodpeckers and chickadees quarry the smaller holes, which, in succeeding years, are occupied by other birds, including nuthatches and tree swallows. Wood ducks and screech owls are among the birds that excavate larger nest holes; squirrels, in turn, may take up housekeeping in some of these.

Some birds excavate in trees holes that are unrelated to nesting. Pileated woodpeckers quarry generally rectangular, although sometimes egg-shaped, holes in trunks (Figure 22) usually a foot long or less and up to eight inches wide and six inches deep. Some of these holes may be connected up to a length of about six feet. All this work is the result of a quest for largely carpenter ants. Sapsuckers peck out small, circular, or squarish holes, about one-fourth inch wide or less, arranged in rings around a trunk. These birds, as their name implies, seek the sap and the insects it attracts.

Insect Sign

Because insects are cold-blooded, your chances of seeing them in winter—especially active—are relatively slim. (This is one reason why some outdoorsy people camp out, insect-free, in winter.) Much of their sign, however, is all around you. Insects overwinter in all stages—egg, larva, pupa, and adult. Learning them in a specific way, however, is more difficult than with mammals and birds because there are so many of them. One estimate is that there are more than a million species—and many are discovered each year.

Galls depict conspicuous sign of insects in winter. They are caused mainly by insects, but viruses, bacteria, fungi, and certain worms induce them as well. Insects irritate plants physically, as by biting or burrowing, or by a chemical secretion. Plants grow around the insects and, in so doing, provide them with food and protection. More than 15,000 kinds of galls are known in the world; insects make more than 2,000 of them in North America alone. The main gall-producing insects are gall wasps, gall midges, and gall aphids or lice; the non-insect gall mites also contribute significantly to gall formation.

Oak galls are more common than insect galls produced on any other group of plants. Galls form mostly on the leaves and twigs but also on branches, buds, flowers, roots, and acorns. Most are induced by gall wasps.

Leaf oak galls form on the leaf stem, the base or surface of the leaf, and on the midvein or side veins. They vary in size and form, from slight swellings to ball-like enlargements and other shapes; most often smooth, they may also be faceted or spiny. Conspicuous are the oak apple galls (or simply oak apples), which usually appear like tan balls up to one or two

Figure 22. Pileated woodpecker excavations in a dead tree trunk. These birds usually seek carpenter ants.

inches in diameter. Enclosed by a firm, outer shell is a hard central part separated from the shell by either spongy or fibrous material. Most oak apples are smooth, but some are rough, hairy, or spiny.

Twig and branch oak galls are usually slight enlargements to irregular swellings on twigs and branches, but some may be knotty and egg shaped and even ball-like. Among them are: oak potato galls, gouty oak galls, mealy oak galls, oak fig galls, and oak bullet galls. Oak bullet galls, conspicuous in winter, are egg shaped and pointed or round, and occur singly or in clusters. They are solid inside, and each contains a single, white grub.

Willow galls, of numerous types, form on leaves, buds, and twigs. Sawflies, gall midges, and gall mites produce most of them.

Most distinctive is the willow pine cone gall, shaped like a closed pine cone, an inch or more long, that hangs from the tips of willow branches. Gall midges lay eggs on growing buds; the hatched larvae incite growth of the gall and overwinter in it. In the spring, the larvae transform to pupae and eventually emerge as adult midges. If you cut open a willow pine cone gall, don't be surprised if other insects besides the larval midge that induced it are present. It's common for non-gall-forming insects to occupy galls.

Another bud willow gall, often seen on the same individual willow as the willow pine cone gall, is the willow petaled gall. It resembles an open, gray rosette at the tips of willow branches. Gall midges also cause this gall to form in spring and summer.

A gall formed strictly on willow twigs is the easily recognized willow potato gall, truly reminiscent of a miniature, potatolike swelling one-half inch to an inch in diameter. A midge is also responsible for this gall. Each gall contains several maggots, each in its individual cell.

Goldenrod galls are caused mainly by gall midges, but moths, flies, and wasps also play a part. All parts of goldenrods are affected: flowers, flower and leaf buds, leaves, stems, and roots. Of the numerous types of galls, two durable ones are commonly seen in winter.

The goldenrod ball gall, about an inch in diameter, appears as a round stem swelling. Found at about the same height, more than one may occur on a single stem. It's not unusual to find this gall with a reddish blush in autumn. The larval stage of a fly with brown markings on its wings creates this gall as it burrows into the stem. Overwintering in the gall, the larva becomes a pupa in the spring and later emerges as a full-fledged adult fly. Various insects may eat the larva and interrupt the life cycle.

Elongate and spindle shaped rather than round, the elliptical goldenrod gall is a less conspicuous stem swelling than the goldenrod ball gall. It is induced by the larva (caterpillar) of a moth. Hatching in spring from eggs laid the previous fall, the larva burrows into the end buds of goldenrod shoots and eventually into the stem; the plant forms the gall around the emplaced larva. This larva bores a later-to-be-used exit hole near the top of the gall; it becomes a pupa and finally an adult moth in late summer and early autumn. So, you won't find the instigator of the gall inside it in winter; what you should find, however, is the reddish-brown skin of the pupa.

The resin of cone-bearing trees doesn't deter many insects from forming galls on them. Gall midges and gall aphids, especially, are prolific gall formers. Needles, twigs, cones, buds, and pitch masses are all affected.

An easily recognized gall of evergreen trees

is the spruce cone gall or spruce pineapple gall. Formed at the developing shoots of branch tips, this gall, one-half to one inch long, resembes a pine cone or perhaps a miniature pineapple because rudimentary needles extend from it. As immature gall aphids feed on the developing needles in the spring, the needles swell and grow together to form the gall.

Other insect sign besides galls is observable in winter. We'll examine three other kinds: engravings in wood, galleries in wood, and wasp nests.

Engravings in wood occur on the underside of tree bark and on the surface of the wood beneath the bark. These form interesting patterns and are the work of bark beetles that may overwinter as larvae, pupae, or adults. The engravings, though, are actually egg tunnels and larval "mines." Female beetles cut the tunnels—straight, winding, forked, radiating, cavelike, or irregular—to lay their eggs in them. Hatched larvae elaborate the pattern by excavating "mines" outward from the egg tunnels. You are unlikely to see the stubby adult beetles, usually about one-eighth inch long or less, but may notice tiny exit holes in the bark left by them. You might remember that some bark beetles spread a fungus that causes Dutch elm disease.

Galleries in wood, resembling a kind of latticework, are usually the work of carpenter ants. You may find the excavations in dead trees, logs, fence posts, telephone poles, and buildings. The galleries are actually nests and burrows to protect the ant colony and raise young, as the ants don't eat the wood as do termites. You might recall that pileated woodpeckers mine pits in dead tree trunks in their search for carpenter ants.

Wasp nests are made of paper or mud. Paper nests are more conspicuous but less durable.

The globe-shaped or egg-shaped paper nests, up to about a foot and a half high but frequently shorter, are most likely to attract your attention. They hang from the branches of trees and shrubs or from the eaves of buildings. These nests are covered with a paper wrapper of several layers. Inside, you will find a few tiers of egg cells. Look for an entrance opening at the base of a nest. Hornets and yellow jackets manufacture the paper nests by chewing wood and adding a fluid to hold the fine wood bits together. A queen initiates the colony by building a few cells and laying eggs in them. In time, males and female workers appear. Don't worry about approaching a paper nest in winter; its occupants abandon it before the onset of below-freezing temperatures.

Another kind of smaller paper wasp nest consists of a single layer of egg cells. This nest is basically like a single tier inside a globe-shaped nest without an outside wrapper. It usually hangs from branches or eaves by a single thread. Paper wasps, forming a colony similar to that for the globe-shaped nest, inhabit the single-tiered nest.

Some wasps build nests of mud. Best known are the mud daubers, which construct egg cells singly or in groups. You can find these cells attached to trees, rocks, bridges, and the sides of buildings. Each cell is usually stocked with an insect or spider, paralyzed or stung to death, to serve as food for the hatched young. Eggs are usually laid on the prey, and the entrance to the cell is sealed. Winter is usually passed as a larva or a pupa in a cocoon. Some mud daubers don't build mud cells but simply repair those made by others. Simplified, a mud dauber society differs from a paper wasp society in consisting of only males and females.

EIGHT

Winter Wildlife Survival Techniques

Animals, collectively, have a wider range of strategies than plants when confronted with winter's cold and snow. Some leave their summer habitats or migrate. Others become dormant or hibernate. Many simply die, as do innumerable plants. Still others remain active, cope with the rigors of winter, and adapt. I'll dwell mostly on this last group.

Appropriate for this chapter, I'll place animals into cold-blooded and warm-blooded groups. In both groups, some pass the winter in a dormant state, others endure it while active.

Cold-Blooded Animals

Cold-blooded animals cannot regulate their body temperature and essentially must assume the temperature of their surroundings. They include invertebrates, fishes, amphibians, and reptiles.

Invertebrates

Usually relatively small, *invertebrates* (in-VURT-uh-bruhts) are those animals without backbones; that is, they lack a *vertebral* or spinal column. Among them are the numerous insects, clams, snails, and crayfish.

Of the aquatic invertebrates, some are dormant or nearly so during the cold season. Snails burrow into the mud or plant debris. Clams generally rest in the bottom mud or sand.Whirligig beetles, which live on the surface of the water in summer, hibernate as adults or larvae in mud or plant debris; they are joined by adult leeches and by larval mosquitoes, dragonflies, and damselflies. Water striders, also surface-film inhabitors, hibernate in and under plant debris near the water. Freshwater sponges die or partly disintegrate in winter, but survive as minute, ball-shaped, resting cysts that can survive even when water freezes to the bottom. In spring, the cysts release vital cells that initiate new colonies.

Many invertebrates, including scuds, water mites, and crayfish, remain active under the

100

ice but are less so than in summer. Some diving beetles, backswimmers, and water boatmen, which overwinter as adults, are also active. Caddis flies, mayflies, midges, stone flies, and blackflies tend to overwinter as active larvae; some of these may survive as adults and others may hibernate.

Some aquatic invertebrates simply die as winter approaches. Not only the sponges but also water fleas, rotifers, copepods, and protozoans—single-celled animals—commonly die as well.

On land, most invertebrates that do not die beforehand survive the winter by hibernating. Insects overwinter as eggs, larvae, pupae, and adults—as mentioned in chapter 7—in leaf litter, under bark, or in galls. These animals often adjust to the cold by supercooling their bodies or secreting an antifreeze, commonly a *glycerol* (GLISS-uh-rawl), a sugary alcohol. Before winter sets in, insects "migrate" short distances to warmer places, such as into grasses, under leaves, or into the surface of the soil.

A few insects migrate, in the true sense, great distances. The monarch butterfly is one great migrator. Western monarchs, inhabiting parts of the western United States, have been known for some time to migrate to the Monterey Peninsula in California. Migration of the eastern monarchs, occupying the region from Texas to New England and Florida to Minnesota, was a puzzle until the mid-1970s. It is now known that the eastern monarchs, flying at speeds of ten to thirty miles per hour, mostly overwinter in central Mexico; some also go to such places as Central America. Although not living beyond a year, some return to their summer grounds from their overwintering place.

Land snails hibernate in leaf litter, in the soil, or under logs and stones. They seal their shell openings to prevent their bodies from drying out.

Fishes, Amphibians, and Reptiles

Fishes are active in winter, as anyone fishing through the ice can attest. Besides coping with cold water, fishes must often endure low levels of oxygen that can lead to their "winter kill." Some adjust to the cold by supercooling, others by producing antifreezes, such as glycerol or *glycoprotein*, which is produced by some arctic fishes.

Among the largely aquatic amphibians, most frogs hibernate in or on the mud, although some may be active occasionally under the ice. They breathe through the skin or the mucous membrane lining the mouth. Wood frogs, residing in moist woods and often some distance from water in summer, range farther north than any other amphibian or reptile. They extend northward from Labrador through much of Canada and into Alaska. Wood frogs, known to freeze solid and recover, can flood their bodies with *glycogen* (GLY-kuh-juhn), a sugar that acts as an antifreeze. Adult newts and mud puppies are other aquatic amphibians that stay active during the winter in much the same way as do the fishes. Other salamanders and toads hibernate under logs and stones; tiger salamanders spend most of their time in burrows, winter or summer.

Aquatic turtles ordinarily hibernate in the mud like frogs. Besides breathing much like frogs while hibernating, they can also respire by blood-filled tissues in the anus and extract oxygen from the muddy water. Snapping turtles may also settle under logs or other plant debris or occupy muskrat, beaver, or other holes in banks. Occasionally you may glimpse turtles swimming under the ice.

Land turtles, lizards, and snakes hibernate under decaying logs and stones, in burrows and other holes, and in rock dens.

Garter snakes live farther north than any other reptiles in North America. Among them,

Figure 23. Bobwhites conserve warmth by huddling.

red-sided garter snakes extend the farthest north, to at least northern Alberta. One of the largest concentrations of snake hibernating dens or "hibernacula" in the world occurs in the Interlake region of southern Manitoba north of Winnipeg. Here, hibernacula include fissures, caverns, and sinks in limestone. Highly communal, tens of thousands of garter snakes congregate in the fall; this activity begins in early September with the last snakes going underground in about late October. The concentrations, at times, resemble writhing masses of giant spaghetti. The snakes withstand cold through supercooling and creating antifreeze solutions. In spite of these defenses, many snakes still die in their dens from the cold.

Warm-Blooded Animals

Warm-blooded animals, the mammals and birds, can control and maintain their body temperatures independent of surrounding air or water temperature. In winter, warm-blooded animals must continually maintain body temperatures above that of their surroundings, analogous to setting the furnace thermostat of a dwelling to maintain inside temperature above that of the outside.

Mammals and birds share several cold-coping strategies. Some are tied to behavior, others are purely involuntary or inherent within the body. These include huddling, curling, fluffing of fur or feathers, shivering, increasing insulation, desensitization to cold, and heat exchange to prevent freezing of extremities.

Huddling, or the close grouping of individual animals, cuts down on exposed surface area and reduces heat loss. Some small mammals, such as certain voles, mice, and shrews, become social in winter and huddle in communal nests to conserve heat. Coveys of bobwhites (Figure 23) and quails also huddle at night.

Curling into a curved, compact shape, combined with retracting the extremities, reduces surface area and conserves heat in a manner

Figure 24. A red fox waiting out the cold by curling.

similar to that of huddling but can be done alone. Foxes, coyotes, and wolves all curl when cold; foxes, especially, can go further by wrapping their bushy tails, like muffs, around their heads (Figure 24). Crouched squirrels in exposed places may curve their bushy tails toward their bodies to protect their back and neck.

The fluffing of fur or feathers is a natural response to cold. Fluffing makes the fur or feathers more erect, thereby trapping more air, which increases the thickness of the insulating layer and reduces heat loss.

Shivering, induced involuntarily, provides for heat generated by muscles contracting. It is a last-resort heat-generation process for mammals, but a primary one for birds.

Warm-blooded animals increase their insulation by adding fur, feathers, or fat. More insulation means having to produce less heat. Such mammals as red foxes and porcupines mostly add noticeable underfur when winter approaches; smaller mammals, such as deer mice and red squirrels, aren't able to add much fur. Harbor seals enhance their insula-tion mainly with additional fat. Mainly the larger birds, notably ptarmigans, produce thicker plumage; the smaller birds generally possess little capability for this.

Most warm-blooded animals tend to desensitize to cold with greater exposure to it; their tolerance to cold, thereby, becomes greater with time. One result of this is delayed shivering with repeated exposure to cold. A body's system is reset by the *hypothalamus*, an organ at the base of the brain significant for temperature control, and by changing the balance of hormones. A laboratory study of goldfinches in southern Michigan showed that birds captured in winter could endure more cold than those captured in summer.

Have you wondered how animals' extremities, especially the thin, frail feet of songbirds with no obvious insulation, keep from freezing? It has to do with the constriction of blood vessels, the exchange of heat between close or touching blood vessels, and the *shunting* or diversion of blood flow. At a critical low temperature, the near-surface veins of a foot, let's say, constrict to reduce heat loss. This constriction causes blood returning from the foot to shunt or divert through deeper veins lying close or next to arteries carrying warm blood in the opposite direction toward the foot. Heat is readily exchanged between the close or touching veins and arteries carrying blood with opposite flow. Venous blood (carried by veins) is gradually prewarmed on its way toward the main body, and arterial blood (carried by arteries) gradually precools on its way to the foot.

With a foot in danger of freezing, more blood under higher pressure is pumped into an artery, which becomes enlarged and constricts the surrounding deeper veins. This constriction forces or shunts more blood to return from the foot through near-surface veins. In effect, warmer blood reaches the foot because heat is not released to the returning blood in the deeper veins. The network of deep veins surrounding an artery precools the foot and reduces the loss of heat.

Before leaving cold-coping strategies for warm-blooded animals, we might ask "Is it better to be large or small in cold climates?" A straightforward answer doesn't come easily. Smaller animals have a larger body surface area in relation to their body volume than larger animals, so they cool faster. But larger animals, even with a smaller body surface area relative to their volume, lose more heat to their surroundings. Further, large animals require more food overall to maintain their body temperature.

A. N. Formozov, a Russian ecologist, classified warm-blooded animals according to their tolerance to snow. He coined strange—but logical—Greek-derived names for his three groups. You may wish to impress—or depress—your friends with them.

Chionophobes (kye-AHN-uh-fobes), from *chion*, "snow," plus *phobos*, "fearing," are largely unable to adjust to snow or do so with considerable difficulty. Among the snow fearers or snow haters are most insect-eating and ground-feeding birds and waterfowl that migrate south in winter. Some that remain in cold regions include ring-necked pheasants and the opossums.

Those that make adjustments to snow and survive readily are the *chioneuphores* (kye-AHN-you-fourz), from *chion* plus *euphoros*, "healthy." These snow tolerators include such animals as moose, elk, deer, foxes, voles, shrews, and mice.

The relatively few snow-loving animals, the *chionophiles* (kye-AHN-uh-files), from *chion* plus *philos*, "loving," have evolved definite adaptations for snow. Among them are the snowshoe hares, lynx, weasels, caribou, and ptarmigans.

Animals surviving through winter may also be grouped according to whether they live *above* the snow or *beneath* it. I'll follow this approach as I discuss how some mammals and birds adapt to winter.

Mammals

Hoofed mammals, mostly snow tolerators, live primarily above the snow cover, although their legs pierce through part or all of it. They wade through the snow, their legs carrying them along like stilts (Figure 25). Soft snow is fine, but crusty snow may cut their legs. Critical snow depth is about three feet for moose and generally less for other hoofed mammals.

Deer and moose, particularly, yard up in valley bottoms or small groves when snow deepens and makes their movement difficult. Frequent use keeps the trails packed for ease in

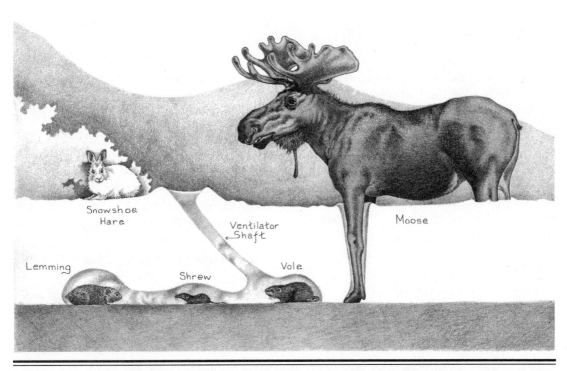

Figure 25. Three adaptations to living with snow. Moose wade through snow on long, stiltlike legs. Snowshoe hares travel on the snow surface with snowshoelike feet. Small mammals, such as lemmings, shrews, and voles, live beneath the snow. They may excavate ventilator shafts to the snow surface when the carbon dioxide level builds up. Animals are not drawn to scale.

feeding. But during storms the animals may starve in their yards when extremely deep snow prohibits their movement.

A study of hoofed animals shows that chest height, foot loading, and behavior give a good idea of how these animals can cope with living in snow. (Foot loading refers to the amount of weight in a given area of the foot; low foot loading means greater ease of traveling over snow.) Of those animals studied—bison, caribou, moose, elk, Dall sheep, bighorn sheep, white-tailed deer, and pronghorn—caribou cope with snow best and bison and pronghorn the least. Caribou exhibit lower foot loading because of their large dewclaws.

Hoofed mammals often migrate, both vertically and laterally. Driven by snow, when midcalf height or so, elk of the Teton-Yellowstone National Park region move down from the high country to the National Elk Refuge in Jackson Hole, Wyoming. Deer migrate first, followed by elk and moose. Caribou abandon the hard-packed snow of the tundra in autumn for the soft, light snow in spruce forests to the south. They prefer snow less than two feet deep for ease in searching for lichens. Desirable snow areas for caribou are bounded by "fences" of hard, dense snow more than two feet thick.

Most hoofed mammals change diets in winter. Moose deviate from especially aquatic plants, with grasses and browse, to a diet of essentially all browse. White-tailed deer make a similar change, but also feed on tree lichens; mule deer food alters from browse and grasses in summer to essentially all browse in winter. Feeding on mostly grasses with some broad-leaved plants and little browse in the warmer seasons, elks' diets change to about one-half browse in winter.

Hoofed mammals vary in their response to preying wolves in winter. Caribou, when pursued by wolves, head for deep, soft snow to discourage their attackers. Moose often stand their ground and fight. Apparently relatively easy prey for wolves, elk and bison usually flee. Bison are probably easier prey for wolves than moose.

Other, smaller, mammals live wholly or largely above the snow. Among them are the doglike mammals, snowshoe hares, lynx, and weasels.

The foxes, coyotes, and wolves, also snow tolerators, develop longer and thicker fur in winter, fluff their fur for greater insulation, and rely on the habit of curling to lessen heat loss from their bodies. In stormy weather, they burrow partly in the snow and wait it out.

Doglike mammals employ some diet-related strategies. Supplementing their largely meat diet with berries, foxes and coyotes rely on prey slightly less in winter. Wolves and coyotes achieve greater success in bringing down larger prey on harder-packed or crusty snow than on soft snow. Recall how caribou strike out for soft, deep snow when pursued by wolves.

The aptly named, snow-loving snowshoe hares grow fur on the bottoms of their hind feet that literally function as snowshoes for easier walking on the snow surface (Figure 25); the additional fur also provides added warmth. In soft, deep snow, snowshoe hares hop up and down to forge feeding trails.

Snowshoe hares' pelts change from brown to white, as winter heralds its approach, to make them nearly invisible to predators. The lighter underbelly softens the shadows and allows the body to blend better with the snow.

Besides snowshoe hares, white-tailed jackrabbits, weasels, arctic hares—in the southern part of their range—and ptarmigans also transform to white in winter. Diminishing day length, lowered temperatures, and snowfall all affect the timing of the color change, but shorter day length triggers hormones that set it off.

Complementing their foot hairs and color change, snowshoe hares also maintain another strategy in their snow-adapting arsenal. They shift from eating leaves and seeds to twigs and bark (Figure 26).

With mops on their snowshoelike feet, lynx are well fitted for walking and running on snow in pursuit of their preferred prey, snowshoe hares (Figure 27). Tufts on their ears help prevent their freezing and may also amplify sound.

Weasel pelage modifies to white—all except the black tip, which seems to offer survival value. Predators, unattracted to the white body, focus on the obvious black tail tip and not the more vulnerable torso. Weasels spend time above the snow, but their slim, sleek body adapts them nicely for burrowing beneath the snow as well. They prey mostly on voles, mice, and shrews but occasionally take small birds and even cottontails.

Now, let's look at some of the mammals preferring winter life beneath the snow. Some of these are active, others wait out winter as hibernators.

Figure 26. A snowshoe hare nibbling bark.

Figure 27. A lynx in hot pursuit of a snowshoe hare, its favored food. Both lynx and snowshoe hares have added fur on their feet in winter for ease in traveling on the snow surface.

In wooded regions receiving little or no wind, such small mammals as voles, mice, lemmings, and shrews disappear beneath the snow when its depth reaches about six inches (see Figure 25). A major challenge for these small mammals is how to cope with winter's rigor between the onset of subfreezing temperatures and a snow cover of about six inches,.

Once under the snow, these small mammals are relatively secure. They build tunnels for access to food and nests in which they huddle for warmth. Although relatively safe from predators, weasels and minks still find them.

How might you, as a vole, for instance, perceive your new environment at the base of a snowpack? It's cool, but warm by winter's standards—generally about 15 to 25 degrees Fahrenheit—and the temperature remains relatively constant. Further, you would find it quiet, highly humid, the air calm, and dark—at two feet only about one percent of the natural light reaches your domain. As you scurry about your tunnels, you might hear the crystals of depth hoar (remember this from chapter 2?) tinkle as you brush past them.

A common problem in living under the snow, especially if the snow loses some of its pore space, is the buildup of carbon dioxide. Small mammals tend to avoid places with high carbon dioxide. Some small mammals construct ventilator shafts (Figure 25) to allow fresh air to reach the base of the snowpack. These shafts, of course, place the animals in further jeopardy from attack by predators.

In open places wind reworks snow and makes it harder and denser. Small mammals must then expend more energy to move about, and the depth hoar is less developed under hard-packed snow. Under these conditions small mammals favor filled cavities in the wind-beaten snow.

Pocket gophers, burrowing rodents with small eyes and ears and short, usually naked tails, leave peculiar evidence of their winter activities. In summer, they transport soil from their excavated tunnels to surface mounds. Continuing their burrowing in winter, pocket gophers now dispose of excavated soil by packing it in snow tunnels. Upon spring melt, earth cores or "ropes" filling the snow tunnels are let down on the ground surface and attest to pocket gophers' winter burrowing.

During winter pocket gophers feed largely on roots and tubers stored in underground caches. They also resort to gnawing tree and shrub bark buried beneath the snow.

Red squirrels are normally above-snow animals. But when temperatures drop to about

−25 to −30 degrees Fahrenheit, they leave the trees to tunnel beneath the snow. Other, larger, tree squirrels generally remain in trees even when temperatures plummet.

Hibernators pass the winter under the snow largely in a torpid state. Their metabolism, or the series of chemical changes required for life processes, alters to conserve energy and reduce the need for food. Biologists group the hibernators as deep versus shallow or those relying on body fat versus those relying on stored food.

Deep hibernators include mainly small mammals, such as bats, ground squirrels, and jumping mice; the smallest are bats, the largest marmots and woodchucks. They're called deep hibernators because of their settling into a deep sleep, with eyes tightly closed and legs rigid. Their body temperature descends to near freezing, blood pressure drops, and the heartbeat slows. In ground squirrels, breathing may change from a hundred breaths per minute to four, body temperature from 97 degrees to 39, and heartbeat from two hundred and fifty beats per minute to ten.

Among the shallow hiberators are generally the larger mammals—bears, badgers, skunks, raccoons, and the much smaller chipmunks. Their hiberation is more a state of drowsiness rather than a deep sleep, and they may wake up periodically. Body temperature is usually near normal, but breathing rate, heart rate, and blood pressure are all lower.

Black bears, shallow hibernators, sleep for months without eating, drinking, urinating, or defecating. They subsist on body fat stored up before entering their dens. Body temperature is generally within about 12 degrees of normal summer temperature. Their heart rate may descend as low as about ten beats per minute; this compares to about forty beats per minute for sleeping bears in summer.

In northern Minnesota black bears inhabit their dens from late September or early October to mid-April. During this time most lose about 15 to 30 percent of their body weight. Bear dens, generally a few degrees below freezing even when covered by much snow, are in burrows, caves, hollow trees, depressions under trees, and other places. Den floors are usually covered with leaves, grasses, or other insulative material. Most black bears survive by using their stored fat and by developing thicker fur in the autumn.

I mentioned earlier that some hibernators rely on stored fat, others on food stored outside of their bodies. Those that store fat, such as bears, spend more time in a sluggish state. Larger animals can store more body fat than smaller animals. Those that store food, chipmunks for example, spend less time in a sluggish state and awaken frequently; the more food stored, the less time an animal spends in torpor.

Man, a Naked Mammal

Without shelter and clothing, humans are generally extremely vulnerable to cold. At −40 degrees Fahrenheit and subjected to a wind of thirty miles per hour, a naked human dies in about fifteen minutes. Further, a naked human can maintain a normal body temperature of 98.6 degrees only down to an air temperature of 73.4 degrees. Below that, the body automatically attempts to add heat by shivering.

In spite of that, some peoples show rather high tolerances to cold. These include the Tierra del Fuegans, Australian aborigines, Ama (Korean female pearl divers), and the Inuit, whose hands are particularly tolerant of cold.

The main tactic for heat production is any form of muscle activity. It can boost heat production by as much as ten times. Shivering, a form of muscle activity, may, itself, raise heat production up to five times. Goose bumps, accompanying shivering, represent a pitiful attempt—a leftover of evolution—to fluff hairs, as in other mammals or the feathers of birds. Fluffing, of course, is of no consequence in humans.

Though minor compared to muscle activity, a rise in metabolic rate with oncoming cold temperatures can contribute some body heat. This rise is probably caused by hormones secreted by the thyroid, pituitary, and adrenal glands.

Concomitant with a rise in metabolic rate is a desire to eat more as temperatures drop; this desire is nourished by a better appetite. These changes are fortified by a greater craving for fat, which is a better source of energy to combat heat loss than carbohydrates or proteins.

The best strategy of the body to reduce heat loss is the concerted effort of blood vessel constriction, heat exchange between blood vessels, and shunting, which was also discussed earlier. As freezing of the extremities becomes imminent, blood vessels first constrict and then intermittently dilate, which allows more blood to flow and warm the extremities. This dilation or expansion of the blood vessels is evidenced by reddening skin. In some people living in cold climates, such as the Inuit, dilation is a normal, early response that allows them better-than-average dexterity of their fingers in cold water or air.

A change in posture that reduces surface area and, thereby, heat loss might be called hunching. You know what that means. When you enter the cold, you have a tendency to hunch your shoulders. Garrison Keillor, the well-known radio humorist broadcasting over National Public Radio, has held audiences spellbound with his stories of fellow Minnesotans living in his fictitious hometown of Lake Wobegon. He labeled this curious habit of raising the shoulders while walking outdoors in cold winters as the "Minnesota Hunch."

Birds

A major cold-coping approach for birds is simply to leave. It's been estimated that about one-half of the species of birds in northern regions migrate south for the winter.

Of the several strategies already mentioned for withstanding cold, shivering seems to be the primary one for birds, especially for small birds. Except when flying, it seems likely that most birds *shiver all winter*, which provides heat by muscle contractions.

A strategy that lessens the need to produce heat is roosting at night. Roosts, in dense vegetation, cavities in trees or rocks, or burrows in the snow, cut down on the heat radiated to the night sky.

Some birds reduce the need for body heat through *hypothermia*, a lower-than-normal body temperature. Occurring at night, this tactic requires less energy to maintain body temperature. Black-capped chickadees, perhaps the most studied of winter songbirds, can drop their nighttime body temperature nearly 20 degrees below that of the daytime temperature, which is about 108 degrees Fahrenheit.

What does winter mean to black-capped chickadees? They require the equivalent of more than 250 sunflower seeds per day when the temperature drops to zero. These birds constantly search for insect eggs and seeds. Their body fat changes during the day from essentially none in the morning to considerable in the afternoon. When temperatures drop to

−20 degrees Fahrenheit, they slow down drastically, fluff, and wait out the cold snap. Chickadees protect their feet by raising them one at a time into the breast feathers or by sitting on them. In spite of numerous precautions, many do not survive the winter.

Differing from mammals, essentially all birds live above the snow. The few exceptions include the ruffed grouse, which may roost in the snow, alluded to earlier, and bobwhites and quails, which may huddle on or partly within the snow. Apparently no birds live for long periods beneath the snow.

Few birds have evolved specific adaptations for life on the snow. Among those that have are ptarmigans and ruffed grouse. Ptarmigans change their plumage to white. Ruffed grouse grow combs on each side of their toes to walk more easily on the snow, in a manner similar to snowshoe hares growing additional fur on their hind feet.

A bald eagle resting on a snow-covered branch.

NINE

Winter Birding

Birding is not strictly the same as bird-watching. Less inclusive than bird-watching, birding may involve the serious identification of birds, the listing of birds seen, the recording of migrations, the ups and downs of bird populations, and the enthusiastic noting of rare birds. Jack Connor, in his book *The Complete Birder,* called birding a "sporting science"—half sport and half science. In the early days, birders routinely *shot* birds—even John James Audubon. In the early part of this century, people gradually began to "glass" birds more frequently than shoot them. Today, most birders are good all-around naturalists and ecologists.

Bird-watching is more of a blanket activity. It ranges from simply looking at birds, or feeding them, to intensive ornithological study of them. We might even consider a waterfowl or upland bird hunter as a kind of bird-watcher— or a birder in the old sense—who is concerned only with a few species.

Why bird? It is a recreational activity enjoyed by one out of every four Americans that can be treated as a game or sport, and, under the right circumstances, might even be considered a religious experience. In the process, though, you become enmeshed in another aspect of nature. Birding also enables us to monitor the environmental health of our region, country, and planet as we keep track of the fluctuations of bird species and populations. As Roger Tory Peterson phrased it, birds are a kind of "ecological litmus paper."

Identification

What Birds to Expect in Winter

A first step in identifying winter birds is realizing which species to expect. Winter in northern regions pares down tremendously the number of possible candidates.

It takes a while for a winter assemblage of birds to establish itself in northern climates. The resulting assemblage is governed largely by available food, not cold. About the first to leave the middle latitudes after cold weather sets in are many birds that eat flying insects, such as flycatchers, vireos, swifts, and most warblers. They leave because their insect prey have all but disappeared, becoming dormant for the winter. (Insect-eaters that don't leave include woodpeckers, nuthatches, and brown creepers equipped with long bills to probe insect larvae and eggs from the bark of tree trunks and limbs.) Departure of the flying insect-eaters is followed by the arrival of water birds—swans, geese, and ducks—from the north. With some exceptions, water birds tend to linger only until most water bodies freeze up and then proceed south. Sandwiched between the insect-eaters and water birds are "half-hardy" birds whose numbers fluctuate with cold temperatures. Among them are such land birds as catbirds and brown thrashers, and such shorebirds as willets, marbled godwits, and great blue herons.

With the autumn migration complete, a residual winter assemblage remains in the middle latitudes. It consists of regular, year-round residents and drifters from the far north—such as Lapland longspurs and snow buntings—all of which may be grouped as "snow tolerators," as mentioned in chapter 8.

Contrary to humans known by the same name, true avian "snowbirds" are those generally highly tolerant of winter. I am following Kit and George Harrison, in their *The Birds of Winter*, in considering "snowbirds" as those bird species wintering in significant numbers north of 40 degrees north latitude. The fortieth parallel runs through central New Jersey, southern Pennsylvania, south-central Ohio, central Indiana and Illinois, northern Missouri, the southern edge of Nebraska, northern Colorado and Utah, north-central Nevada, and northern California. Table 6 lists these snowbirds in North America, exclusive of those in coastal areas, and the willow and rock ptarmigans, which will not be seen by many people because of their far northern ranges. This list of about 100 species is a far cry from some 650 species known to nest in North America north of Mexico.

What Features to Look For

To identify a bird, it helps to ask yourself questions as you observe it. The following questions will help you evaluate the basic features for identifying birds:

1. How large is the bird? Is it large, crow-sized or larger; medium-sized, like a robin; or small, like a sparrow? (Table 6)

2. What is its shape or silhouette? Is it dumpy like a dipper or slender like a mockingbird? Does it have a crest like a blue jay, cardinal, or the waxwings?

3. What shape are the wing tips? Are they rounded like a northern goshawk's or pointed like an American kestrel's?

4. How is the tail shaped? Is it pointed like a black-billed magpie's, keel-shaped like a common grackle's, squared off like a gyrfalcon's, or notched like a mountain bluebird's?

5. What is the shape of the bill? Is it hooked downward like a hawk's or an owl's, crossed like a crossbill's, short and stout like an evening grosbeak's, or long and slender like a brown creeper's?

6. What of the bird's color and markings?

    a. Is the color pattern solid like a crow's, heavily speckled like a European starling's, or barred (markings at right angles to the body) like a great horned owl's? How does the color of the breast compare with that of the back?

    b. Does the tail show a flash pattern—white sides as a dark-eyed junco's or meadowlark's, white outer corners like the rufous-sided towhee's, or yellow tips like a waxwing's?

    c. Is there a light rump like a common flicker's or a red-bellied woodpecker's?

    d. Are there wing patterns? If so, are they patches like a mallard's or stripes (also patches) like a mockingbird's?

    e. When perched, do the wings show light wing bars like a blue jay's or a kinglet's?

    f. Does the bird have an eye stripe through, above, or below the eye? Is the crown striped?

    g. What about a light eye ring around the eye like a ruby-crowned kinglet's or a robin's?

7. How does the bird behave?

    a. Does it soar like a hawk, fly in an undulating, up-and-down fashion like a common flicker, or fly straight out like a crow?

    b. When perched, does the bird hold its tail quietly like a house sparrow or flick it from side to side like a northern mockingbird?

    c. If it climbs trees, does it jerkily use its tail as a prop like the woodpeckers, ascend spirally from the trunk's base like the brown creeper, or go down headfirst like the nuthatches?

    d. If it enters water, does it dabble and upend like a surface-feeding duck, dive like a deep-water duck, or walk under water like a dipper?

TABLE 6 Birds Commonly Expected in Winter in Parts of Inland North America North of 40 Degrees North

Bird Species	Body Length (Inches)	Expected Feeding at Bird Feeder (Y = Yes, N = No)
Large Birds: Crow-sized or Larger, Mostly 12 Inches or Longer		
WATERFOWL		
1. Canada Goose	25–43	N
2. Mallard	20–28	N
3. Black Duck (E. N.Am.)	21–25	N
4. Green-Winged Teal	14	N
5. Common Goldeneye	20	N
6. Barrow's Goldeneye	21	N
7. Bufflehead	13–15	N
8. Common Merganser	20–27	N
HAWKS AND EAGLES		
9. Northern Goshawk	20–26	N
10. Sharp-Shinned Hawk	10–14	N
11. Cooper's Hawk	14–20	N
12. Red-Tailed Hawk	19–25	N
13. Rough-Legged Hawk	19–24	N
14. Gyrfalcon (rare in U.S.)	20–25	N

(continued on next page)

Bird Species	Body Length (Inches)	Expected Feeding at Bird Feeder (Y = Yes, N = No)
15. American Kestrel	9–12	N
16. Northern Harrier	18–24	N
17. Golden Eagle	30–40	N
18. Bald Eagle	30–43	N
GROUSE AND RELATIVES		
19. Blue Grouse (W. N.Am.)	18–21	N
20. Spruce Grouse	15–17	N
21. Sharp-Tailed Grouse	15–20	N
22. Sage Grouse	22–28	N
23. Greater Prairie Chicken	17–18	N
24. Willow Ptarmigan	16	N
25. Rock Ptarmigan	13	N
26. White-Tailed Ptarmigan	12–13	N
27. Northern Bobwhite	8.5–10	N
28. Chukar (W. N.Am.)	14	N
29. Ring-Necked Pheasant	30–36	N
30. Gray Partridge	12–14	N
31. Wild Turkey	36–48	N
DOVES		
32. Rock Dove	13	Y
33. Mourning Dove	12	Y
OWLS		
34. Great Horned Owl	18–25	N
35. Long-Eared Owl	13–16	N
36. Short-Eared Owl	13–17	N
37. Barn Owl	14–20	N
38. Snowy Owl (rare in U.S.)	20–27	N
39. Barred Owl	17–24	N
40. Great Gray Owl	24–33	N
41. Northern Hawk Owl (rare in U.S.)	14–18	N
JAYS, CROWS, AND RELATIVES		
42. Blue Jay	11–12	Y
43. Steller's Jay (W. N.Am.)	12–14	N
44. Scrub Jay	11–12	Y
45. Pinyon Jay (W. U.S.)	11–12	Y
46. Gray Jay	11–13	Y
47. Black-Billed Magpie (W. N.Am.)	18–22	Y
48. Clark's Nutcracker (W. N.Am.)	12–13	N

Bird Species	Body Length (Inches)	Expected Feeding at Bird Feeder (Y = Yes, N = No)
49. Common Raven	22–27	N
50. American Crow	17–21	Y
BLACKBIRDS		
51. Common Grackle	11–14	N
WOODPECKERS		
52. Common Flicker	12–14	Y
53. Pileated Woodpecker	16–20	Y

Medium-Sized Birds: Robin-sized, Mostly 7–12 Inches Long

Bird Species	Body Length (Inches)	Expected Feeding at Bird Feeder
OWLS		
54. Screech	7–10	N
55. Boreal Owl	9–10	N
56. Saw Whet Owl	7–8.5	N
57. Pygmy Owl (W. N.Am.)	7–7.5	N
WOODPECKERS		
58. Red-Bellied Woodpecker (E. U.S.)	9–10	Y
59. Red-Headed Woodpecker	8.5–9.5	Y
60. Yellow-Bellied Sapsucker	8–9	Y
61. Hairy Woodpecker	9.5	Y
62. Downy Woodpecker	6.5	Y
63. Three-Toed Woodpecker	8–9.5	N
64. Black-Backed Woodpecker	9–10	N
LARKS		
65. Horned Lark	7–8	Y
DIPPERS		
66. Dipper (W. N.Am.)	7–8.5	N
MOCKINGBIRDS		
67. Northern Mockingbird	9–11	Y
BLUEBIRDS AND ROBINS		
68. Mountain Bluebird (W. N.Am.)	7	N
69. Robin	9–11	Y

(continued on next page)

Bird Species	Body Length (Inches)	Expected Feeding at Bird Feeder (Y = Yes, N = No)
WAXWINGS		
70. Bohemian Waxwing	8	N
71. Cedar Waxwing	7	N
SHRIKES		
72. Northern Shrike	9–10	N
STARLINGS		
73. European Starling	7.5–8.5	Y
MEADOWLARKS		
74. Eastern Meadowlark	9	Y
75. Western Meadowlark	9	Y
BLACKBIRDS		
76. Red-Winged Blackbird	7–9.5	Y
77. Brewer's Blackbird	9	Y
78. Brown-Headed Cowbird	7	Y
CARDINALS AND GROSBEAKS		
79. Cardinal	7.5–9	Y
80. Evening Grosbeak	8	Y
81. Pine Grosbeak	8–10	Y
TOWHEES		
82. Rufous-Sided Towhee	7–8.5	N

Small Birds: House Sparrow-sized, Mostly Less than 7 Inches Long

Bird Species	Body Length (Inches)	Expected Feeding at Bird Feeder (Y = Yes, N = No)
CHICKADEES AND TITMICE		
83. Black-Capped Chickadee	4.8–5.8	Y
84. Boreal Chickadee	5–5.5	N
85. Chestnut-Backed Chickadee	4.5–5	Y
86. Mountain Chickadee (W. N.Am.)	5–5.8	Y
87. Tufted Titmouse (E. U.S.)	6	Y
NUTHATCHES AND CREEPERS		
88. Red-Breasted Nuthatch	4.5	Y
89. White-Breasted Nuthatch	5–6	Y
90. Pygmy Nuthatch (W. N.Am.)	4.5	Y
91. Brown Creeper	5	Y

Bird Species	Body Length (Inches)	Expected Feeding at Bird Feeder (Y = Yes, N = No)
KINGLETS		
92. Golden-Crowned Kinglet	3.5	N
93. Ruby-Crowned Kinglet	4	N
FINCHES, REDPOLLS, CROSSBILLS, SPARROWS, AND RELATIVES		
94. Purple Finch	5–5.6	Y
95. Cassin's Finch (W. N.Am.)	6–6.5	Y
96. House Finch	5–5.8	Y
97. Rosy Finch (W. N.Am.)	5.8–6.8	Y
98. Common Redpoll	5	Y
99. Hoary Redpoll	5	Y
100. Pine Siskin	4.5–5	Y
101. American Goldfinch	5	Y
102. Red Crossbill	5.2–6.5	Y
103. White-Winged Crossbill	6–6.8	Y
104. Dark-Eyed Junco	5.5–6.8	Y
105. House Sparrow	6	Y
106. White-Crowned Sparrow	6.5–7.5	Y
107. White-Throated Sparrow	6.5–7	Y
108. Fox Sparrow	6.5–7.5	Y
109. Song Sparrow	5–6.5	Y
110. American Tree Sparrow	6–6.5	Y
111. Field Sparrow	5	Y
112. Lapland Longspur	6.5	Y
113. Snow Bunting	6–7.2	Y

Aids for Identification

Bird calls, of course, are a great aid in identification. In winter, calls tend to be simpler and more repetitive. The lack of deciduous foliage makes the tie with call and bird easier. Among the birds having distinctive calls in winter are crows, jays, chickadees, titmice, nuthatches, and most woodpeckers. One call that I clearly remember, although I heard it years ago, was a barred owl's, issuing from deep woods on a cold, wintry, moonlit night as I shoveled thick snow off my house roof.

An easy way to learn bird calls is by listening to recordings on cassette tapes or compact discs (CDs). A good source for bird call recordings is the Cornell Laboratory of Ornithology (159 Sapsucker Woods Road, Ithaca, NY 14850). Some recordings are tied directly with field guides.

Sonagrams, literally diagrams or pictures of bird songs, are produced electronically. They depict pitch and frequency of a bird call. These visual bird call reproductions are best viewed while listening to tapes or CDs of bird call recordings.

Lacking recordings or sonagrams, you will probably resort to mnemonics to help you identify bird sounds. Translate bird calls into English words or phrases. So, the rufous-sided towhee's song is "Drink your teeee," or maybe "Drink tow-hee" and the black-capped chickadee says "Chick-a-dee-dee-dee" or "dee-dee-dee." You might also try acoustic analogies. A hairy woodpecker's voice, for example, might be likened to a baby's rattle or sound like the chatter of a tree squirrel.

After you tick off many features of a bird, and maybe acquire a good sense of its call as well, reach for a field guide. (If you reach too soon, you may miss crucial features before the bird flies off.) Standard field guides (see Selected Readings), identified by my abbreviated names, include: Peterson East, Peterson West, Audubon East, Audubon West, Audubon Master, National Geographic, and Robbins.

Instead of using field guides and bird song recordings, you might find videotapes an easier way to go. The Audubon Society, as one source, markets a set of videotapes with still photographs of birds and their sounds. A precursor to its videotapes, and still available, is "Audible Audubon," a combination of birds illustrated on cards and songs delivered from a tiny, battery-powered phonograph. Videotapes with moving color images of birds accompanying their sounds are becoming more available.

At Your Bird Feeder

A good place to learn to identify birds is at your bird feeder. You don't have to seek out the birds—they concentrate naturally about the food. And you can observe the birds and flip through field guides in comfort.

Although birds overlap somewhat in their attraction to feeders, they tend to "sort out," to a degree, by the type of feeder. This general "sorting out" can help you reduce the possibilities in bird identification.

Birders generally recognize three main kinds of feeders: sunflower seed feeders, cracked corn and mixed seed feeders, and suet feeders. Besides varying in type of food and type of container, each is placed somewhat differently.

Sunflower seed feeders are stocked only with sunflower seed, preferred by most songbirds. Most seed-eaters favor the smallest, all-black sunflower seeds, which have a higher percentage of oil for their weight and thinner husks than the other two kinds of striped sunflower seeds. Sunflower seeds are placed in either hanging or pole-mounted feeders. "Snowbirds" attracted to sunflower seed feeders include black-capped chickadees; tufted titmice; white- and red-breasted nuthatches; cardinals; American goldfinches; purple and house finches; pine siskins; downy, hairy, red-bellied, and red-headed woodpeckers; common flickers; evening grosbeaks (Figure 28); redpolls; starlings; house sparrows; and blue and scrub jays.

Cracked corn and mixed seed feeders are generally simple trays above the ground, or the seed is scattered on the ground. Such feed may, of course, be also placed in hopper-type feeders hung or mounted on poles. Cracked corn should dominate with less white or red millet and sunflower seed. Avoid such seeds as wheat, milo, oats, rye, or rice that birds tend to ignore. Additional birds attracted to cracked corn and mixed seed feeders, beside those at sunflower seed feeders, include dark-

Figure 28. Evening grosbeaks feasting on sunflower seeds from a feeder attached to a window sill.

eyed juncos; white-throated, white-crowned, fox, American tree, and song sparrows; mourning and rock doves; crows; brown-headed cowbirds; common grackles; rufous-sided towhees; red-winged blackbirds; ring-necked pheasants; and northern bobwhites.

Suet feeders contain suet, the hard fat about the kidneys and loins in beef and mutton. Pick up suet at the meat counter. (In winter you can use raw beef fat.) Place the suet in wire, nylon, or plastic mesh containers hung or attached to tree trunks. Or, press the suet in holes bored in a short suet log that can be easily hung. An easily acquired container is a plastic onion bag. Peanut butter alone, or mixed with lard or cornmeal, may be offered as a suet subsititute,

simply spread on a tree trunk. Suet especially attracts the insect-eaters remaining in winter, including the downy, hairy, red-bellied, and redheaded woodpeckers and white- and red-breasted nuthatches (Figure 29); such birds as chickadees, starlings, and mockingbirds, who vary their insect diet with plant food, also are attracted to suet.

Other feeding methods are possible besides the three just mentioned. One uses the thistle seed feeder, fitted with tiny holes to allow the small seed to pass through, which attracts finches. Thistle seed is really niger seed imported from Ethiopia and India.

Feeding should begin in the early autumn and continue uninterrupted until spring—or

Figure 29. A white-breasted nuthatch gripping a suet feeder.

longer. Some feed birds throughout the year. If you must stop feeding, do so gradually so the birds can shift to other sources of food.

Water is not a must when feeding birds in winter because they can eat snow. But drink-ing water is easier than eating snow, and water especially attracts birds. You can carry warm water out to them, which may require many trips, or use a submersible water heater to maintain open water.

Christmas Bird Count

Another, perhaps easier, way to learn to identify birds is by participating in the Christmas bird count, sponsored by the National Audubon Society. Don't be shy about signing up for a count because you feel inadequate in your identifications. Experienced birders team up with novices and intermediate birders.

Each year, bird groups in the United States, Canada, Central and South America, and the West Indies choose a twenty-four-hour period within two weeks of Christmas to survey birds, both the species and the numbers of birds within each species. The search takes place within a circle fifteen miles across.

The count, the ninety-second in 1991, is the world's oldest and largest wildlife survey. More than 40,000 birders tally birds at more than 1,500 locations. Results of the count each year are published in the journal *American Birds*.

Why a Christmas bird count? Although not strictly a scientific survey, it provides a good idea of population and species changes in birds: What are the early winter population trends of certain species? How do the populations change from winter to winter? Are some species shifting their ranges? How does the general health of bird assemblages reflect environmental changes? What rare birds—those far from their normal range—have wandered into a region?

Behavior

Some birders are satisfied with feeding birds or listing those they identify. But many progress to the next level—observing birds' behavior to gain insight into their lives.

You can become engrossed in four kinds of bird behavior in winter: feeding, social, territorial, and courtship.

Feeding, of course, is the primary activity. Birds must constantly fortify themselves with sufficient food to maintain their body temperatures. An easy place to observe feeding behavior is at a home feeder, but look carefully in the wild as well. Watch for how, what, when, and where birds feed. Knowing what a bird feeds on gives you an intimate sense of a bird's role or *niche* within its community of plants and animals and within the greater interacting complex of the living and nonliving known as the *ecosystem*. Notice particularly how the bill, feet, and tail feathers might be adapted for feeding.

Social behavior deals with the interactions between individual birds of the same species or between birds of different species. You can often witness social behavior better in winter because many birds group into flocks. Some behavior is passive, other behavior is aggressive.

A bird territory is usually an area that a bird or group of birds defends. But many birds have territories in winter that they don't defend, perhaps better called ranges. Although we might think of territories as surrounding nests or breeding areas, many territories are of the nonbreeding type. Once a territory becomes established, it tends to remain throughout the winter—and sometimes even into the summer.

Courtship behavior in winter? Yes, many bird species participate in courtship activities in the middle of winter. Love does not die in the cold. Examples include several ducks and hairy woodpeckers.

To give you some specific ideas about bird behavior to watch for, I've selected intimate glimpses into four common species: black-capped chickadees, starlings, mallards, and hairy woodpeckers. These four encompass the four main kinds of winter behavior.

Many black-capped chickadees form social flocks in late summer or early fall; these flocks are stable and remain intact until the breeding season in spring. Each flock, of about six to ten birds, consists of paired or single adults and some juvenile birds; it is built around a dominant pair that bred the previous season. A flock moves slowly through the woods, maintaining contact by tseet-calls and chicka-deedee-calls. Perhaps strangely, chickadee flocks are often joined by birds of other species to form mixed flocks; common joiners include downy woodpeckers, tufted titmice, kinglets, brown creepers, and white-breasted nuthatches.

Chickadee flocks circulate within nonbreeding, feeding territories that may be twenty acres in size. The flocks stop to feed at selected spots within their territories as they move about. The territories are defended by chasing, other signs of aggressiveness, and calling.

You'll learn a lot about chickadee feeding behavior at a home feeder. They favor sunflower seeds but also appreciate suet. If two flocks arrive at the same feeder, expect much scolding between members of each flock. You will see competing members holding their bodies horizontally, heads thrust forward, and beaks often gaping. Within each flock look for a hierarchy of feeders; the two members of the dominant pair eat first, followed by those that dominate over still others. A chickadee places a sunflower seed between and under its feet and rat-a-tat-tats the edge of the shell with its bill until the inner morsel comes into view.

Starlings change their dress as winter approaches. Upon molting in late fall they become speckled as new feathers are tipped in white. An added change occurs in midwinter when the bill turns yellow.

Most birders don't favor starlings, which are cast in the same light as house sparrows. Starlings are noisy and drive away birds from nesting sites and feeders where they seek seed and suet. In spite of these shortcomings, they consume many ground insects and their social behavior is particularly worthy of study.

Starlings congregate in communal roosts throughout the year. Up to two hours before sunset, they gather at the tops of trees and buildings and often whistle, click, and chuckle noisily. They then head for the main roosting sites—trees, buildings, and bridges—along established flight lines followed day after day. They might dive into the roosting sites before settling down. Roosting birds may number in the few hundreds to a few hundred thousand; congregations are smaller in winter.

In the morning, starlings leave their roosts and disperse into small flocks to feed. They may assemble into smaller roosts around noon and then resume feeding once again before returning to the main roosting sites before nightfall. You can locate the roosting sites by noting birds flying away from the roosts in the morning and toward them in the evening.

Mallard courtship behavior peaks in November and December but generally lasts from September to April. What you learn about mallard courtship can be generally applied to other related ducks, especially black ducks. Although most mallards migrate south in winter, many remain in northern regions with open water and available food.

In mallard flocks courtship behavior begins with males undergoing what may be called competitive courting. Two or more males churn about in the water with their heads drawn closely to their bodies; they frequently exhibit head shakes and tail shakes. Later, they may add the following to their repertoire: grunt-whistles (back of the neck is raised while the bill is directed down), head-up-tail-ups (head, tail, and wing tips are rapidly raised and lowered), and down-ups (bill is dipped into the water and raised quickly). Each of these maneuvers lasts one to a few seconds and is accompanied by a whistle-call. Each male directs his display toward a particular female. A female may acknowledge a group of males by nod-swimming—swimming toward them with her head low in the water; this excites the males to other displays.

Group displays eventually lead to pair formation involving a single male and female. In the inciting display, a female follows her mate, repeatedly flicking her bill backward over one side of her body as she emits a distinctive call. Another accepting display is mock preening, where the wing is lifted vertically with the feathers fanned, exhibiting the distinctive blue patch or speculum; the bill is placed behind the wing in a simulation of preening. Both male and female may display mock preening. Actual mating is usually preceded by "pumping" as the two birds face each other and bob their heads up and down repeatedly.

Distinctive about woodpeckers is drumming, the loud, rapid, continuous hammering of their bills on hard surfaces for a few seconds. On trees no wood is excavated, and sometimes they drum on drainpipes, gutters, and other metal objects. Woodpeckers drum to attract mates and announce their territories. (Pecking for food is quieter and irregular as a bird searches for food or excavates a nest hole.)

Hairy woodpecker courtship behavior begins in midwinter, and drumming initiates pair formation. Both males and females drum, most frequently in the early morning and each from their own drumming trees.

Peculiar interactions take place when mates meet. One is the still-pose, where one or both freeze for tens of seconds to maybe up to twenty minutes. The still-pose may be preceded or followed by fluttering-flight, a kind of hovering just before landing or after takeoff. They exchange a many-noted soft call after forming their pair bond. During pair formation they may interact aggressively with other birds.

Hairy woodpeckers also drum to make their territory known to competing birds. Thus they can assert themselves without having continually to defend their territory. The largely non-defended territory, or range, throughout the year may be six to eight acres in size, but the defended, nesting territory in spring is much smaller.

Primarily insect-eaters, hairy woodpeckers especially like suet at home feeders but will also consume peanut butter, sunflower seeds, and cracked nuts. Because of their consciousness about territory, you can expect only one pair of hairy woodpeckers to a feeder. Look, however, for territorial interactions as well as courtship behavior at your feeder.

If you become engrossed in bird behavior from this introduction, I highly recommend reading the three volumes of *Bird Behavior* by Donald and Lillian Stokes, fully cited in the Selected Readings.

Birding Equipment

Binoculars

For meaningful birding, or any nature observation at some distance, we all require eye extenders, most frequently in the form of binoculars. Selecting a pair best for you is not always easy.

A first consideration is magnification or

power, indicated by a number followed by a times sign: 7X, 8X, 9X, 10X. Although thought of as how many times larger an object appears through binoculars as compared with the unaided eye, the mind and eye perceive an object as closer rather than larger. Realize that each step up in power gains you less than you might expect. Ten power binoculars reduce the apparent distance by 90 percent as compared to 80 percent for 5X binoculars, so the 10X seems just 10 percent more powerful than the 5X.

Higher power has its drawbacks. It costs more. It makes binoculars, above about 9X, harder to hold steady, even though weight is also a factor in holding binoculars steady. And higher power cuts down on the light that reaches your eye.

How do you choose the "right" power? Any power below 7X is of little value for nature observation. How high you go depends on your preference, keeping the pros and cons in mind.

"Exit pupil size," an index of the light reaching your eye, is important if you intend to bird under low-light conditions. Calculate it by dividing the diameter of the larger (objective) lens—the larger number stamped on binoculars next to the power—by the power. For binoculars stamped as 7X35, 8X42, 9X30, and 10X40, the exit pupil size is 5, 5.2, 3.3, and 4 millimeters. Holding binoculars away from you, the "exit pupil" is the small circle of light you see through the smaller (ocular) lens or eyepiece.

The exit pupil size should be as large as the pupil of your eyes or larger. Your pupils are three to four millimeters in diameter in normal light but about seven millimeters in extremely low light. Depending somewhat on your specific use, select binoculars with an exit pupil size of three millimeters or larger.

Field of view is another feature of binoculars to consider. A wider field of view enables you to pick up objects faster and track moving birds and mammals easier. Bear in mind that the higher the power, the narrower the field of view. Stamped on binoculars are such field of view values as 350 or 450 feet at 1,000 yards. More important for birding is the field at 10 yards, so think of it at this distance. It may also be given in degrees; one degree equals 52.5 feet. A desirable field of view is 7 degrees or more or 368 feet or more.

Check the focusing. You want binoculars that focus quickly and finely with a central control. Most often with a ring or wheel, some use a rapid-rocking gizmo that can be easily worked, even with mittens on. Some binoculars are equipped with autofocusing powered by batteries, similar to cameras. This approach may not be a good choice for winter use. For birding be also concerned with the closest focusable distance, best if about fifteen feet or less.

Weight should not be taken lightly. If you always bird from a vehicle, this may not be important. But if you like to hike well off roads to observe nature, any additional weight mounts with each step. Settle on how much binocular weight you are willing regularly to carry. A viable option here is using lightweight, compact binoculars. But with the less weight you usually sacrifice losses in exit pupil size and field of view.

Once you decide on binocular specifics, buy the best pair you can reasonably afford. Buying the cheaper ones usually means buying binoculars again and again as you become dissatisfied and wish to upgrade them. Some companies that make middle-priced binoculars include Nikon, Bushnell, Bausch and Lomb, and Swift. Zeiss, Leitz, and Leica are among those that have demanded high prices.

Binoculars are a must for nature observation, but higher powered spotting scopes are, for many, in the category of nice-to-have. They are especially useful to see detail on more or less fixed birds and for stargazing. You may not appreciate setting up a scope on a tripod in snow in the cold, although car window mounts are less trouble. Realize that a 20X scope is only 5 percent stronger than 10X binoculars, and has a narrower field of view. If you get a scope, it's best to stick with one having a standard sixty-millimeter objective lens and not one smaller.

Field Notebook

For meaningful birding and other nature observation, a field notebook is a worthy piece of "equipment." No one can possibly remember a myriad of desirable details experienced on a field excursion or at a home feeder from one week to the next. The notebook really becomes significant when you wish to compare details of observations over time.

A notebook in a three-ring binder style with filler paper is probably most versatile. For each trip you can take notes on paper fastened to a clipboard and leave the binder at home. If you lose the clipboard, the notes of previous trips are still intact. A three-ring binder allows you to insert maps, checklists of bird species, and magazine and newspaper clippings at will. For sketching, pages of unlined paper can be slipped in. If you always take notes in your vehicle, an eight-and-one-half-by-eleven-inch size is fine; otherwise, a smaller six-by-nine notebook for your pack is more appropriate.

Enter information in your notebook that you wish to retain for later use and believe will be significant. Preliminaries include a field number, locality description, date, and weather. A field number is handy for later reference and can be applied to maps, checklists, and anything collected. A simple field numbering system I use is the year followed by a consecutive number for each observation episode. So, for the fifteenth observation stop in 1993, I would jot down *93-15*. Write with a simple, telegraphic style. For birds, you might record features of unidentified birds, abundances of identified birds, and various aspects of bird behavior. Even in winter, take notes as soon as possible after making the observations.

Some take audio notes with a tape recorder. This seems simple and straightforward, but it has its drawbacks. Batteries may not work well in the cold. It is not easy to locate a specific bit of information unless you faithfully label each tape completely and record the meter readings continually. Transcribing the tapes later requires additional time. And you can't make sketches with a tape recorder.

For comparing birds lists from month to month, season to season, or year to year, you might call upon a personal computer. Bird lists from your backyard, favorite park, or other region can be entered on a conventional data base program or menu-driven listing program. Quickly and efficiently you can recall species' lists and look for trends.

TEN

Winter Astronomy

Humans likely have marveled at and wondered about the innumerable, mysterious points of light in the night sky since they could first contemplate. What illuminates the night sky? How far are the lights from Earth? Will they ultimately extinguish? The stars seemed fixed in position, and, in time, humans perceived outlines of animals, people, and objects within star groups and gave them names. Astronomers systematically amassed information and probed many of the secrets of brightly lit bodies in space. But much remains unknown, and night sky observers continue to marvel and wonder.

Winter stargazing can be a fascinating activity, for much can be seen on clear, winter nights—with little or no equipment. Besides numerous stars and constellations, Earth's moon and four planets are clearly visible with the unaided eye. Details to heighten your interest can be seen with simple binoculars used for birding.

The Celestial Sphere

It's useful to perceive the sky as a huge imaginary bubble or shell, the *celestial sphere*, with Earth at its center. Imagine further that stars are attached to the inside surface of this sphere—as portrayed in a planetarium. At any place on Earth, you see only half of this sphere—as a huge dome or hemisphere. The point directly above you on this dome is the *zenith*.

Now, mentally extend Earth's equator and the ends of its axis of rotation onto the celestial sphere. The projected equator becomes the *celestial equator*. Projected ends of Earth's axis, at right angles to the equator, become the north and south *celestial poles*.

Motions in the night sky result from Earth's rotation. A counterclockwise rotation produces an apparent east-to-west motion of bodies in space. Stars passing near the zenith seem to make half-circles as they rise in the east and set in the west. Those stars closer toward the southern horizon move in east-to-west arcs rather than half-circles. In the northern sky of the Northern Hemisphere, stars follow circular paths: smaller circles if close to the celestial pole, larger circles if farther away. Those stars closest to the pole never "rise" or "set."

Stars speed along at 360 degrees in twenty-four hours or 15 degrees per hour. (A trip around the horizon is 360 degrees; that halfway is 180 degrees. The angle from any point on the horizon to the zenith is 90 degrees.) They rise near the eastern horizon about four minutes earlier each night—or two hours earlier each month or a day earlier each year—because of Earth's revolution about the sun. This revolution causes a lag of the sun relative to the stars.

Selected Stars and Constellations of the Northern Sky

Before taking up some common stars and constellations, be aware of how stars differ visibly from planets. Stars twinkle, that is, they flash rapidly as starlight is bent in passing through the turbulent hot and cold air of Earth's atmosphere. Planets that are much closer to Earth glow steadily as they emit light more like disks rather than points, as do stars.

Earliest astronomers named constellations, groups of stars, after their assumed resemblance to animals, characters from Greek mythology, and inanimate objects. In some cases, the resemblance was close, in others, not. During the Middle Ages, constellations were named in Latin, a nearly universal language.

Individual stars are designated in more than one way. The brightest are designated by name, several of which I shall describe. Modern astronomers also apply an elaborate system of arabic numerals and Greek letters for the fainter as well as for the brighter stars.

One of the best known and easiest group of stars to recognize in the Northern Hemisphere is the Big Dipper (Figure 30). It consists of seven major stars, four making up the bowl and the remaining three the handle. All are of the same relatively high brightness except for the one connecting the bowl to the handle. The bowl is about 10 degrees across, equal to the width of a fist—including the grasped thumb, while held at arm's length. It's useful to measure sky distances in degrees as gauged by the fist or fingers; three fingers equal about 6 degrees. Binoculars, however, are more accurate. Those with a 7-degree field of view, for example, show a circle diameter of 7 degrees against the sky. (You learned how to convert field of view from feet to degrees for binoculars in chapter 9.)

The handle of the Big Dipper tends to hang down, attaining this position earlier as the winter wears on. It hangs essentially straight down around midnight at the beginning of December and around 10:00 P.M. at the end of the month; from 10:00 P.M. to 8:00 P.M. during January; and from 8:00 P.M. to 6:00 P.M. during February.

Not a true constellation, the Big Dipper is but part of the constellation Ursa Major, the Great Bear. The Dipper's handle forms the bear's tail, and the bowl is within its back.

Two stars at the outer edge of the Big Dipper, the Pointers, point to Polaris—the Polestar or North Star. To reach Polaris (puh-LAIR-uhs), follow a line from the Pointers directly out of the bowl about three fist widths (about 30 degrees). This distance also equals about five times that between the pointers. Polaris is not particularly bright but is brighter than other stars in its part of the sky, and about as bright as the Pointers. The north end of Earth's axis

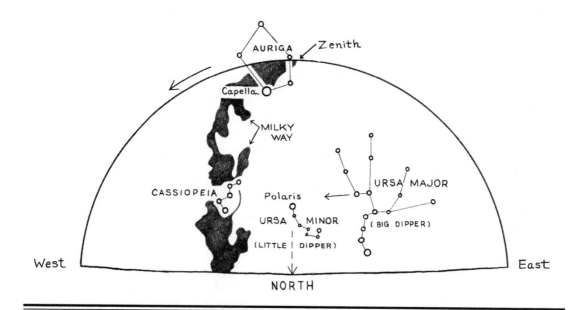

Figure 30. Selected stars and constellations (capital letters) of the northern winter sky. Brighter stars are shown by larger-sized dots. The arrow indicates the apparent movement of the stars during the night as they rotate about Polaris. This is the amount of sky you would see from 40 degrees north latitude. Stars are positioned as if you were viewing them on January 1 at 11:30 P.M., January 15 at 10:30 P.M., and January 30 at 9:30 P.M. (local standard time), or at other days or times with the same relative spacing, keeping in mind that stars seem to rise one hour earlier each half-month.

points toward the Polestar, which is within one degree of the North Celestial Pole.

From Polaris extends the tip of the handle of the Little Dipper, also known as Ursa Minor, the Little Bear. Stars of the Little Dipper are relatively faint, none as bright as the five brightest within the Big Dipper. Bowls of the two dippers oppose each another, as if emptying their contents into each other.

Opposite the Big Dipper, and about the same distance from Polaris as is the Big Dipper, is Cassiopeia (cass-ee-uh-PEE-uh), shaped like a crooked W or M, depending on the season or the time of night that you view it. Made up of five stars, either the top of a W or the bottom of an M faces the Big Dipper. This constellation symbolizes Cassiopeia,

queen of Ethiopia and wife of King Cepheus, seated on a chair. Here's a constellation shape to really stretch your imagination!

Cassiopeia resides within the Milky Way galaxy, of which we are a part, one of millions of galaxies in the universe. Our galaxy is a faint, hazy gigantic band of dust, gas, and about a trillion stars, light in places, dark-splotched in others. It is disk-shaped, and Earth is about halfway out from its center. When you gaze at the Milky Way you are looking along the plane of the disk. That's why it appears as a narrow band.

Bear in mind that the Big Dipper, Little Dipper, and Cassiopeia all rotate (counterclockwise) completely around Polaris each twenty-four hours and so arrange themselves in various positions. You see these star groups only in certain positions because they are visible only during the winter night.

Having bracketed Polaris by the Big Dipper, the Little Dipper, and Cassiopeia, you can use it in direction finding and in determining your latitude (Box 5).

BOX 5   How to Tell Direction and Latitude from Polaris

If Polaris is covered by clouds, you can still locate it if both the Big Dipper and Cassiopeia are visible. Remember that it is about halfway between the two star groups. Now, place it on the midpoint of a line connecting the middle star of Cassiopeia with that star on the Big Dipper where its bowl and handle join. Even if you cannot actually see it, you should have Polaris rather accurately positioned.

Once you locate Polaris, project its position directly down to the horizon. That point on the horizon marks true north (Figure 30), or is actually within one degree of it. So you see why Polaris is also aptly named the North Star.

If you are north of 10 degrees north latitude, you can use Polaris to determine your latitude. That is, Polaris's altitude in degrees is equal to your latitude. You can better understand this by realizing that, at the North Pole, the Polestar is directly above you or at an angle of 90 degrees. At the equator, however, this star is on the horizon or at an altitude of zero degrees. You might first approximate the angular dis-

tance of the North Star at your location, using your fist, fingers, and binoculars as measuring devices.

To measure Polaris's angle in the sky more accurately, use a protractor. Attach it upside down to a straight, flat, foot-long stick. To serve as sights, tap in a small nail near each end on the side of the stick toward which the base of the protractor faces. With a bolt, fasten the midpoint of the stick to a straight, flat staff so that the stick readily tilts up and down. Tack a plumb line to the stick at the midline of the upside-down base of the protractor. (When the stick is horizontal, the plumb line on the protractor will read 90 degrees.) Hold the staff upright and sight up at the true north point of the horizon. Tilt the stick up and sight directly on Polaris. The new angle under the plumb line, reading down from the 90-degree mark, will be equivalent to your latitude. A reading of 42 degrees from the 90-degree mark, then, signifies that you are at a latitude of 42 degrees north.

Selected Stars and Constellations of the Southern Sky

Most obvious in the southern sky are three stars in a line, inclined to the east, that make up the belt of Orion, the Hunter. This constellation rises in the early evening as December begins and dominates the sky all winter (Figure 31). Hanging down seemingly from the middle star in the belt is a string of stars representing Orion's sword. The fuzzy, central "star" in the sword is actually the Great Orion Nebula, a mass of dust, gas, and stars condensed from the dust and gas. Use your binoculars to get a better look at the nebula and the Trapezium, a trapezoid cluster of four stars within it.

Four bright stars trace a stretched, squarish outline about the three belt stars of Orion, whose upright body faces you. The reddish star in the upper left, Betelgeuse (BEET-uhl-juice), marks Orion's right shoulder. Diagonally opposite is bluish-white Rigel (RYE-juhl) in Orion's left foot. Fainter stars delineate his raised right arm holding a club and his left arm grasping a shield.

Star colors indicate star temperature. From cooler to hotter, the colors range over red, orange, yellow, white, and blue. Reddish stars, like Betelgeuse, have surface temperatures of about 3,000 degrees Centigrade, whereas bluish stars, like Rigel, are around a hot 12,000 degrees. Visualize the star colors as similar to those seen in intensely heated iron: reddish when cooler, whitish when very hot.

Similar to Polaris, Orion serves as a useful direction finder (Box 6).

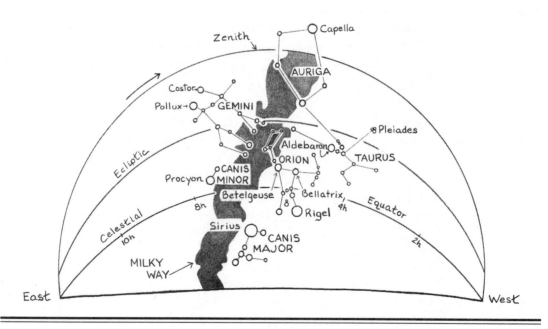

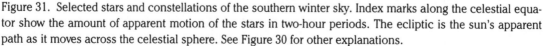

Figure 31. Selected stars and constellations of the southern winter sky. Index marks along the celestial equator show the amount of apparent motion of the stars in two-hour periods. The ecliptic is the sun's apparent path as it moves across the celestial sphere. See Figure 30 for other explanations.

BOX 6   How to Tell Direction with Orion

You know first of all that Orion generally exists in the southern sky. But shortly after it rises, you see it in the southeast, titled toward the east; and before it sets, you see it in the southwest, tilted toward the west. When upright, Orion is more or less due south. This is the case at about 1:00 A.M. at the beginning of December and about 11:00 P.M. at the end of the month; from 11:00 P.M. to 9:00 P.M. during Jan-

uary; and from 9:00 P.M. to 7:00 P.M. during February.

For more precise direction finding, check the uppermost, right star on Orion's belt. Because this star lies directly on the celestial equator, it rises directly east of you and sets directly west of you anywhere on Earth. You can rely on this star as readily as you can on Polaris.

Above and to the right or west of Orion is his presumed adversary, Taurus (TORE-uhs), the Bull. Its head is outlined by a V-shaped group of stars, the brightest being the orange Aldebaran (al-DEB-uh-ruhn), a cooler star representing Taurus's right eye. Imagine the bull's horns extending above Orion.

Above and to the right of Aldebaran rests a faint cluster of stars, the Pleiades (PLEE-uh-deez), within Taurus's body. Known also as the Seven Sisters (after the seven daughters of Atlas, who held the world on his shoulders), most people can see six with the naked eye. Those with good eyesight can discern several more—that arrange into a tiny teacup, clearly seen with binoculars. In fact, though, hundreds of stars constitute this cluster.

Near Orion's right heel, below and to the left, is the brightest star in the sky, Sirius (SEAR-ee-uhs). Bluish-white, it is a hot star with a surface temperature of about 10,000 degrees. Although one of the closest stars, it shines from a whopping nine light-years away or about 53,000,000,000,000 miles! Sirius is much larger than the sun, as a tennis ball compares to a Ping-Pong ball.

Also called the Dog Star, Sirius marks the

head of the constellation Canis Major, the Great Dog; a smaller star pinpoints its nose, and still other less well seen stars make up the body.

Not only does a large dog trail the Hunter's right heel, but a small dog follows behind his right shoulder. Canis Minor, the Little Dog, is evidenced by the relatively bright, yellowish-white star Procyon (PROH-see-on) and a fainter star. Procyon rises in the east before Sirius. You might have already surmised that neither Canis Major nor Canis Minor look much like dogs.

To help you spot three bright stars, note the arrangement of Betelgeuse, Sirius, and Procyon. Together they form a nearly equal-sided triangle.

Above and to the left (east) of Betelgeuse are two stars about three finger widths (6 degrees) apart: the brighter, reddish Pollux (PAHL-uhx) and the fainter, more northern Castor (CASS-tuhr). These two stars position the heads of the twin sons of the god Zeus and help make up the constellation Gemini (GEM-uhn-eye), the Twins. Bodies of the twins extend toward Orion. Gemini is mostly disposed on the opposite side of the Milky Way from Orion and Taurus.

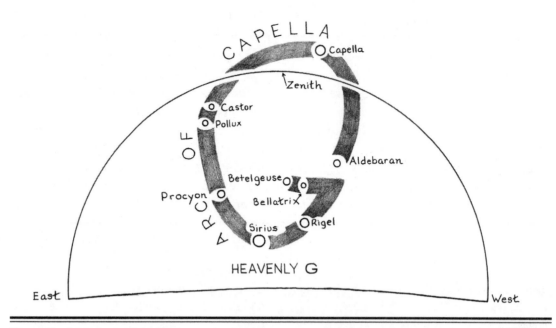

Figure 32. Bright stars of the southern winter sky trace, counterclockwise, an imaginary Arc of Capella (Capella through Sirius) and a Heavenly G (Aldebaran through Betelgeuse). Times and dates are the same as those for Figure 31.

High in the sky above Orion and to the right of Gemini is the bright, yellow star Capella (kuh-PELL-uh). It forms part of the five-sided constellation Auriga (Aw-RYE-guh), the Charioteer.

Now, I'll give you a wrap-up of the major stars in the southern winter sky and two approaches to help you remember them easily. First, think of six stars—Capella, Castor, Pollux, Procyon, and Sirius—arranged alphabetically in a huge arc, the Arc of Capella (Figure 32). The two brightest stars, Capella and Sirius, punctuate each end of the arc. Go farther and continue both ends of the arc to outline a letter G—the Heavenly G: Add Orion's Rigel and Bellatrix to the base and Taurus's Aldebaran to the upper part of the G. You could also add Aldebaran to the beginning of the Arc of

Capella and not upset the alphabetical order of stars within the arc.

If you master the stars and constellations I've outlined, you will have a solid beginning to winter stargazing. To learn more, check the references in the Selected Readings. An especially useful aid is a star chart with one or two rotating disks. (One source is Edmund Scientific Company, C942 Edscorp Bldg., Barrington, New Jersey, 08007.) Such a chart enables you to set up a star map for different days of the year and for different times during the night, as well as quickly visualize star pathways across the sky. By covering your flashlight with red plastic or cellophane you need not continually adjust your eyes as you illuminate the star chart. For best viewing, avoid places with lights that mask the light from the stars.

Zodiac Constellations

An imaginary line on the celestial sphere, actually a great circle, that traces the sun's yearly path through the stars is called the *ecliptic* (see Figure 31). (It can also be thought of as the plane of Earth's orbit projected onto the celestial sphere.) It is named after the eclipse of the sun or moon, which can occur only when the moon is on the ecliptic and lined up with Earth and the sun. During the winter solstice (chapter 1), the December day with the fewest hours of daylight, the sun reaches its southernmost point on the ecliptic or is as close to the southern horizon as it gets.

A belt or zone 8 degrees wide on either side of the ecliptic, or a total of 16 degrees wide, is known as the *zodiac*. Paths of the moon and all planets except Pluto, along with that of the sun, pass through the zodiac.

The zodiac is divided into twelve constella-

TABLE 7   Signs of the Zodiac with Astrological Dates

Zodiac Sign	Astrological Dates*
Spring	
1. Aries, the Ram	Mar. 21–Apr. 19
2. Taurus, the Bull	Apr. 20–May 20
3. Gemini, the Twins	May 21–June 21
Summer	
4. Cancer, the Crab	June 22–July 22
5. Leo, the Lion	July 23–Aug. 22
6. Virgo, the Virgin	Aug. 23–Sept. 22
Autumn	
7. Libra, the Balance	Sept. 23–Oct. 23
8. Scorpio, the Scorpion	Oct. 24–Nov. 21
9. Sagittarius, the Archer	Nov. 22–Dec. 21
Winter	
10. Capricorn, the Goat	Dec. 22–Jan. 19
11. Aquarius, the Water Bearer	Jan. 20–Feb. 18
12. Pisces, the Fishes	Feb. 19–March. 20

*First date for each sign is when the sun enters each constellation.

tions or signs (Table 7), each occupying 30 degrees of longitude. I've already mentioned two of the zodiac signs, Taurus and Gemini.

Astrologers believe that the stars, moon, sun, and planets influence human affairs. People born under different signs are influenced differently: A Pisces, for example, has a different destiny than a Leo. The positions of the sun, moon, and planets relative to one another and to the signs are determining factors. Most newspapers carry horoscopes either summarizing the positions of heavenly bodies at specific times or provide astrological forecasts.

The Moon

Earth's moon is the most prominent object in the sky for the greater part of each month; look for it within 5 degrees of the ecliptic.

The moon is a little more than one-fourth the size of Earth and averages about 239,000 miles away. The moon revolves counterclockwise in an elliptical path about Earth in 29½ days in respect to the sun and in 27⅓ days in respect to the stars.

Astronomers speak of the moon's phases (Figure 33). Although the moon is always half-lit by the sun, as viewed from space, you see different parts of the lighted half from Earth as this satellite pursues its orbit. Phases include: new moon (not lit, all in the sun's shadow), crescent (less than half-lit), first quarter (right half lit; a half moon), gibbous (more than half-lit), full (fully lit), gibbous, third quarter (left half lit; another half moon), crescent, and the next new moon. The first quarter is one-fourth of the way around the monthly moon cycle,

about one week after the new moon, and the third quarter is three-fourths of the way around after about three weeks.

The moon waxes and wanes. A waxing moon, gradually becoming more illuminated, transforms from the new moon to the full. A waning moon, gradually becoming less illuminated, passes from the full moon to the new. You can often see part of the moon even when in shadow because of *earthshine* or *earthlight*—sunlight bounced from Earth onto the moon.

It helps to know how moon phases relate to its rising and setting. A full moon must rise when the sun sets and sets when the sun rises; a new moon, conversely, must rise when the sun rises and set when the sun sets. A first-quarter moon rises at noon and sets at midnight; a third-quarter moon, oppositely rises at midnight and sets at noon. On average, the moon rises about fifty minutes later each night, but it varies considerably.

It's best to view the moon between the last and first quarters. At these times you experience less glare, and shadows are longest to emphasize features, especially along the line separating the lighted and shadowed areas.

The moon is surfaced with two main kinds of features. The highlands or *terrae* (TEAR-ee; singular, terra) are light-colored and heavily cratered from the impact of numerous meteorites and comets. Rock samples picked up by Apollo astronauts indicate terrae are made up largely of *anorthosite* (un-NORE-thuh-sight), a rock mostly of the mineral feldspar and formed by the slow cooling of molten rock material. Lowlands, the *maria* (MAR-ee-uh; singular, mare, MAR-ay), are dark-colored and sparsely cratered. Apparently maria represent large craters filled with *basalt,* a dark rock formed by the relatively rapid cooling of volcanic lava. Besides hard rock, the moon, in

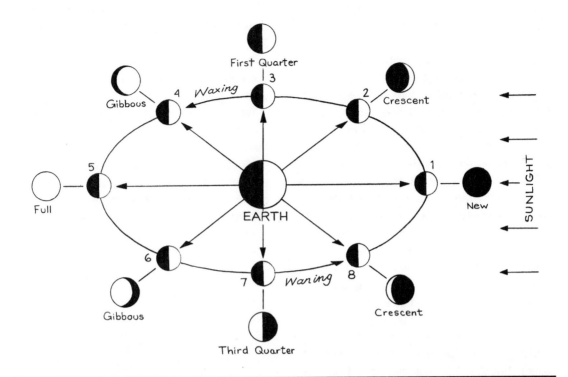

Figure 33. Phases of the moon as they change in the Northern Hemisphere. Half of the moon is actually always lit by the sun, viewed from space as it revolves about Earth. But if you view it from Earth, it is variably lit as it constantly changes position to present its phases: new (totally in the sun's shadow), crescent, first quarter, gibbous, full (fully lit), gibbous, third quarter, crescent, and again new. As the moon changes from new to full—gradually becoming more illuminated—it is waxing; while changing from full to new it is waning.

places, is veneered by a thin coating of dust that resembles pulverized cement.

Geologists believe that the moon's birth dates back to 4.6 billion years ago—the time also for the beginning of Earth and other bodies in the solar system. (Oldest rocks from the moon date at 4.4 billion years old.) Intense bombardment by meteorites followed, as evidenced by the heavily cratered terrae. The outpouring of lava that formed the maria ceased possibly about 3 billion years ago. Since that time relatively few meteorites have struck the moon, as shown by relatively few craters in the maria.

The Planets

You can tell planets from stars because they shine with a steady light—don't twinkle as stars do—and they continually change position. They, consequently, are sometimes called "wandering stars" in contrast to true stars or "fixed stars." ("Fixed stars" also change position but so slowly that it may take centuries clearly to notice a change.)

Where do you look for the wandering planets? First, remember to look for them within the zodiac. But you will need help. Some places to check are local newspapers, the Celestial Events section of *Natural History* magazine, and the Celestial Calendar section of *Sky & Telescope* magazine. (Both magazines also publish star maps.) Planets are located by their placement in particular constellations at particular times. It's best to look for them on moonless nights or when they are opposite the moon and highest above the horizon.

The search for planets is simplified by knowing that only four can be easily seen with the unaided eye or binoculars: Venus, Mars, Jupiter, and Saturn.

Silvery Venus appears as the brightest planet, brighter than any star—ten times as bright as Sirius. You see it near the sun only during a few hours before dawn (as a "morning star") or during a few hours after sunset (as an "evening star"). It is nearly the same size as Earth and remains seemingly suspended at an average distance of 67 million miles. Venus's surface is obscured by a thick layer of clouds, but space studies have shown it to have few craters and a surface similar to that of Earth's.

Mars looks like a bright, reddish, nontwinkling star, about four times as bright as the star Rigel. It is only a little more than half the size of Earth, and farther than Venus, at an average distance of 142 million miles. Mars is heavily cratered; has volcanoes, dust storms, and polar ice caps that change with the seasons; and lacks thick clouds.

Yellowish Jupiter is brighter than any star, second to Venus in brightness of the planets.

As the largest planet, its diameter is more than eleven times larger than Earth's, and it extends 390 million miles from us. Jupiter is mostly a ball of gas—especially hydrogen—and liquid, but holds many solid moons within its gravitational grasp.

Yellowish Saturn appears about as bright as the brightest stars. As the second largest planet, its diameter is more than nine times that of Earth's; it graces our view from 793 million miles away. Saturn is truly a ball of gas, mostly hydrogen and helium, but, like Jupiter, has many solid moons. It is well known for its numerous, conspicuous rings, visible through a telescope.

ELEVEN

Winter Photography

Photographically, winter should not be thought of as the Spartan season. Subjects certainly are not in short supply; in fact, new subjects materialize. Your camera equipment won't let you down and neither will your cold-sensitive hands—if you take the right precautions. So, on winter trips, don't leave your camera(s) at home.

Keeping the Camera Working in the Cold

Modern cameras, unfortunately at times, are powered by batteries to drive the shutter and exposure meter, and advance and rewind the film. Batteries usually work fine down to about 20 degrees Fahrenheit, but they may lose their power drastically in colder temperatures. Of the kinds of batteries available, nickel cadmium batteries probably work best in cold weather.

Winter photography requires that batteries be kept warm. The easiest way is to keep your camera, most comfortably on a chest harness, under some clothing to take advantage of body heat. A good place is beneath an oversized parka provided with many pockets for ancillary camera gear. A better, but more expensive, approach is a pocket battery pack—stowed in a warm pocket—connected to the camera by a silicone rubber cable.

Shutter operation is the main camera concern in frigid weather. You might be able to bypass other difficulties, but a sluggish or inoperable shutter cancels any intent for photography.

One good way to lessen shutter operation problems is to use a camera with a mechanical shutter, that is, one not dependent upon batteries for its operation. Cameras with a mechanical shutter offering several speeds include the Nikon FM2, the Canon New F-1, and the Pentax K100. Most cameras with electronic shutters offer, at best, usually only one speed mechanically.

Even mechanical shutters may slow in the cold, causing some photographers to "winterize" their cameras, which means replacing the normal lubricants with thinner ones. (Lenses may also be winterized.) This may not necessarily be a good choice because the process is expensive, and after the cold season, the camera must be "dewinterized" or the mechanisms may wear out prematurely. Most modern cameras contain synthetic lubricants that don't stiffen except in severe cold, so winterizing is usually unnecessary.

If you expect to have difficulty with your camera's shutter under low temperatures, check its operation after a stay in the refrigerator or freezer. Don't forget to test *all* the shutter speeds.

All exposure meters self-contained in cameras, as well as most off-camera meters, are battery operated. A few off-camera meters, however, are driven by non-battery-operated selenium cells. These provide a good option for winter photography without the worry of unreliable meter operation because of cold-affected batteries.

Film becomes brittle when cold and may snap if you wind or rewind it too rapidly. Avoid motor drive and automatic wind and rewind if possible; slowly transporting the film manually from frame to frame is best.

Rapid rewinding in dry, cold air may also set up electrostatic discharges. These discharges may create distracting branchlike or lightninglike markings on the developed film, which, of course, will appear in the finished print.

Condensation is a leading problem when using your camera in winter. Your breath may condense on your lens as you attempt to set the lens opening manually or blow off snowflakes. (Snowflakes melt from your warm breath and refreeze.) Instead of blowing, remove the snowflakes with a camel's hair brush or a squeeze-bulb blower. Condensed breath

may also fog up the eyepiece of the viewfinder as you frame the image or focus manually. Try holding your breath while sighting through the eyepiece. If condensation forms on the lens or eyepiece, wipe it off quickly with chamois or a soft cloth after breathing on the cold surfaces once again.

Bringing a cold camera inside and exposing it to warm, moist air compounds the condensation problem. Condensation forms not only on the outside but on the inside of the camera mechanisms and lenses as well. Even the film is not spared. To avoid this insidious moisture, place the camera inside a sealed plastic bag with most of the air removed before bringing it inside. Or, wrap it in a sweater or place it in an ice chest.

Exposing a warm camera to blowing snow can also cause trouble. Snowflakes melt on contact and refreeze. If this happens, bring the camera back inside. For a better approach, allow the camera to cool before baring it to the cold; then the snowflakes don't stick upon striking the camera.

Keeping Your Hands Working the Camera in the Cold

Protect your hands with the layered system of insulation. Your first layer might be thin gloves of silk, nylon, or cotton. (I prefer thin woolen gloves, but these may leave unwanted fibers on film when you change it.) Slip larger leather gloves over the undergloves and large mittens over the leather gloves. All coverings should fit loosely for most warmth. Use the hand coverings singly or in different combinations, depending on the temperature and the job at the moment. To shed the mittens easily but still retain them securely and conveniently, join them with a cord that passes through your coat sleeves.

Tape insulative materials to the camera to avoid freezing your skin to exposed metal or simply to lessen the discomfort of handling a cold camera. Try chamois, moleskin, felt, or sponge rubber. Even cotton or canvas tape alone is of some benefit. Especially protect yourself from freezing your facial skin around the viewfinder eyepiece.

Carrying tripods can be especially cold on the hands. You definitely need some form of insulation on the tripods. A good choice, for the upper parts of the tripod legs, is foam pipe insulation cut lengthwise and held in place with cloth tape; you might also cover the knobs and handles with the tape. Other choices are the heavy, cloth tape wound around bicycle handlebars or bicycle handlebar foam pads. The foam pads can be slipped on with the aid of liquid soap, which keeps the pads in place as it dries.

Spare your hands from the cold by cutting down on the time spent changing lenses. You can accomplish this best by using a few zoom lenses instead of several fixed focal length lenses. I would suggest two zoom lenses for most winter photography: a wide-angle to normal zoom (about 24 to 50 millimeters) and a moderate to longer telephoto zoom (about 70 to 210 millimeters).

Exposing Snow Scenes

Exposing film correctly with snow about can be tricky. I'll give you some useful tips for three methods: reflected-light metering, incident-light metering, and using the sunny f/16 rule.

Reflected-light meters, as are all built-in camera meters, measure the light reflected from the subject. They are set up assuming that the light reflected from all subjects is of average brightness (middle gray or middle-toned), or equal to the light reflected from a standard gray card having a reflectance value of 18 percent. If the subject is grayish, the meter reading should be okay; if not, you must make some adjustments. Light subjects require adding more light (increasing the exposure), dark subjects call for subtracting light (decreasing the exposure).

Reflected-light meters *underexpose* snow scenes if read directly off snow. The meter calls for the exposure to look like middle gray, of average brightness. White snow, consequently, will look grayish in the final image or underexposed. To outfox the meter, take a reading off the snow and *add to* or *increase* the exposure by 1½ to 2 stops; 1½ stops usually works best for me. For frost, you might increase the exposure by about one stop. (Increasing the exposure by one stop means opening the lens aperture twice as much—such as from f/11 to f/8—or halving the shutter speed, such as from ⅟₁₂₅ to ⅟₆₀ of a second; either approach allows twice as much light to reach the film.) You can also take a reflected meter reading off the palm of your hand and increase the read exposure by about one stop; that is, for many people the palm of the hand is about one stop brighter than middle gray. (This guide applies most closely to a Caucasian hand.)

Wherever possible, though, try to expose snow correctly without having to adjust for the medium (middle) tone readings of reflected light meters. Swing your camera away from the

Figure 34. Under the ice, a scuba diver's view—looking up—of his entrance hole. The radiating light streaks mark the spokes of a safety wheel design—with the hole at its center—shoveled in the snow. Bubbles rising from me muddle the right part of the photograph. Exposure here was tricky. I began with the sunny f/16 rule before submerging and guessed at an increase in exposure because of the ice ceiling.

snow scene and take your readings off *gray* objects, such as gray tree trunks, gray clothing, and the like. You might even consider sewing a gray patch (best if of 18 percent reflectance) on a sleeve of your parka.

Hand-held incident light meters measure the light falling on the subject rather than the light reflected from the subject. Such meters, therefore, are not usually fooled by unusually light or dark subjects. Hold the meter in front of the subject and point its translucent diffuser dome toward the camera's location. If you can't reach the subject, orient the meter as if you were standing by the subject.

If you don't have use of an exposure meter, don't despair. You can always resort to the "sunny f/16 rule" (Figure 34). It says that on a bright sunny day the correct exposure is f/16 at a shutter speed most closely equal in number to the ISO rating of the film speed. (Actually, the shutter speed is the reciprocal of the ISO film speed.) For ISO 50 or 64 film, use a shutter speed of $\frac{1}{60}$ of a second; for ISO 100 film, use a shutter speed of $\frac{1}{125}$ of a second.

The sunny f/16 rule applies from two hours after sunrise to two hours before sunset.

Bear in mind that the sunny f/16 rule applies strictly to average or middle-tone (grayish) subjects that are lit from the front. Exposure must be increased or decreased for other conditions (Table 8). For light subjects, such as snow, you *decrease* the exposure by one stop for sidelight and two stops for backlight; for dark subjects, you *increase* the exposure by one stop for sidelight and two stops for backlight. Notice the direction of the correction is exactly opposite from that when using reflected-light meter readings off nongray subjects.

Even under nonsunny light conditions, the sunny f/16 rule can be generally applied with the appropriate corrections. I've listed these in Table 8.

When exposing snow scenes with any of the three exposure methods, it's always a good idea to bracket your exposures to ensure some good shots. This means shooting additionally at least one-half or one stop on both sides of a determined exposure, keeping in mind that black-and-white film has a greater latitude for exposure than does color film.

Some Winter Subjects

As I mentioned at the beginning of this chapter, there is no dearth of photographic subjects during winter. You can be kept busy with the so-called record shots that simply record photographically, without attempting to stir emotions or portray nature's moods meaningfully. But look for these more meaningful shots, too. In time, you may desire to attempt the artistic and even the abstract. Stay aware. These subjects await your capture.

Most persons prefer to shoot in color. But shooting in black-and-white can also be very rewarding, particularly in winter, when color is less obvious. Besides, some shots are more effective when done in black-and-white, such as dark tree trunks, tracks, and long, dark shadows against white snow (Figure 35).

Ice and Snow

Ice and snow features are best photographed when fresh, just after they form. You may wish to review ice and snow features in

TABLE 8   Exposure by the Sunny f/16 Rule

Natural Lighting	Average Subject	Light Subject	Dark Subject
Bright, front	f/16 at 1/ISO*	− 1 stop	+ 1 stop
Bright, side	+ 1 stop	f/16 at 1/ISO*	+ 2 stops
Bright, back	+ 2 stops	+ 1 stop	+ 3 stops
Weak, soft shadows	+ 1 stop	f/16 at 1/ISO*	+ 2 stops
Weak, no shadows	+ 2 stops	+ 1 stop	+ 3 stops
Heavy overcast, no shadows	+ 3 stops	+ 2 stops	+ 4 stops

*Exposure is at a lens opening of f/16 and a shutter speed as close as possible to the reciprocal of the ISO film speed. With a film having a speed of ISO 100, the shutter speed is 1/125 of a second.

Figure 35. A winter stream-scape interrupted by snowshoe tracks on new snow. On a bright day, capitalize with black-and-white film on the dark tree trunks and long shadows contrasted with the light snow.

chapter 3 before setting out on a photography trip. If unaccompanied by wind, snow piles and drapes interestingly, giving new form to old objects. Just settling on trees, tufts of grass, and fence posts, snow presents fascinating shapes. In the aftermath of wind playing with snow, search for such intriguing features as snow dunes, sastrugi, and snow cornices. If the snowflake bug bites you hard, you may wish to try photographing snowflakes in interesting clusters (Figure 36) or as close-ups. (The book by E. R. LaChapelle listed in the Selected Readings tells you how to photograph individual snowflakes.)

Ice in its many forms offers almost an endless variety of photographic adventures: frost on leaves, twigs, nests, grass, berries, spiderwebs, and windowpanes (Figure 37); rime on trees and shrubs, particularly striking against a dark blue

sky; glaze on twigs and berries; icicles (Figure 38); wave-washed ice plastered on lighthouses and rocks along the shores of large lakes; and buckled ice slabs, to name a few. The clear ice forms can be particularly exotic as bright sunlight plays through them and reflects off their surfaces.

With ice and snow, look creatively for the artistic and the abstract—a strong, graphic impact is possible with these materials. Be alert for the unusual forms, patterns, and especially appealing long, blue shadows. Don't forget that shadows, themselves, may be the subjects.

Plants

Plants offer a stark beauty, in a dormant state, as they project above the snow. You might try to capture scraggly branches or bark patterns against the snow. Or the nice blend of white birch bark, with black blotches, against freshly fallen snow. Or erect flower stalks of mullein or evening primrose against a field of white. Let your mind wander freely, searching for other plant-snow subjects (Figures 39, 40).

Think of color within the interplay of ice and snow and plants. Accents of plant color can enhance your images, particularly colorful splotches produced by berries.

Birds and Mammals

We usually get more indirect rather than direct photographic opportunities with birds and mammals—from their sign. Most obvious are the numerous tracks that become distinct with reasonable snow cover. The keys to good track photos: Seek only fresh tracks and photograph them in bright light for strong shadows to set them off. Track images lack snap when taken in soft light. Don't ignore other interesting bird and mammal sign for photography, such as grouse nesting burrows, wing and tail impressions in the snow of a bird of prey, gnawings of twig bark by rabbits, and entrances to weasel snow burrows.

A good place to photograph birds, and sometimes squirrels and rabbits, is in your backyard. Mount your camera with a telephoto lens on a tripod. Place the lens close to your window of choice to eliminate reflections. For

Figure 36. Freshly fallen snowflakes resting lightly on balsam fir twigs.

Figure 37. Seaweedlike frost artistry on a windowpane.

the same reason, keep the room dark while photographing. For birds, place feeders near your chosen window and close to a perching branch where birds can contemplate feeding. For a natural setting, photograph birds at the perching branch. Guard against a distracting background, or throw it out of focus with a larger lens opening that lessens the depth of field.

Away from home, you probably have the best chance of photographing birds and mammals from your vehicle, which doubles as a good blind and shelter. On warmer outings, roll a window down part way and place your camera equipped with telephoto lens on it, cushioned by a jacket, sweater, pillow, or bean bag. You might also support your equipment with a window mount used for supporting a spotting scope. To lessen distraction of your

subject, hold the camera with a shoulder stock or mount it on a monopod, away from the window.

When camera shooting birds and mammals, particularly in winter, be careful not to interfere unduly with their feeding or other activity. They are stressed sufficiently by the cold and their continual need to seek food without having to contend also with your interference.

Hints for Good Composition

Average photographs can become good and good photographs ascend to great simply by paying attention to composition. Many persons, unfortunately, don't take the time or recognize the necessity for good composition when shooting. Extra time devoted to composition while you are freezing is most difficult, but it pays off in considerably better photographs.

Keep each photograph simple, with a single center of interest. Any critic viewing a photo should know immediately the subject of interest; his or her eyes should go to that subject directly and not flit about to other distracting objects.

Move in as closely as possible to most subjects. A deer photograph should not depict that animal as a rather insignificant speck; it should fill much of the viewfinder. (The deer *may* be a relatively small part of the photograph if the intent is a landscape with the deer simply relating to it.) Think of cropping—trim-

ming unwanted parts—of a photograph before taking it. This will help you isolate desired subjects and omit extraneous ones. A good habit is to scan your critical eye around the entire margin of the field before snapping the shutter.

Look constantly for busy backgrounds that detract from your intended subjects. Clean up backgrounds two ways: Become more discriminate in your choice of them, or select a lens of longer focal length or a larger lens aperture to throw a distracting background out of focus.

Watch the light. Light affects the kind and amount of shadow. Sidelight and backlight make a subject more appealing than front light—sometimes called "flat light" because it flattens out the subject, making it less interest-

Figure 38. Water drips off a small icicle in company with a massive brother. A shutter speed of $\frac{1}{125}$ of a second was chosen to show drop movement.

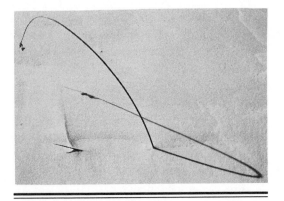

Figure 39. An arching bulrush stem outlines its arcuate shadow in the snow.

ing. Sometimes you want bright, contrasty light to depict tracks and interesting shadows, for example; but at other times soft, subdued light is best—such as if you wish to capture the moody spell of fog or falling snow (Figure 41).

An old composition rule that still applies is the rule of thirds. Mentally divide the field of view in the viewfinder, both horizontally and vertically, into three regions. Two horizontal and two vertical thirds lines intersect in four places. Place your center of interest at one of the intersections. If a bird or animal occurs at one of the intersections, have it look into ample space and not have its view cut off abruptly near one edge. If you don't adhere strictly to the rule of thirds, at least avoid placing the center of interest in the center of the photograph.

Consider both horizontal and vertical formats for most subjects. Some subjects clearly call for one or the other, but for other subjects either selection may be an artistic choice. A horizontal format tends to evoke serenity, a vertical format action or tension.

Strive to arrange lines or linearity pleasingly.

Repetitive linearity, such as sastrugi or patterned shadows, portray greater snap if passing diagonally through a photograph, rather than trending parallel to a side. Arrange a road or a stream as an S curve if possible. Some features may be arranged as a triangle to add unity to a photograph; here, the lines connecting them are simply imagined.

Balance is another aspect of composition. It may mean arranging colors or shapes in a pleasing way. But neither need be symmetrical in terms of shape or size. The whole idea is for the colors or shapes to unify the image.

Avoid both merging subjects and strange corners. Merging subjects include trees seemingly arising out of someone's head, or a human's legs, minus the rest of the body, behind a team of horses hooked up to a sleigh. Strange corners refers especially to linear features cutting across the corners of a photograph that should not be there: power lines, telephone lines, fence lines, and door frames are examples.

Try varying the perspective. Change your view up and down or from side to side. If still dissatisfied, broaden or restrict the perspective by switching to lenses of shorter or longer focal length.

A Few Filters for Winter

You may not wish to bother much with filters in the cold. But a few are worth the trouble because they can clearly strengthen the impact of your images.

For both black-and-white and color photos, using a polarizer filter markedly will darken the sky and deepen snow shadows; for black-and-white photos alone, a red or orange filter accomplishes much the same. Screw on a polarizer also to saturate all colors, and reduce haze, glare from snow and ice, and reflections.

If the blue of shadows in snow is a bit much for you, mount an ultraviolet or skylight filter in front of the lens. Both filters also cut down on the bluishness of light in open shade, under an overcast sky, at high altitudes, and at a distance. You can also diminish haze in both black-and-white and color photos with these filters.

Bluish light not correctable to your taste with an ultraviolet or skylight filter can be further reduced by a yellowish warming filter. You "warm up" the image by adding some color from the yellowish or "warm" end of the color spectrum. Warming filters come in more than one shade.

Figure 40. Early spring snow covers newly opened lilac flower and leaf buds.

Improving Winter Photos in the Darkroom

If you have access to a photographic darkroom and like working with photos in one, you can usually improve the prints received from a commercial photographic laboratory. All it requires is patience and the willingness to expend some effort. Working with black-and-white film is less expensive and necessitates less equipment. If you are new to print making, check on the basic chemicals and procedures in a darkroom manual. I wish to focus here on improving the prints, especially those depicting snow scenes.

Some may think that manipulating prints in the darkroom is a form of "cheating," that is, altering a print in some way that shouldn't be. This could not be further from accepted procedure. Every good photographer strives to produce the best possible image he or she is capable of creating. If darkroom manipulation is necessary, so be it. Well-known landscape photographer Ansel Adams approached darkroom manipulation of photos as necessary and standard practice. He thought nothing of six manipulations for a single photograph.

I wish to emphasize two common procedures: burning and dodging. Burning is selectively adding light—more than the basic exposure—to a print to bring out more detail or darken a region intentionally. (One time I received black-and-white prints from a commercial laboratory and saw no clouds in one print—just bleached sky. I was sure clouds were present when I snapped the landscape, and a glance at the negative proved this. In the darkroom I burned in the sky considerably, and the clouds appeared!) Burning on a print is frequently necessary to bring out detail in snow. You usually burn with a cardboard

Figure 41. Old trees and a hip-roofed barn within a whiteout created by gently falling snow.

sheet, larger than any print you intend to make, in which you cut a small hole somewhat off-center. Extra light passes only through the hole onto the print. Keep moving the cardboard up and down during the added exposure so no distracting, well-defined margins of burned areas appear on the print.

Dodging is the opposite of burning; here, you attempt to hold back light from a darker-than-normal part of the print. Perhaps you wish to de-emphasize the darkness of shadows in a snow scene. For large areas, you might use part of your cardboard sheet for burning. For small areas, attach small pieces of rounded black paper to thin, stiff wires or narrow plastic sticks. Continually move the

dodger up and down as you expose the print. Dodging is trickier than burning because it is harder to control.

How much time to burn or dodge? It's in the realm of guesswork. But with experience, you learn to guess more closely each time you do it. Figure the amount of burning and dodging in terms of the basic exposure (Figure 42).

Figure 42. A snow-fringed, open stream in later winter. Raccoon tracks mark the foreground and middistance. The light snow and dark stream make for tricky film exposure as well as tricky print exposure. The snow was metered in the right middistance, and the exposure was increased by 1½ stops. During printing, the darker, upper left part of the photograph was dodged for the duration of the exposure. The main snowy areas were additionally burned for four times the basic exposure.

WINTER PHOTOGRAPHY

Looking through a glass patio door into a snow-covered backyard. A red squirrel contemplates seeds, amid bird tracks, dropped below a feeder. Tracks of a cottontail, hopping from left to right, pass the trunks of a white birch.

TWELVE

Exploring Nature
in Winter:
Excursions Near and Far

Home is not only our domicile but a larger place or setting very familiar to us—that which we know best. I think of home as extending into a community, out to at least a few miles from our place of residence.

Exploring nature in winter is easiest at home. Nature is at our fingertips, so to speak, albeit hampered to varying degrees by our presence and our constructions. And, in our home territory, we can easily and frequently duck inside to escape from the cold. No need to brave unnecessary hardship from the weather here.

Important, too, home is an ideal *training ground* for more ambitious excursions. Close to comfort, we can become proficient on skis and snowshoes, and condition our bodies to cold and for longer, more demanding treks. We can experiment with winter clothing. We can become intimate with ice and snow, and try our hand at igloo or snow shelter building—even test these snow houses by sleeping in them. And where is a better place to

sharpen our skills at identifying plants and animals and animals' winter sign?

Three out of four Americans inhabiting the United States live in urban areas, that is, communities with 2,500 or more people. My comments that follow, therefore, relate more directly to urban rather than rural dwellers. But if you live in a rural area, you have the opportunity to experience nature so much more fully.

In Your Backyard

Most of us freely relate to birds at feeders in our backyards in winter. In chapter 9 we considered the kind of feeders and food, the ease of identifying birds at feeders, and how we may learn some kinds of bird behavior at feeders. In chapter 11, I touched on how to photograph birds in winter at or near feeders.

But you can learn much more at bird feeders. Observe the kinds of foods your bird visitors savor. At what times do various species feed? Do some birds avoid conflict with others by timing their visits during the day? Record the species that come to your feeder(s) on a regular basis. How do the species vary during the winter season, especially near its beginning and near its end? What species vary from winter to winter? How does weather affect bird visitations? Try to distinguish ground-feeding birds from their tracks. What kinds and how many squirrels come by for their handouts? How do they interact with the birds? What foods do squirrels favor? (It won't take you long to discover that sunflower seeds and various nuts are among the foods that they relish.)

Don't restrict your viewing of animal activity to bird feeders, even though such activity seems most feverish there. Birds, when satisfied, frequently perch well away from feeders, especially in trees and bushes facing south and protected from wind. Watch them fluff, preen, and interact with their neighbors. I particularly recall a flock of house sparrows in my backyard several winters ago. Withstanding a January temperature of more than 20 degrees below zero, they markedly fluffed themselves while perched in a lilac bush, seemingly squeezing every last bit of warmth from the low rays of the late afternoon sun. Backlight marked my indelible impression of these birds. As a bird defecated, its droppings descended in a plume of steam in the frigid air, resembling an incendiary bomb igniting prematurely and encased in a flaming trail on its rapid trip down. I witnessed several of such "attacks."

Look for mammal sign in your backyard. You can usually expect at least tracks of tree squirrels and cottontail rabbits. To your dissatisfaction, you might stumble on other sign: the chewed bark and neatly nipped twigs of a fa-

vorite shrub—the telltale work of rabbits! Remember that both rabbits and squirrels leave four-print patterns but those of squirrels are smaller and squarish; front prints form side by side. Rabbit fore prints, on the other hand, are arranged with one slightly behind the other. Squirrel prints tend to begin and end at trees or fences. You might also see the much smaller four-print track patterns of mice and voles. If you live at the edge of a town or city, you can also expect the tracks of deer and other mammals.

Plants in your backyard, native or otherwise, offer insight into how they tolerate winter, how they accommodate to its onset, and how they respond to its end, followed by new growth. You can witness changes by a daily glance. As mentioned in chapter 6, you are often rewarded by their winter beauty, depending on which woody plants you selected and which nonwoody plants you left standing in a garden. My sedum, dull red in autumn, faded to an attractive rusty bronze in January touched with a light coating of snow.

A backyard weather station can be a source of continual interest, not only to record winter weather but also to learn how to forecast it (chapter 2). Such a station need not be elaborate. A thermometer, preferably mounted on the north side of your dwelling, is the simplest of equipment. It should bear large, easily read numerals and, conveniently, be calibrated in both degrees Centigrade and Fahrenheit. You might get in the habit of recording temperatures a few times each day, say, in the morning, at noon, and again in the evening. A maximum-minimum thermometer is a useful addition to your weather station, allowing you easily to establish daily high and low temperatures without continually watching a standard thermometer. (Several outdoor-equipment firms sell maximum-minimum thermometers.)

Wind direction is of considerable value in weather forecasting, and a simple weather vane, mounted away from obvious wind obstructions, is worth considering. A device for measuring wind speed could be added, but this is of lesser value.

A rain gauge can round out your weather station paraphernalia. Place it in the open as much as possible, away from the sheltering effect of buildings, trees, or shrubs. Depending on your winters, a rain gauge may be of limited use. Measuring snow depth with a graduated stick, however, is always appropriate.

Inside, you really should have a barometer for recording changes in atmospheric pressure. You can go a long way into weather forecasting with only a thermometer, barometer, and weather vane. Besides recording values, however, it's easiest to visualize weather changes when they are plotted on graph paper. One time, I recorded temperature, barometer readings, and wind direction for about a year and plotted them on the same graph. Eventually, I began to sharpen my weather forecasting skills by perceiving some obvious relationships, such as rain or snow frequently accompanying falling barometer readings and easterly winds.

Besides various experiments with ice and snow in your backyard, a unique and easy activity is studying and photographing frost crystals on windowpanes. Here is an opportunity to create truly artistic photographs. You must come in close with your camera and watch composition. Light, of course, is also critical; experiment with the best light direction to set off your selected crystals. In addition, watch the background. You might want to provide an artificial black or colored background. Or, throw it out of focus with a longer lens or a wider lens opening, highlighted by natural, yellowish, low-level sunlight.

Indoor Life

Besides gardening indoors in winter (chapter 6), most of us can also interact with animal life indoors. No, I'm not talking about pets. I'm referring to several native insects that may have taken up winter housekeeping with you.

In summer, with prodigious insect life all around us—much of it in the category of pests—we take insects for granted. In winter, with fewer active animals in our midst, we may become more receptive to insects in our homes and find them most fascinating. We might respect any winter survivors, even those surviving within the protection of our homes. Some of the insects that you may find sharing your home include ants, spiders, silverfish, cockroaches, and fruit flies. Admire their tenacity and ingenuity and observe their behavior.

In Your Community

In your community, within a few miles of your domicile, you can usually find several special places to observe nature in winter. In urban areas, this may be a favorite park, bike path, or cemetery—yes, even a cemetery. Cemeteries, parks for the dead, also constitute parks for the living—places where you can enjoy plants, birds, and sometimes other animals. But, of course, you must be respectful of the dead as you roam any cemetery, and take care where you walk.

One of the places near home that I enjoy walking through in winter—and in summer as well—are alleys in residential areas. Alleys offer you the opportunity to peer into numerous backyards and much expand upon the variety of birds and perhaps other animals seen in your own backyard. You will also gain a valuable perspective about the possibilities of different kinds of bird feeders, landscaping, and gardening—elaborations that may attract more wildlife. Along the alleys, too, you may spot interesting alien and wild plants that may have dispersed through garbage pickup and removal. Alleys are especially attractive to those persons who prefer the somewhat unkempt character of these places over that of manicured, less natural-looking front yards.

Special places within an urban community, apart from alleys, can provide a wide diversity of wildlife. Among the possible sightings are birds of prey, so-called upland game birds, scavenging birds, deer, moose, foxes, and—near water—waterfowl, muskrats, and raccoons. With the added species comes more animal sign.

If you live in a rural area, your possibilities for viewing nature in winter in a community are nearly endless. If you have dogs that roam freely, however, they tend to keep wildlife at some distance from a residence, and you may have to roam farther than the dogs. As a child growing up on a Great Plains farm, I needed some distance from my dogs to approach, for example, jackrabbits in their snow burrows and gray partridges huddled in snow-choked tree-and-shrub shelter belts. Later, in adult life, I lived for a year on a small farm along a stream at the edge of woods. While snowshoeing or skiing on the ice-covered stream, a new bit of winter natural history seemed to await me at nearly every meander—provided I scolded the dogs and commanded them to remain at home.

Testing Winter Clothing at Home

Experiment with winter clothing combinations at home in order to travel comfortably on foot in your community and especially on extended excursions. Make your mistakes where a poor choice is not apt to become damaging.

A systematic approach to clothing versus cold works best for me. I've taken this to the extent of plotting clothing items on graph paper on one scale and wind chill (in degrees Fahrenheit) on the other. So, some clothing for comfort at 25 degrees might include a pair of polyester socks with a pair of woolen socks, leather hiking boots, light polyester underwear, polyester pants, a cotton and a woolen shirt, a polyester parka, and leather gloves with woolen inserts. But with a wind chill of −50 degrees, a different tack is required for comfort: a pair of polyester socks and two pairs of woolen socks, pac boots with felt liners, lightweight and middle-weight polyester underwear, thick woolen or polyester pants with nylon windbreaker pants, two woolen or polyester shirts, a down-filled parka, and leather mittens with thick woolen or polyester inserts. Of course, what works best for me may not work best for you. Depending on weight, frame, and other variables, some people are more susceptible to cold than others, and so clothing requirements differ. But experiment fully; discover what truly works for you—at any temperature or wind chill you are likely to encounter.

Winter Excursions in Open Terrain

Winter excursions on foot away from home vastly broaden your outlook of nature as you immerse yourself in a variety of habitats. Only by visiting many kinds of habitats can you truly expand your backlog of experience. These excursions also allow you meaningfully to apply what you have learned about nature in winter so far. As you ramble, look for snow barchans, rime, weasel tracks, twigs chewed by cottontails, grouse snow burrows, mulleins spearing their flower stalks above the snow, willow pine galls, and the like.

In this section and the next, my approach will be the same. For each group of habitats, I'll introduce you to what general conditions and some plants and animals to expect. The large region I'm particularly thinking of for both sections is southernmost Canada and the northern United States north of about 40 degrees latitude; I'll also stick to inland habitats, those away from coastal areas.

You might wish to keep a road log while heading out to and returning from an excursion site. For greatest safety while driving, choose less traveled roads and proceed at moderate to slow speeds—conditions that also allow you to see more. In your vehicle, place your notebook at a comfortable height for easy writing, perhaps on a box, and fasten it so it doesn't shift around when you make turns. Use a shorthand style of note taking to reduce the number of glances at your notebook. A safer method, of course, is to have a companion record the observations. Here's a sample of how a nature road log might look:

Home to Heron Wildlife Refuge   1/7/93
Cold (5 degrees), moderate NW wind, clear

Miles	Item
0.0	Home (7:30 a.m.)
5.2	Hwy [Highway] 4
7.3	Snw bntgs [Snow buntings] (est 20) [estimated 20 birds]
7.7	Crws (4) [Crows, 4 birds], etng crrn [eating carrion]
10.0	Snw brkns [Snow barchans] in fld [field]
19.6	PARKVILLE
22.4	Rk dvs [Rock doves] near farm
24.3	Jct [Junction] Hwy 3
29.2	Lvng glcl lk pln [Leaving glacial lake plain]
33.7	Elk River, fx? trks [fox? tracks] on ice
34.0	Wte tld [White-tailed] deer (DOR) [Dead on road]

What to Expect

Open habitats are those in which nonwoody vegetation predominates. Grasses, sedges, and broad-leaved nonwoody plants, therefore, dominate the landscape, although scattered scrubs and trees may occur.

Exposure to wind is nearly omnipresent. This means snow tends to gather in drifts and blocks roads even when snow depth is slight. Humans and other animals must contend with wind chill.

Five main kinds of open habitats not generally associated with water include lowland meadows, shrub-sapling openings, plains grasslands, mountain meadows, and sagebrush grasslands; two associated with water are lowland sedge meadows and inland marshes. Each habitat harbors characteristic plant and animal life in winter (Table 9).

Lowland meadows in the eastern United States are grassy openings in forests caused by fire, high winds (that blow down trees), clearing for farming, devastating insects or disease, or flooding by dam-building beavers. These meadows may remain for a time if continually grazed, mowed for hay, or if their encroachment by woody vegetation is checked by frequent fires. If left unchecked, they develop thickets and eventually become forested.

Meadows with scattered trees are called savannas, if located inland, or barrens, if near coasts. In the north-central United States and southernmost Canada is a transition belt of natural grassland with scattered aspens called aspen parkland. It lies between the eastern forests and the western plains grassland.

Meadows, like other grass-dominated habitats, are among the first habitats to lose snow cover. In spring, the grasses of open habitats tend to become green and show new growth before other plants.

Think of a shrub-sapling opening as a habitat in transition as meadow evolves into forest. If fires, cattle grazing, or hay mowing are held back, this transition habitat will develop and ultimately become a forest. In the progression of plant replacement, grasses yield to annual exotic "weeds" that give way to such perennials as goldenrods, asters, milkweeds, and raspberries. In time, shrubs—such as hazelnuts and dogwoods—and tree saplings gradually thicken and eventually predominate, and a forest ensues. Expect to witness more life above the snow in a shrub-sapling opening than in a meadow.

Plains grasslands, or western prairies, occupy the Great Plains, a low-relief region more than 500 miles wide east of the Rocky Mountains.

Three kinds of prairie regions, in roughly north-south bands, reflect the greater precipitation from west to east across the Great Plains. Tallgrass prairie, the wettest, lies adjacent to the eastern forests; it originally covered eastern parts of the Dakotas, Nebraska, Kansas, and Oklahoma; western Minnesota and northwestern Iowa; and southernmost Manitoba, Saskatchewan, and Alberta. Key grasses include tall bluestem—up to eight feet tall with roots up to six feet—switch grass, and Indian grass. Today, little tallgrass prairie exists, and the region is a leading grain-producing area.

Midgrass prairie, of medium-height grasses two to four feet high, lies to the west of tallgrass prairie. This belt originally spread over much or most of the Dakotas, Nebraska, Kansas, Oklahoma, and Texas and parts of southernmost Manitoba, Saskatchewan, and Alberta. Little bluestem, western wheatgrass, and June grass are among the characteristic grasses.

Shortgrass prairie, of the shortest grasses, about sixteen inches and less, forms the western and driest belt of the Great Plains, butting up against the east flank of the Rockies. It encroaches over eastern and central Montana, eastern Wyoming and Colorado, northwest Texas, and parts of Arizona and New Mexico as well as small parts of southern Saskatchewan and Alberta. Buffalo grass and blue grama grass typify shortgrass prairie. Shortgrass and midgrass prairie today harbor the western cattle-raising empires.

Mountain meadows of the West are grassy regions found at higher elevations. Many form in ways similar to those of the eastern, lower-elevation meadows. Others, however, may originate from the filling of former lake basins or from avalanches. Still others are naturally treeless places because of their being too wet,

TABLE 9   Selected Open Terrain Inland Habitats and Characteristic Observable Life in Winter

Habitat	Plants	Animals
Not Generally Associated with Water		
Lowland Meadows (E)*	Grasses, mulleins, milkweeds, goldenrods, thistles, yarrows, asters, roses	Red foxes, cottontails, meadow voles, short-eared owls
Shrub-Sapling Openings (E)	Hazelnuts, sumacs, chokecherries, grapes, dogwoods, raspberries, aspen, birch, and pine saplings	White-tailed deer, coyotes, weasels, skunks, white-footed mice, screech owls
Plains Grasslands (W)*	Grasses, coneflowers, sunflowers, yuccas, prickly pears, sagebrush, rabbitbrush, junipers	Bison, mule deer, pronghorns, coyotes, red foxes, jackrabbits, deer mice, prairie chickens, snowy owls
Mountain Meadows (W)	Grasses, sedges, rushes, horsetails, cow parsnips, yarrows, willows, heaths	Mule deer, elk, mountain goats, bighorn sheep, montane voles, white-tailed ptarmigans, northern goshawks
Sagebrush Grasslands (W)	Sagebrush, saltbushes, rabbitbrush, gooseberries, snowberries, Mormon teas, grasses, goldenrods, yarrows, prickly pear cacti	Pronghorns, mule deer, coyotes, black-tailed jackrabbits, sagebrush voles, long-eared owls
Associated with Water		
Lowland Sedge Meadows (E, W)	Sedges, grasses, sweet gales, willows	Meadow voles, short-tailed shrews, northern harriers, short-eared owls
Inland Marshes (E, W)	Cattails, bulrushes, reed grasses, sedges, wild rice, willows	Muskrats, minks, cottontails, meadow voles, short-eared owls

*E = part of primarily eastern North America north of about 40 degrees latitude. W = part of primarily western North America north of about 40 degrees latitude.

too dry, or too cold. Some meadows in basins between mountain ranges are called "parks." Dry meadows, such as those on ridge tops or on south-facing mountain slopes, are larger than wet meadows, which are usually in high, subalpine regions. Alpine tundra, the highest marshy grassland with permanently frozen subsoil, is included with the other mountain meadows.

In intermontane regions, drier than that in which you find shortgrass prairie, is sagebrush grassland. This mostly covers parts of western Wyoming, southern Idaho, northern Nevada, northeastern California, eastern Oregon, and southeastern Washington. Sagebrush grassland appears as expanses of gray-green shrubs—particularly sagebrush—with grasses and broad-leaved nonwoody plants. In winter, pronghorns and sage grouse feed almost exclusively on sagebrush, an important source of protein. (In winter, pronghorns assemble in larger herds, of a hundred or more animals.) Mule deer feed on sagebrush but browse also on other shrubs.

Lowland sedge meadows occur in much of Canada and the northern United States where the action of glaciers has left depressions. Look for them where the ground is too dry for marshes and too wet for grass meadows; frequently you see their beginnings along the edges of older lakes and sluggish streams. In places, particularly the Far North, these wet sedge meadows border bogs and nonwoody peat forms in them.

Sedge meadows can withstand considerable fluctuation in water level, but not major changes, such as those brought about by human-induced draining or flooding by beaver dams. Depending on the change, sedge meadows may evolve into marshes, ponds, shrub swamp forests, or dry grass meadows.

The dominant sedges of sedge meadows

differ from grasses in usually having solid, three-sided stems. They grow in clumps or tussocks on which you might step across a sedge meadow in summer.

Widespread inland marshes are wet places characterized by nonwoody plants. They exist on their own but may flank old lakes and ponds and sluggish streams or occur within inundated parts of sedge meadows. As they dry up, inland marshes evolve into sedge meadows, bogs, or shrub swamp forests.

Muskrats are particularly good marsh indicators. In colder regions, you'll consistently see their lodges above the ice if the water is at least about three to four feet deep so it doesn't freeze to the bottom. Muskrats especially savor cattails and bulrushes. You might see some of these plants in piles pushed up through holes in the ice gnawed by the muskrats. Cavities within these piles, usually large enough to prevent the ice from freezing over them, allow the muskrats places to rest, eat, and breathe. Watch for mink tracks in the snow covering marshes. They continually prey on muskrats.

Marshes adjoining woods may be inhabited by beavers (Figure 43).

Winter Excursions in Woods

The section on open terrain fixed the pattern I've set up for winter excursions: discussing the kinds of specific habitats to expect, with their characteristic plants and animals. Let's continue the pattern, this time in wooded habitats.

What to Expect

Unlike habitats in open terrain, wooded habitats, with some exceptions, are signifi-

Figure 43. Looking over a beaver lodge in a marsh giving way to woods.

cantly protected from the onslaught of wind. Snow tends to pile up rather than shape into drifts, and animals, including humans, are less affected by wind chill.

In wooded places, expect a greater variety of plants projecting above the snow, as well as more kinds of wildlife. Animals inhabiting woods find more places protected from the cold and from their enemies.

Nine main kinds of wooded habitats, not associated with water, and four, associated with water, can be experienced in the colder regions of North America. In each habitat you can expect characteristic plant and animal life in winter (Table 10).

Northern coniferous forests cover much of

Canada south of the tundra away from grasslands and extend into Alaska. They also occur within New England and the northern parts of most of the Great Lakes states. These forests tolerate low temperatures and a short growing season well. Two main kinds of northern coniferous forests are clearly recognizable: spruce-fir and pine.

Spruce-fir forests are especially characterized by white spruces and balsam firs.

Northern pine forests are made up of several kinds of pines, including: eastern white and red in the East; ponderosa, lodgepole, and western white in the West; and jack pine in both the East and West.

Light-favoring pines have thick bark and spe-

TABLE 10 Selected Wooded Inland Habitats and Characteristic Observable Life in Winter

Habitat	Plants	Animals
Not Associated with Water		
Northern Coniferous Forests (E, W)*	Balsam firs, white and black spruces, jack and other pines, hemlocks, huckleberries	Moose, white-tailed deer, martens, red squirrels, snowshoe hares, porcupines, fishers, deer mice, red-backed voles, long-eared owls, red crossbills, spruce grouse
Aspen-Birch Forests (E, W)	Quaking aspens, paper birches, hazelnuts, dogwoods, alders, bracken ferns	Moose, white-tailed deer, snowshoe hares, long-tailed weasels, deer mice, ruffed grouse, yellow-bellied sapsuckers, northern goshawks
Sugar Maple Forests (E)	Sugar maples, American basswoods, eastern hemlocks, yellow birches, gooseberries, wood ferns	Gray foxes, deer mice, gray squirrels, blue jays, sharp-shinned hawks, tufted titmice
Oak-Hickory Forests (E)	Bur, northern red, white, and black oaks, bitternut, mockernut, pignut and shagbark hickories, wild grapes, blackberries	Gray foxes, gray squirrels, white-footed mice, Cooper's hawks, wild turkeys, red-bellied woodpeckers
Ponderosa Pine Forests (W)	Ponderosa, western white and limber pines, common and Rocky Mountain junipers, dwarf mistletoes	Elk, mule deer, Abert's squirrels, deer mice, black-billed magpies, Clark's nutcrackers, blue grouse
Douglas Fir Forests (W)	Douglas firs, lodgepole and western white pines, grand firs, western hemlocks, western red cedars, Pacific rhododendrons	Elk, mule deer, deer mice, northern flying squirrels, spotted owls, blue grouse, pileated woodpeckers
Lodgepole Pine Forests (W)	Lodgepole and western white pines, Engelmann spruces, subalpine firs, common junipers, manzanitas, heartleaf arnicas	Elk, mule deer, snowshoe hares, porcupines, martens, fishers, deer mice, black-backed and three-toed woodpeckers, pine grosbeaks

Habitat	Plants	Animals
Subalpine Fir Forests (W)	Subalpine firs, Engelmann spruces, white-bark, foxtail, and bristlecone pines, white rhododendrons, huckleberries, bear grasses, fireweeds	Mountain goats and sheep, northern pocket gophers (burrows), martens, red-backed voles, Clark's nutcrackers, Cassin's finches
Pinyon-Juniper Woodlands (W)	Pinyon and ponderosa pines, common and Utah junipers, skunk-brush, antelope bitterbrush, prickly pear cacti, Mormon teas, yuccas	Elk, mule deer, coyotes, black-tailed jackrabbits, pinyon jays, golden eagles, common bushtits

Associated with Water

Habitat	Plants	Animals
Forests Along Streams (E, W)	Cottonwoods, willows, alders, ashes, maples, dogwoods, scouring rushes, ferns	Deer, raccoons, otters, minks, beavers, muskrats, eagles, owls
Forests Along Lakes and Ponds (E, W)	Willows, aspens, birches, spruces, cattails, bulrushes, sedges, and wild rice along edges of lakes and ponds	Moose, deer, raccoons, otters, minks, beavers, muskrats, eagles, owls
Bog Forests (E, W)	Black spruces, tamaracks, Labrador teas, leatherleafs, cotton-grasses, sphagnum mosses	White-tailed deer, moose, lynx, snowshoe hares, bog lemmings, great gray owls, spruce grouse
Shrub Swamp Forests (E, W)	Alders, willows, dogwoods, gooseberries, ferns, sedges	Moose, white-tailed deer, snowshoe hares, weasels, common redpolls

*E = part of primarily eastern North America north of about 40 degrees latitude. W = part of primarily western North America north of about 40 degrees latitude.

cial buds, which make them resistant to fires; some, however, such as jack pines, rely on the heat of fires to open their cones and spread seeds.

Pine needles pile up on pine forest floors and are not readily recycled in the soil. Shrubs and nonwoody plants have difficulty in establishing themselves in a pine forest because of the thick mat of needles and poor light.

Northern coniferous forests provide a haven for wildlife. Red squirrels and red crossbills have the means to extract seeds from cones. Porcupines like to gnaw on the inner bark of conifers. Spruce grouse, white-tailed deer, moose, and snowshoe hares relish coniferous twigs in winter. Many animals benefit from the dense branches, which offer good protection from the wind and snow buildup below.

Aspen-birch forests range widely in area and elevation. Quaking aspens, dominant trees of these forests, cover most of northern North America.

Although some aspen-birch forests are stable, most enter other forests as pioneers after some annihilating disturbance, such as fire, logging, and insect or disease outbreaks. When you spot a patch of aspen-birch forest within a larger coniferous forest, for example, you know that a mortal disturbance of the conifers has allowed opportunists a foothold. Aspen roots remain alive after fires, and suckers from them quickly establish a new forest.

Look at the understories of aspen-birch forests to tell if such forests will persist or others will take their place. If the understory is largely of aspen and birch saplings and various shrubs, the aspen-birch forest likely will continue. If the understory consists of saplings of shade-tolerant firs, hemlocks, spruces, sugar maples, beeches, or basswoods, some type of longer-lived coniferous or hardwood forest will replace the shorter-lived aspen-birch forest.

Ruffed grouse are at home in aspen-birch forests. Among their principal foods are aspen buds and catkins.

Sugar maple forests inhabit mostly the northern part of the eastern United States but extend into a part of southeastern Canada. These forests intermingle with northern coniferous forests from the north and oak-hickory forests extending from the south.

Sugar maples make up more than half the trees in most places, but you can expect to see other hardwoods, as well as conifers. Maple seedlings constitute most of the understory. This means that sugar maple forests are long lasting and usually are not replaced by other forests. Fire, logging, or other disturbances only temporarily hinder their growth.

You find oak-hickory forests mostly south of the sugar maple forests. They cover one-fourth of the forested land east of the Mississippi River. Shade-tolerant trees, such as the northern red, white, and black oaks, eventually tend to take over these forests. Many oaks can survive fires because of their resistant roots.

Oak-hickory forests provide numerous nuts for birds and mammals. Wild turkeys and squirrels, in particular, consume great quantities of acorns and hickory nuts.

Ponderosa pine forests spread over much of the western United States and part of southwestern Canada. Expect them in the foothills as well as in the mountains. They vary from savannas in the foothills to shady thickets to mixtures of aspens, cottonwoods, and other conifers at higher elevations. Deep-rooted, ponderosa pines are highly resistant to drought. Young ponderosas have difficulty in gaining a foothold because of shade from their own kind.

Douglas fir forests populate much of the mountainous western United States and part of southwestern Canada. Douglas firs, the domi-

Figure 44. Dried ferns project above the snow. As you travel in winter woods, mentally note such ferns; in spring, you might return to feed on the tender fiddleheads.

nant trees, predominate on middle elevation slopes in the Rockies; here, they take over such pioneers as ponderosa pines, lodgepole pines, western larches, and aspens. In the moist Pacific Northwest, Douglas firs grow larger and behave as pioneer trees to be eventually replaced by western hemlocks and western red cedars.

Look for fallen Douglas fir logs, which frequently serve as nurseries for tree seedlings. Seedlings' roots grow on either side of the fallen logs. When the logs fully decay, the now-grown seedlings are left supported on once-straddling prop roots.

Spotted owls depend on old-growth Douglas fir forests in which to nest and will not return if their nesting grounds are burned or logged. These birds of prey hunt various birds and mammals, but especially northern flying squirrels.

Lodgepole pine forests can be seen in much of the mountainous West of the United States and Canada. Inland, they frequently occur with Douglas fir forests or at elevations above them.

Trees of lodgepole pine forests grow tightly packed—so much so that lower branches die, making these pines look like power line poles. These dense stands result from fires heating cones and causing them to release great numbers of seeds quickly.

In understories of lodgepole pine forests, you are likely to notice seedlings of Engelmann spruces, Douglas firs, and subalpine firs. These shade-tolerant trees frequently take over lodgepole pine forests.

In places, you might see many rusty-looking crowns of old lodgepole pines, signifying they are dead. They have succumbed to the joint effects of mountain pine beetles and the blue stain fungus. Beetle larvae girdle the bark, and the fungus clogs a tree's water vessels.

Subalpine fir forests live at high elevations in much of the mountainous West of the United States and Canada. Above them is the alpine tundra. Their makeup varies from region to region. In the Rockies, for example, subalpine firs and Engelmann spruces are the dominant trees. In the Great Basin region of Nevada and closely surrounding regions, though, limber pines and bristlecone pines—the oldest living plants—dominate.

The subalpine fir forest habitat is a rigorous one. Winter may last nine to ten months, leaving little time for new growth and reproduction. Winter winds, armed with abrasive snow crystals and ice pellets, relentlessly prune branches and strip bark. At the higher elevations, many trees display strange and contorted shapes. Near timberline, trees are very short because of the severe winds and heavy snowpack, and some have been forced to grow horizontally.

Pinyon-juniper woodlands occupy much of the arid Great Basin and Colorado plateau. For a characteristic snowy winter excursion, however, you would encounter them mostly in northern Utah and Nevada and northwestern Colorado. They lie at elevations just above grasslands and just below ponderosa pine forests.

Also called pygmy woodlands, the pinyon-juniper woods are actually a mixture of small trees, shrubs, grasses, and nonwoody broad-leaved plants. The pinyon pines and junipers usually rise less than thirty feet. Trees space themselves widely at lower elevations, where they compete severely for moisture. They grow more clustered together at higher elevations, where greater moisture exists.

Mammals and birds spread pinyon-juniper woodlands by carrying pinyon nuts and juniper berries to their caches or disseminating them through their droppings. Rock squirrels, pinyon mice, pinyon jays, and Clark's nutcrackers are among the distributors.

Four forested habitats associated with water are: forests along streams, forests along lakes and ponds, bog forests, and shrub swamp forests.

Forests along streams vary widely in their makeup of plants, although cottonwoods, willows, and alders are nearly universal; and both coniferous and deciduous broad-leaved trees can be expected. So, for example, expect eastern cottonwoods, black ashes, and silver maples along streams in parts of the eastern United States; plains cottonwoods, green ashes, and peachleaf willows along plains grassland streams; and narrowleaf cottonwoods, balsam poplars, and blue spruces in the Rockies.

Some animals inhabiting woods flanking streams are found in much of colder North America. These include deer, raccoons, otters, minks, beavers, and muskrats. A few, such as dippers and northern water shrews, are especially characteristic of high mountain streams with swift rapids separated by intervening pools. Expect to see both dippers and water shrews in winter: dippers walking and diving in open streams—as in summer—and water shrews hiding under overhanging ice shelves left by lowered water levels.

The widespread forests along lakes and

ponds are similar to those along streams, but some differences exist. Cottonwoods, for example, are usually lacking. And, fringing the standing water of lakes and ponds are such characteristic nonwoody plants as cattails, sedges, bulrushes, and reeds—all of which you can readily see projecting above the ice.

Visible animals in winter along the wooded shores of lakes and ponds are also very similar to those along streams.

Bog forests are found in most of Canada, part of Alaska, and parts of the northernmost United States where melting glaciers have dumped rock debris unevenly. Depressions in the terrain often formed when blocks of glacial ice, trapped under insulative rock debris, melted more slowly than exposed ice. These depressions evolved into *bogs*, places of wet, spongy ground or cold, acidic water unfed by streams. With open water, floating mats of sedges topped with sphagnum (SFAG-nuhm) moss begin at the bog's margin and spread inward; the mats keep the water cold. Peat accumulates along the margins of the floating mat and beneath it because the cold acidic water promotes litle plant decay. Acids formed by the sphagnum and accumulating peat stain the water the color of strong tea.

Besides the ever-invading floating mat, other changes take place in bogs. Leatherleafs, Labrador teas, and other small shrubs take root where the mat is thick enough. Black spruces and tamaracks, particularly characteristic, begin to grow where the mat meets the bog bottom.

If bog forests are left undisturbed, they may transform. As the soil becomes less acidic, a northern coniferous forest may take over, possibly one dominated by northern white cedars.

Bog forests may be difficult to traverse. Even with snow cover, the lumpy ground may slow your travel. And fallen logs and leaning trees may hinder you further.

Shrub swamp forests occur in low places in much of the territory occupied by bog forests. The rich, wet soils in which they live, however, are less acidic because flowing water dilutes them and carries in nutrients for the plants. These forests may develop from drained beaver ponds, dried up marshes or sedge meadows, bog forests, and along the edges of streams and lakes.

Speckled alders are the most obvious trees—actually most often shrubs—in the shrub swamp forests of southeastern Canada and the northeastern United States. They are efficient nitrogen factories, extracting it from the air and making it available to other plants when they shed their nitrogen-loaded leaves.

A P P E N D I X

A Winter Survivalist's Handbook

Most of us don't expect to be caught in a winter survival situation, and probably most of us won't. But we don't know. The uncertainty of it happening is enough for us to be prepared. It's something like death—with death, however, we know it will happen, but not when.

Here you will find useful information to help you survive in a winter emergency, whether on foot or in a vehicle. Assimilate this information before you set out on a winter trip. It will give you added confidence in your travels, may help you avoid some discomfort, or may help save your life.

Survival Psychology

Survival as a State of Mind

Mostly your mind dictates whether you will be a survivor. Sure, subzero temperatures, strong wind, and heavy snow may highly complicate your predicament, but the way your mind functions under these stresses will usually be the deciding factor. As the mind can affect the body, so can it affect the mind. Control your mind so that it works for you, not against you.

Mother Nature could care less about you; she is simply indifferent—but she is *not* out to get you. We suffer at her hand when we use poor judgment in her midst. We temporarily forget or lose respect for the power she has, or our uncontrolled mind panics.

You are aware that you must have a good grasp on your will to live in order to survive. Some persons have a greater grasp on that will than others. Why the difference? It depends a great deal on your self-image.

Self-image is how you view your importance as an individual. It reflects your values, habits, and attitude. Your self-image mirrors your subconscious mind. If your self-image is good and healthy, it will foster a positive or "can do" attitude, one that nurtures self-reliance, self-confidence, and utmost patience. A good self-image prevents a negative "give-up-itis" attitude from taking control.

Armed with a positive attitude and the

strong will to live, you will not be swayed by temporary, uncomfortable events. You will believe that highly unpleasant experiences seldom last long. You expect that being lost is usually short-lived and that moderating weather should develop within a few days or less after a cold snap.

Fears and How to Cope with Them

Fears often confuse the need to survive. Become aware of your fears and learn how to overcome them. I've identified four main fears related to winter survival: Fear of Death, Fear of Harm, Fear of Fear, and Fear of Society, listed in order of importance.

Fear of Death depends on your personal convictions and religious beliefs. But whatever the degree of your fear of death, remember that having little or no fear of death is contradictory to survival! Some fear of death, then, is good to help ensure your survival. Just don't allow this fear to gain the upper hand and become all-absorbing.

In winter, most people probably fear death primarily by freezing; other likely causes in winter include hypothermia, avalanches, and carbon monoxide poisoning. But they could also die from heart attacks, strokes, vehicle crashes, and a number of other causes. Don't blow death "by winter" out of proportion, and don't blow the fear of death out of proportion.

Fear of Harm refers to physical discomfort or suffering arising from the same trials that may lead to death. This fear can cause you to push on in a storm to reach the warmth of your home or vehicle when the best approach for survival is to remain where you are. Modern humans are accustomed to instant comfort, and many fear being cold, wet, or otherwise miserable. At times, we must tolerate discom-

fort or suffering, and we must recognize that either is temporary and not the major difficulty. It is better to experience discomfort or suffering than to die.

A specific fear of harm is that caused by wild animals. This fear has been overplayed in movies and television. In winter, the only animals likely to concern you are wolves, coyotes, and polar bears. Your chances of encountering a polar bear are less than being bitten by a rattlesnake or struck by lightning. And the chances of being harassed by wolves or coyotes are very remote. If you've started a wood fire, stick by it. In the unlikely event that a wolf or coyote attacks you, bash it on the nose or head with a club.

Fear of Fear is anxiety over phobias or exaggerated fears that defy explanation or logic. Phobias arising from winter survival include fear of closed places (claustrophobia, such as fear of heavily wooded areas or sleeping in snow shelters), fear of open places (agoraphobia, such as fear of open grasslands or marshes), fear of darkness, and fear of being alone. Phobias may be acquired from a frightening happening, from childhood experiences, or from depression.

You have to work hard to shake phobias, but it can be done. If you have a phobia, the first step is to admit it. Try to allay a fear of darkness by spending more time in the wilderness at night through stargazing, listening and identifying animal sounds, and the like. Extroverts may have more difficulty with the fear of being alone. If you have this fear, spend time alone in everyday life, so you become comfortable with your own company.

Fear of Society includes the fear of ridicule, loss of face, personal guilt, or inconveniencing or worrying others. You might fear what others will think if you become lost, fail to arrive at a designated rendezvous on time, or fall through the ice. Just remember that this fear is pointless relative to your own survival. If confronted with real winter survival, you will also quickly realize that the Fears of Death and Harm will heavily outweigh the Fear of Society.

A Survival Approach

Upon realizing you are in a survival situation, you first STOP.

S = Stop moving. If on foot, sit down, for this forces you to stop moving.

T = Think. Evaluate your immediate and future danger. Tell yourself that you *will* be a survivor.

O = Observe. Look about for resources around you, in your vehicle, pack, or pockets. Try to determine if the weather will remain as it is, or how it might change.

P = Plan. Formulate a plan for survival, using your resources and your available energy. Be creative to *improvise with anything* available to you.

Second, seek or construct a shelter. If stranded in a vehicle, you are usually better off remaining in it. If you need to construct a shelter, become familiar beforehand with a later section of this appendix dealing with shelter construction.

Third, if you have sufficient reserve energy and especially some food to replenish it, signal for help.

If stranded in a vehicle in snow, tie colored—particularly red or orange—cloths or pieces of plastic to the antenna. You might try three blasts from your vehicle horn, but don't run down the battery. If you carry flares, set them off at night.

On foot, good choices of signaling are by mirrors, shadow signals in the snow, and signal fires.

Besides mirrors, such reflective materials as shiny metal, aluminum foil, Mylar, and glass also work well, even without full sunlight. Face the reflector about halfway between the sun and an apparent rescuer who is on the ground or in the air. Sweep the horizon if no rescuer is in sight.

For a good shadow signal to attract an air rescuer, tramp a large **X** twenty feet high in the snow; this is an international symbol that means "unable to proceed." (A large SOS is also effective, but requires more energy.)

With signal fires, use smoke by day and fire at night. Three fires offer the most meaningful signal. If in the open, you might even try setting a coniferous tree on fire.

Another easy means of signaling, for rescuers close by, is a high-pitched whistle, which you can always readily carry with you. Three blasts from it, periodically, might be enough to attract attention.

Staying Warm

Heat Loss

An important part of staying warm is knowing how you lose heat. You lose it by radiation, convection, conduction, evaporation, and respiration.

Generally the leading cause of heat loss in still air is by *radiation,* whereby heat is directly released from your body's surface. Your unprotected head, for example, may radiate up to one-half of your body's heat at 40 degrees Fahrenheit and up to three-fourths at 5 degrees.

Heat lost by *convection* means it is removed by the wind. Here's where *wind chill* comes into play. You've seen wind chill charts that are virtually impossible to memorize, and you've heard weather forecasters caution you incessantly about wind chill. Knowing the "rule of thirty" is enough to drive the point home: A thirty-mile-per-hour wind at −30 degrees Fahrenheit will freeze exposed flesh in thirty seconds; wind chill is about −100 degrees. The best approach against heat loss by convection is simply to stay out of the wind as much as possible.

With *conduction,* you lose heat by your body's direct contact with cold solids (including metal, rock, plastic, leather, and rubber) and liquids (including water, gasoline, and kerosene). You likely have heard of children touching cold metal with their tongues; not only do they lose heat, but their moist tongues may freeze to the metal. The rate at which water conducts heat away is many times that of air. If your body becomes wet from perspiration or falling through ice, you lose heat through *water chill.* Avoid sitting on heat-draining materials in the cold. Sitting on insulative materials, such as closed-cell foam, is wiser.

You lose heat by *evaporation* as the perspiration on your skin evaporates. Try hard, therefore, not to perspire in the cold. But if you do perspire, cover your body with breathable clothing so perspiration is not trapped, which leads to water chill.

Heat loss through *respiration* is a double-edged sword. You exhale warm air and inhale cold air. About all you can do to reduce heat loss by respiration is to breathe through your nose rather than through your mouth.

Clothing Materials and Their Use

Your body generates heat in two ways: by chemical reactions as your food is processed and by muscular contraction, through exercise or shivering. Clothing traps this generated heat and insulates your body against heat loss.

Your clothing's ability to insulate against heat loss relates directly to the amount of still or dead air trapped within it: more dead air means greater warmth. More still air is trapped with loose-fitting clothing and with several layers of clothing. Also, some clothing materials trap more dead air than others.

The common insulative clothing materials for cold conditions include polyester, polypropylene, Thinsulate, wool, and down.

Polyester is a synthetic fiber that absorbs virtually no water, wicks moisture from your skin to the next layer, dries easily, is relatively lightweight, and doesn't hold body odors. Some of its numerous trade names include Dacron, Capilene, Hollofil, Thermax, and Polartec.

Polypropylene, another synthetic fiber, is similar to polyester but doesn't feel as comfortable to some people and retains body odors.

Thinsulate, a synthetic material of polyester and polyolefin fibers, is similar to polyester and polypropylene in not absorbing water and drying easily. Its good insulative power is enhanced by very fine fibers trapping dead air along their length.

Wool, an old standby, is, of course, a natural fiber. Its fibers trap air even when wet, but it absorbs water readily, dries poorly, doesn't wick that well, and is heavy—particularly when wet.

Down, the under feathers of geese and ducks, is a good insulator and lightweight when dry. But when wet, it assumes wool's negative characteristics.

Review the best clothing materials for cold-wet and cold-dry conditions. For cold-wet conditions, down to about 32 degrees Fahrenheit, use polyester, polypropylene, Thinsulate, and possibly wool if you protect if from wetness. For cold-dry conditions, below about 32 degrees, down and wool are definitely appropriate, along with the synthetic materials.

Because many clothing layers trap more still, insulative air, let's see how you might dress in layers, keeping in mind the common materials. In cold weather, think in terms of three or more layers.

Layer one might begin with two-piece polyester or polypropylene lightweight underwear that insulates but also wicks perspiration from your skin to the next clothing layer. Similarly, try thin polyester or polypropylene, knee-length socks on your feet, and polyester, silk, or nylon glove liners on your hands. On your head, choose a stocking cap or the more protective balaclava of polyester, polypropylene, acrylic, or wool. Or try a cap with earflaps made of polyester or Thinsulate.

Layer two could be a midweight, two-piece (with a turtleneck upper) underwear or a thicker, insulated underwear, of either of the materials already mentioned but also of down. A pair of knee-length wool or Thinsulate socks might cover your feet, and thicker glove liners or gloves of various materials—including wool, might cover your hands. Consider covering your head further with a second cap.

Layer three, covering your main body, might be a parka (with attached hood for neck warmth) of pile or fleece, Thinsulate, down, or wool and pants of similar materials except maybe down. (Pile and fleece are thick, knitted, or woven fabrics, most often of polyester.) If relatively warm, forego one of the second underwears mentioned above, and this main body covering may become layer two. A second pair of wool or Thinsulate socks may cover your feet. Protect your hands further with mittens. Your head is additionally protected by the parka hood.

Layer four which may also be layer three if temperatures are relatively warm, may cover your main body with a nylon windbreaker parka (with attached hood) and pants. If you expect wet conditions, select windbreaker clothing that is also waterproof but breathable to allow body moisture to pass through. A good choice laminates Gore-Tex with the fabric. Gore-Tex is a synthetic membrane with pores so tiny that water drops cannot enter but water vapor from your body passes through. Layer four (or three) may be insulated, as well as serving as protection from the wind and rain. If you are wearing pac boots (with leather uppers and rubber bottoms), layer four may be a boot liner of polyester, polypropylene, Thinsulate, or wool; the boot provides a fifth layer. Layer four on your head is the hood of the final parka.

Your feet take a lot of punishment from cold, perspiration, and supporting the weight of your body. Further protect them with gaiters, which prevent snow from working into your boots.

Temperature Regulation

It's important continuously to regulate the temperature in terms of how your body feels. You can both overheat and overchill your body.

Overheating causes perspiration that results in heat loss by evaporation or conduction through water chill. This is a dangerous situation because you cannot readily dry your clothes or body.

You can prevent overheating several ways—but make a correction before you perspire. First try loosening your clothing; partly unzip or unbutton your parka or slip the hood down. If this is insufficient, remove your cap; remember that your head radiates much heat. If you are still warm, shed a layer of clothing. Prevent overheating also by cutting down on physical activity; if you're walking too fast, slow down. A fine adjustment for overheated hands, covered by either gloves or mittens, is spreading your fingers.

If overchilled, you have similar options. Fasten any open clothing, add a cap or an extra hood—as well as another layer on other parts of the body, eat or drink something hot, or increase your physical activity. The last, however, is self-limiting and not a good long-term choice.

Winter Hazards and How to Cope with Them

The main winter hazards include hypothermia, frostbite, falling through the ice, blizzards, carbon monoxide poisoning, snow blindness, and avalanches.

Hypothermia, which is lower-than-normal body temperature, is usually called "exposure" by the news media. Your body loses heat faster than you can produce it. You can get hypothermia at temperatures well above freezing if your body is wet or subjected to wind. Hypothermia saps your strength and inhibits your reflexes. Several symptoms arise as your body temperature drops from a normal of about 98.6 degrees Fahrenheit. One of the first is uncontrollable shivering. With a further drop, you might experience difficulty in speaking, poor muscle coordination and thinking, and drowsiness. Unconsciousness may follow. Below 78 degrees, death is likely, although some people have survived with a body temperature of less than 78 degrees.

Prevent hypothermia with adequate cloth-

ing, but don't overinsulate, which leads to unwanted perspiration. Keep fortified with food and water. Seek shelter well before you actually need it. And avoid falling through the ice.

For treatment, get out of the wind, shed wet clothing, and restore body heat quickly. A good remedy is to crawl into a prewarmed sleeping bag with another person. Hot drinks and fast, energy-producing foods, such as chocolate, help, but avoid alcohol, which tricks the brain into thinking the body is warm and can release cold, near-surface blood to your body core. If you later have access to a modern dwelling, immerse yourself in warm (about 100 degrees Fahrenheit) water. It may take six to eight hours or longer for you to re-warm.

Frostbite is the freezing of skin and underlying tissue, usually on the face, hands, and toes. It happens when you are underinsulated, experience severe wind chill or water chill, or touch cold objects that conduct your body heat away.

Near-surface frostbite shows up as numb gray or white waxy skin; it is stiff on the surface but soft and resilient below. Deep, more serious frostbite is similar but causes stiffness below the skin's surface as well.

A number of steps can prevent frostbite. If your face is threatened, grimace or make faces. You can also warm your face briefly with a bare hand. Wear several insulative layers on your hands and feet, and keep your fingers and toes moving when they feel cold. If truly surviving, stuff dry cattail down in your boots and mittens. Avoid touching cold objects and liquids.

Treat frostbite by getting out of the wind, covering the frozen part with extra clothing, and warming it with your body or someone else's. Place a warm hand over your frostbitten face or toes. Warm your toes against the stomach of a companion. Hold frostbitten fingers under an armpit or in your crotch. *Don't rub the frostbitten parts:* Ice crystals in the frozen tissue may further damage the tissue. If possible, sip hot drinks. Don't let frozen parts refreeze once they've been thawed. If you have access to a modern dwelling, soak the frostbitten parts in warm (about 100 degrees Fahrenheit) water.

Depending on the severity of the frostbite, aftereffects include tingling, stinging, itching, blistering, swelling, and darkening or mottling of the skin. Frostbitten parts become more susceptible to cold. Don't take frostbite lightly: In extreme cases fingers, toes, and larger parts of hands and feet must be amputated if gangrene sets in.

One precaution to avoid falling through the ice is knowing safe ice thicknesses for various loads. Lake ice should be at least four inches thick for walking on it, five inches for snowmobiling, twelve inches for driving a car, and fifteen inches for driving a pickup truck. For added safety, apply even greater ice thicknesses.

Ice strength depends on more than thickness. Lake ice is stronger than stream ice. Clear ice of midwinter is strong than slushy ice of early winter or dark ice of late winter. Clear ice is stronger than white ice with trapped air bubbles formed under windy conditions. And ice near shore tends to be weaker.

Realize that ice can vary on the same water body , and avoid the thinner places. Snow, by its insulating effect, slows down the ice-forming process, so ice under snow is thinner. Ice is thinner where warmer-water springs seep in. On streams, ice is thinner in turbulent places near snags and boulders, and on the outside of stream bends.

Besides watching for weak and thin ice, you can take other precautions. Ski or snowshoe on ice to better distribute your weight. Carry a heavy-duty ice awl in each hand to help pull yourself from the water should you break through the ice. Mine are made from short lengths of thick, hardwood doweling that fit comfortably in my hand. I've force-fitted thick nails in the ends of the dowels, cut off their heads, and ground the cut ends to sharp points. I keep the awls, analogous to single polar bear claws, fastened to my wrists with stout cord.

In spite of precautions, you may fall through the ice. You must free yourself quickly: At a water temperature of less than 40 degrees Fahrenheit the body remains completely functional less than ten minutes. If on foot, pull yourself free with your awls. Lacking awls, keep your body flat and attempt to crawl out, first kicking with your feet. When free, roll away from the break, and stand only after you are on solid ice. Now, roll in the snow to blot up the water, and brush off the water-laden snow.

Head for a protected place and build a fire immediately. (Always carry matches in a waterproof case, a candle, and tinder for a quick fire when traversing ice.) Once the fire is burning well, build a second fire. After both fires are going well, stand between them, shed and dry some of your clothing, and make a hot drink. If you don't warm yourself quickly, you are a prime candidate for hypothermia or frostbite.

If your vehicle breaks through the ice, your best chance of escaping it is while it is still afloat. Your vehicle will float from a few seconds to maybe two or three minutes. Water pressure will prevent you from opening the doors, so open the windows and crawl through them. After the vehicle begins to sink, you have little chance of escaping from it. It will descend steeply, the end with the engine first, and may settle into the bottom upside down.

Although hazards in themselves, blizzards— a combination of a strong wind, low temperature, and blinding, falling, or blowing snow— result in a combination of winter hazards. In a blizzard you could suffer from hypothermia, frostbite, carbon monoxide poisoning, and snow blindness.

The best way to deal with blizzards is not to travel in them. Even in the remotest chance that a blizzard is on its way, *stay put.* Except for an emergency, traveling in a blizzard is simply not worth the risk.

If you are caught in a blizzard, you must wait it out. If in a vehicle, stay with it. This requires a lot of willpower, but remaining with the vehicle is almost always your safest course. Prepare for a long wait and assemble all your supplies and clothing. Keep the exhaust pipe free of snow. Idle the engine for warmth, but only about fifteen minutes every hour to conserve fuel. Crack a window on the downwind side for ventilation. Move your arms and legs from time to time for muscular-generated heat.

On foot, seek shelter immediately and build a fire. You might have to construct one of the shelters described later. If you cannot find or build a shelter, you have a final option: Burrow into a snowbank and crawl into the burrow. Many animals rely on this tactic for survival, and you can, too.

Carbon monoxide is an odorless, colorless, and tasteless gas that results from incomplete burning because of insufficient oxygen. This gas can build up from a vehicle idling in a closed garage, from exhaust seeping into an ice-fishing house or closed vehicle—such as when waiting out a blizzard—or from a camp stove or candles burning in a closed vehicle or snow shelter.

You can die from carbon monoxide poison-ing. At high concentrations, carbon monoxide can kill you in a minute. It cuts off oxygen to your brain.

Symptoms of carbon monoxide poisoning include dizziness, headache, nausea, and blurred vision. Detect it also by a yellow, rather than a blue, flame from candles or camp stoves.

To avoid carbon monoxide poisoning, keep closed places well ventilated. This means idling a vehicle only in an open garage, keeping a window open while waiting out a blizzard, and puncturing a ventilation hole in a snow shelter.

Snow blindness is an affliction of your eyes upon exposure to ultraviolet rays reflected from snow and ice. It's similar but more severe than the pain from not wearing sunglasses in summer. Your eyes become red, burn, water, and take on a sandy feeling. You may experience poor vision and a headache. Strangely, you may become afflicted hours after exposure to the intense light rays.

Prevent snow blindness by wearing dark glasses or goggles whenever you are exposed to the bright, reflected light of winter; wraparound sunglasses or those with side shields offer the most protection. If you are caught without dark glasses or goggles, cut eye shades from birch bark or cardboard and add thin, horizontal slits for your eyes.

If you become snow blinded, cover your eyes from the light and wait it out. Expect a wait of a few to many hours for recovery.

Avalanches are snow and ice slides in mountainous country that happen when unstable surface snow and ice slip on an unstable base. There are two kinds: loose-snow avalanches and slab avalanches. Loose-snow avalanches begin in a small area or at a point, and grow as they descend; they leave a V-shaped path with the tip of the V at the source.

The sliding mass has little form or internal cohesion. Slab avalanches begin with a large mass of snow and ice moving at once, and a wall forms where the large mass or slab separated. The mass has more of a tendency to stick together, but, of course, breaks up. Most persons are killed or injured by slab avalanches.

Imagine an avalanche in motion. It gains momentum as it moves down the slope and may speed along at 200 miles per hour. Clouds of snow dust may roll into the sky hundreds of feet. The avalanche may rise and ride on a cushion of air. Frequently an air blast, great enough to collapse buildings, precedes an avalanche.

Avalanches result from the overloading of snow and ice and unstable conditions at depth. Most avalanches happen during or shortly after heavy snowstorms, especially when snow falls at a rate of one inch per hour or more and thick snow buildup occurs. Compounding this buildup is wind-blown snow accumulating on leeward slopes, perhaps to the extent of forming snow cornices, which may break loose and set off an avalanche. Unstable layers, on which a snow-ice mass can slide, include those with surface hoar, sun crusts (a refrozen snowmelt), and depth hoar, whose crystals act like tiny ball bearings.

If you can't avoid avalanche country, take several precautions. After a heavy snowfall, let the snow consolidate before setting out on a trip. Avoid avalanche paths, indicated by a lack of trees or where trees lean in the same direction. Your safest routes are on the windward sides of high ridges away from cornices or in valleys, well away from the bottoms of slopes. If you must cross an avalanche path, use clumps of trees and prominent rock masses for protection. Listen for snow settling beneath you and watch for rolling snowballs; they often foretell unstable slopes above you. Tie a red, hundred-foot avalanche cord to your waist; it has metal pieces attached to it that indicate the distance and direction to you should you become buried. Consider carrying a small, pocket avalanche transceiver, turned on. Possible rescuers can home in on your signal.

If caught in an avalanche, your actions can help you survive it. Get rid of any encumbering equipment if you have time, such as skis, snowshoes, ski poles, and pack. Try to stay on top of the sliding mass by a kind of backstroke swimming with your head directed up slope. As the avalanche comes to a stop, raise your arms above your face to trap an air space in the congealing snow.

Survival Shelters

Only a few survival shelters are practical in winter, judged by the energy expended and the exposure to cold while constructing them. (I've already mentioned your vehicle as a shelter in a blizzard). I've selected four: the fallen-tree shelter, the lean-to, the snow pit, and the snow cave.

In timbered country, the fallen-tree shelter is probably the fastest and least energy-consuming shelter to construct. If the snow is deep, simply hollow out a space under the trunk with a ski, snowshoe, stout pole, or piece of bark. Cover your sitting or lying surface with evergreen boughs or other insulative material. If there is little or no snow, lay poles or slabs of bark against the trunk or upturned roots of a fallen tree. Cover the intervening spaces with branches, bark, boughs, and snow. You can easily have a fire with this shelter.

The lean-to takes more energy and time to construct but is more comfortable. Lay a horizontal ridgepole in the crotches of two trees spaced about as far apart as the length of your body. Now, lay one end of other poles on the ridgepole and at right angles to it for the roof, sloping to the ground; also lay shorter poles to form sides for the shelter. Cover the poles with sticks, branches, bark, boughs, and snow. Assemble boughs and other insulative materials for your bed. Build a long log fire or two small fires in front of the opening. The shelter should be just high enough to sit up in. Face the opening downwind or crosswind.

You can simplify the lean-to by placing one end of the ridgepole in the crotch of a tree and the other end on the ground. Then proceed as you would with a fallen-tree shelter.

You can make a snow pit shelter in the woods or in the open. In the woods, if the snow is deep enough, enlarge the natural pit around a standing tree trunk. Roof over the pit with poles, branches, boughs, and snow. In timberless country, dig a pit and roof it with reed stems, sticks, or anything available. For both pits, insulate the bottoms. You can build a small fire in either pit shelter but carefully ventilate the roof.

In the deeper snow of nonwooded places, burrow into the side of a snowdrift to make a snow cave. Try to have your sitting or sleeping area, lined with grass, reeds, brush, or cattails, higher than the entrance to take advantage of any rising warmer air. Poke a ventilation hole in the ceiling at an angle (not straight up) and block the entrance only partly with a snow block to allow for good circulation. You can heat this shelter somewhat with a candle.

Water and Survival Food

Dehydration is a serious problem when attempting to survive outdoors in winter. The air is very dry, and you lose water continually by exhaling, urinating, and perspiring. You can live for only a short time without water but for days, and even weeks, without food. In the cold, you should drink two quarts a day. Passing dark urine in small amounts indicates that you need more water.

Melt snow or ice—better than snow—to obtain water, and drink it hot if possible. If the snow is dry, many cups may be necessary to produce a cup of water. When the weather is warm and sunny you can melt snow on a sheet of dark plastic.

Eating snow is unwise because this rapidly cools your body from the inside, and you have to eat a lot to obtain much water. If you have no other choice, melt the snow in your mouth and warm the water before swallowing it.

Survival food is hard to come by in winter, but some is almost always available. I'll only mention plant food because this requires the least energy to gather.

A readily available plant food is the inner bark of many trees. Between the outer bark and the solid wood is a thin layer, the inner bark, that can be scraped with a knife and eaten, either dried or fresh. Possible trees include the pines, balsam fir, eastern hemlock, tamaracks, spruces, and box elder. Pitch from such conifers as balsam fir is a concentrated food but may be disagreeable and difficult to eat.

The fruits of several shrubs linger on them in winter; they will be less tasty then but filling. Most are better when cooked rather than eaten raw. Among the possibilities are the fruits of roses (hips), hawthorns, mountain ashes, wild grapes, highbush cranberries, and nannyberries, all of which you are likely to find above the snow.

Two other possibilities require more energy. The leaf buds of basswood trees can be tasty, but you will require many to satisfy you. The tiny seeds of docks can be cooked into a gruel. But be aware that collecting and separating the seeds consumes considerable energy and time.

Lastly, consider certain plants to brew teas, pleasant-tasting although with little nutritional value. The needles of pines, hemlocks, and balsam firs make good teas, as well as the twigs of yellow and black birches and the bark of sassafras. Boil coniferous needles for full flavor. For pines, also cut the needles to release the flavor. Avoid getting pitch in coniferous teas. In bogs with little snow cover, look for Labrador tea and make tea from the leaves.

Winter Survival Gear and Supplies

Winter survival items to take with you depends largely on whether you are in a vehicle or on foot.

Consider these items when traveling in a vehicle:

1. Vehicle equipment (others given in chapter 4)
   a. Flares
   b. Flashlight with extra batteries
   c. Red or orange cloth or plastic (to attach to radio antenna for rescue)
2. Clothing and bedding
   a. Thick socks, mittens, and balaclava or cap
   b. Lined pac boots or down booties
   c. Thick, long underwear
   d. Thick pants
   e. Thick shirts, sweaters, or jackets and parkas
   f. Thick sleeping bag and liner
3. Food and water
   a. Dried, ready-to-eat foods: jerky, meat bars, nuts, dried fruits
   b. Canned ready-to-eat foods
   c. Crackers, cookies, candy
   d. Foods requiring little heating or hot water: soups, canned vegetables and stews, instant meals, hot drink mixes
   e. Small cooking pot and lid with cup and spoon
   f. Hunting knife or large pocketknife
   g. Two gallon jugs of water
   h. Large plastic bag to bring in snow for melting
4. Heating
   a. Idling vehicle until fuel is consumed
   b. One-burner camp stove and extra fuel
   c. Multiwick candle such as a Dakota heater (also for melting snow)
   d. Sterno stove and canned fuel (also for melting snow)
   e. Matches (household)
5. Other
   a. Small plastic pan with tight-fitting lid (toilet) and toilet paper
   b. First-aid kit and manual
   c. Survival manual
   d. Books for entertainment
   e. Transistor radio with extra batteries

Consider these items when traveling on foot, assuming you have a small day pack:

1. Poncho (serves also as waterproof ground cloth or roof of shelter)
2. Reflective film emergency blanket
3. Matches, in a waterproof container
4. Candles (three), long burning

5. Pocketknife
6. Small pot and lid (with handle)
7. Cup and spoon
8. Emergency food: candy bars, cookies, nuts, dried fruit, jerky, soup and drink mixes
9. Nylon cord (fifty feet)
10. Whistle
11. Compass
12. Signal mirror
13. Pocket first-aid kit
14. Optional
    a. Black plastic sheet (for melting snow in warm weather)
    b. Wire saw
    c. Metal match (to use if matches run out)
    d. Chemical smoke device

could I construct a fallen-tree or a lean-to shelter faster? If I became lost here, I could survive on rose hips, nannyberries, and the inner bark of box elder. By continually evaluating survival resources, you will be mentally ready should the survival moment arise.

Practicing Survival

To be fully aware of the difficulties of winter survival, you must practice it. This doesn't mean intentionally driving or walking out into a blizzard—even if presumably prepared—and hoping that you will survive it.

A good way to ease into practicing winter survival is by winter camping. You gain experience in being thorough in your preparations and bringing additional survival gear. Enhance your experience by constructing and sleeping in a snow shelter. Learn what it means really to live in the cold.

Another way to "practice" winter survival is continually to evaluate winter survival resources around you as you travel. How would I free myself if the ice were to crack here? Would it be best to construct a snow cave on the lee side of those shrubs? In these woods,

SELECTED READINGS

ALLEN, OLIVER E. *Winter Gardens*. Alexandria, Virginia: Time-Life Books, 1979. (Very readable, illustrated in color; includes encyclopedia of plants for winter gardens.)

ALLEN, THOMAS B., and others. *Field Guide to the Birds of North America*. Washington, D.C.: National Geographic Society, 1983. (National Geographic Field Guide; well illustrated.)

ANGIER, BRADFORD. *Survival with Style*. New York: Vintage Books, 1972. (Written by an experienced outdoorsman; covers more than winter survival.)

BALDWIN, NED. *Skiing Cross Country*. New York: McGraw-Hill Ryerson Limited, 1977. (Thorough, well-illustrated manual on all types of cross-country skiing.)

BENYUS, JANINE M. *The Field Guide to Wildlife Habitats of the Eastern United States*. New York: Simon & Schuster, Inc., 1989. (Appealingly illustrated; gives easily read accounts of wildlife habitats and plants and animals expected in them.)

———. *The Field Guide to Wildlife Habitats of the Western United States*. New York: Simon & Schuster, Inc., 1989. (A companion volume.)

BROCKMAN, C. FRANK. *Trees of North America*. New York: Golden Press, 1968. (Illustrated in color with distribution maps.)

BROWN, LAUREN. *Weeds in Winter*. New York: W. W. North & Company, 1976. (Illustrated guide.)

BULL, JOHN, AND JOHN FARRAND. *The Audubon Society Field Guide to North American Birds, Eastern Region*. New York: Knopf, 1977. (Audubon East Field Guide; well illustrated.)

CONNOR, JACK. *The Complete Birder: A Guide to Better Birding*. Boston: Houghton Mifflin Company, 1988. (Appealingly written; not "complete," focuses on birds difficult to identify—warblers, hawks, shorebirds, terns, and gulls.)

EHRLICH, PAUL R., DAVID S. DOBKIN, AND DARRYL WHEYE. *The Birder's Handbook*. New York: Simon & Schuster, Inc., 1988. (Fact-jammed book on the natural history of North American birds breeding north of Mexico; no bird illustrations.)

FARRAND, JOHN, JR., ed. *The Audubon Society Master Guide to Birding*, 3 vols. New York: Knopf, 1983. (Audubon Master Field Guide; well illustrated.)

FELT, EPHRAIM PORTER. *Plant Galls and Gall Makers*. Ithaca, NY: Comstock Publishing Company, 1940. (Illustrated, semitechnical key to hundreds of insect-produced galls in North America.)

FORREST, LOUISE R. *Field Guide to Tracking Animals in Snow*. Harrisburg, PA: Stackpole Books,

1988. (Well-illustrated guide to mostly mammal tracks in snow.)

FRENCH, ALAN R. "The Patterns of Mammalian Hibernation," *American Scientist* 76 (1988): 569–575. (Semitechnical, uses technical jargon.)

GRAY, D. M., AND D. H. MALE, eds. *Handbook of Snow: Principles, Processes, Management & Use*. Toronto: Pergamon Press, 1981. (Technical handbook arranged in four parts: snow and the environment, snowfall and snowcover, snow and engineering, and snow and recreation.)

HALFPENNY, JAMES C., AND ROY D. OZANNE. *Winter: An Ecological Handbook*. Boulder, Colorado: Johnson Books, 1989. (Rather technical.)

HARRINGTON, PHILIP S. *Touring the Universe Through Binoculars: A Complete Astronomer's Guidebook*. Belmont, MA: Sky Publishing Corporation, 1991. (Lists more than 1,100 deep-sky objects visible through binoculars, describes 400 in detail.)

HARRISON, KIT, AND GEORGE HARRISON. *The Birds of Winter*. New York: Random House, 1990. (Easily readable account of many birds wintering north of 40 degrees north latitude in North America.)

INTERNATIONAL ASSOCIATION OF HYDROLOGY, COMMISSION ON SNOW AND ICE. The International Classification for Snow (with Special Reference to Snow on the Ground). Ottawa, Canada: National Research Council, Associate Committee on Soil and Snow Mechanics Technical Memorandum No. 31, 1954.

LACHAPELLE, EDWARD R. *Field Guide to Snow Crystals*. Seattle: University of Washington Press, 1969. (Popular guide to snow crystals: their classification, formation, observation, and photography; illustrated with numerous photographs.)

LUDLUM, DAVID M. *The American Weather Book*. Boston: Houghton Mifflin, 1982. (Highlights of weather in the coterminous United States, arranged by month.)

———. *The Audubon Society Field Guide to North American Weather*. New York: Knopf, 1991.

MARCHAND, PETER J. *Life in the Cold: An Introduction to Winter Ecology*. Hanover, New Hampshire: University Press of New England, 1987. (Rather technical.)

MAYALL, R. NEWTON, MARGARET MAYALL, AND JEROME WYCKOFF. *The Sky Observers' Guide: A Handbook for Amateur Astronomers*. New York: Golden Press, 1985. (Well illustrated.)

MENZEL, DONALD H., AND JAY M. PASACHOFF. *A Field Guide to the Stars and Planets*. Boston: Houghton Mifflin Company, 1983. (Peterson Field Guide; useful with the unaided eye, binoculars, or a small telescope; numerous sky maps; some photographs in color.)

MERRITT, JOSEPH F., ed. *Winter Ecology of Small Mammals*. Pittsburgh: Carnegie Museum of Natural History Special Publication Number 10 (1984):1–380. (Many articles; technical.)

MURIE, OLAUS. *A Field Guide to Animal Tracks*. Boston: Houghton Mifflin Company, 1974. (Classic track book of mostly mammals that also includes numerous illustrations of droppings as well as natural history observations.)

NESTOR, WILLIAM P. *Into Winter: Discovering a Season*. Boston: Houghton Mifflin Company, 1982. (Children's book on nature activities in winter.)

NORDIC WORLD MAGAZINE. *All About Winter Safety*. Mountain View, CA: World Publications, 1975. (Useful winter safety handbook.)

OSGOOD, WILLIAM, AND LESLIE HURLEY. *The Snowshoe Book*. Lexington, MA: The Stephen Greene Press, 1983. (Useful, comprehensive guide on snowshoes and snowshoeing.)

PETERSON, ROGER TORY. *A Field Guide to the Birds*. Boston: Houghton Mifflin Company, 1980. (Peterson East Field Guide covers birds of eastern and central North America; well illustrated.)

———. *A Field Guide to Western Birds*. Boston: Houghton Mifflin Company, 1990. (Peterson West Guide covers birds of western North America; well illustrated.)

PETRIDES, GEORGE A. *A Field Guide to Trees and Shrubs*. Boston: Houghton Mifflin Company, 1972. (For northeastern and north-central United

States and southeastern and south-central Canada; also winter keys to woody plants.)

PRATER, GENE. *Snowshoeing*. Seattle: The Mountaineers, 1988.

RAYMO, CHET. *365 Starry Nights: An Introduction to Astronomy for Every Night of the Year*. New York: Prentice-Hall Press, 1982. (Highly readable, profusely illustrated; 365 essays especially designed for the stargazer.)

ROBBINS, CHANDLER S., BERTEL BRUUN, AND HERBERT S. ZIM. *Birds of North America: A Guide to Field Identification*. New York: Golden Press, 1983. (Robbins Guide; well illustrated; includes sonagrams.)

RUFFNER, JAMES A., AND FRANK E. BAIR, eds. *The Weather Almanac*. Detroit: Gale Research Company, 1987. (Reference guide to weather, climate, and air quality in the United States and its key cities; also world climatological highlights.)

SAKAI, A., AND C. J. WEISER. "Freezing Resistance of Trees in North America with Reference to Tree Regions," *Ecology* 54 (1973):118–126. (Semitechnical, uses technical jargon.)

SIMONDS, CALVIN. *The Weatherwise Gardener: A Guide to Understanding, Predicting, and Walking with the Weather*. Emmaus, Pennsylvania: Rodale Press, 1983. (Weather guide for the coterminous United States from the eyes of a gardener.)

STOKES, DONALD W. *A Guide to Nature in Winter: Northeast and North Central North America*. Boston: Little, Brown and Company, 1976. (Well-illustrated guide to winter weeds, snow crystals, plants, insect sign, winter's birds and nests, mushrooms, and tracks in winter.)

———. *A Guide to Bird Behavior, Volume I*. Boston: Little, Brown and Company, 1979.

STOKES, DONALD, AND LILLIAN STOKES. *A Guide to Bird Behavior, Volumes II and III*. Boston: Little, Brown and Company, 1983, 1989. (All three volumes on bird behavior easily read, illustrated.)

———. *The Bird Feeder Book: An Easy Guide to Attracting, Identifying, and Understanding Your Feeder Birds*. Boston: Little Brown and Company, 1987. (Well illustrated.)

SYMONDS, GEORGE W. D. *The Tree Identification Book: A New Method for the Practical Identification and Recognition of Trees*. New York: Quill, 1958. (Mostly photographs, little text; for mostly eastern half of United States.)

———. *The Shrub Identification Book: The Visual Method for the Practical Identification of Shrubs, Including Woody Vines and Ground Covers*. New York: M. Barrows and Company, 1963. (Mostly photographs, little text; for eastern half of United States and adjacent canada.)

TELFER, EDMUND S., AND JOHN P. KELSALL. "Adaptation of Some Large North American Mammals for Survival in Snow," *Ecology* 65 (1984):1828–1834. (Semitechnical, uses technical jargon.)

UDVARDY, M. D. F. *The Audubon Society Field Guide to North American Birds, Western Region*. New York: Knopf, 1977. (Aubudon West Field Guide; well illustrated.)

U.S. DEPARTMENT OF THE AIR FORCE. *Survival*. Washington, D.C.: U.S. Department of the Air Force, 1979. (Air Force survival manual; covers much more than winter survival.)

UNITED STATES DEPARTMENT OF AGRICULTURE. *Common Weeds of the United States*. New York: Dover Publications, Inc., 1971. (Illustrated guide with descriptions and distribution maps.)

WALKER, LAURENCE C. *Forests: A Naturalist's Guide to Trees and Forest Ecology*. New York: Wiley, 1990.

WEISER, C. J. "Cold Resistance and Injury in Woody Plants," *Science* 169 (1970):1269–1278. (Semitechnical, uses technical jargon.)

I N D E X

Note: References to illustrations are in italics.